MEMORIES OF MIGRATION

SUNY Series on Women and Work
Joan Smith, Editor

MEMORIES OF MIGRATION

*Gender, Ethnicity, and Work
in the Lives of Jewish and Italian Women
in New York, 1870–1924*

Kathie Friedman-Kasaba

STATE UNIVERSITY
OF NEW YORK
PRESS

Front cover photo:
Regina Haimowitz poses with her two brothers, Yzzo and Ben, in Szeged, Austria-Hungary. They will join her father, older sister, and brother in the United States after World War I. Courtesy of the author.

State University of New York Press, Albany

Production by Susan Geraghty
Marketing by Dana Yanulavich

Printed in the United States of America

For information, address State University of New York Press,
State University Plaza, Albany, N.Y., 12246

Library of Congress Cataloging-in-Publication Data

Friedman-Kasaba, Kathie, 1954–
    Memories of migration : gender, ethnicity, and work in the lives
of Jewish and Italian women in New York, 1870–1924 / by Kathie
Friedman-Kasaba.
        p.   cm.—(SUNY series on women and work)
    Includes bibliographical references and index.
    ISBN 0-7914-2761-7 (alk. paper). — ISBN 0-7914-2762-5 (pbk. :
alk paper)
    1. Women immigrants—New York (N.Y.)—History. 2. Jewish women—
New York (N.Y.)—History. 3. Italian American women—New York
(N.Y.)—History. 4. New York (N.Y.)—Emigration and immigation—
History.   I. Title. II. Series: SUNY series on women and work.
F128.9.A1F75 1996
305.48'85107471'09034—dc20   95-6566
                                                                CIP

10 9 8 7 6 5 4 3 2 1

For Reşat

CONTENTS

ILLUSTRATIONS

ACKNOWLEDGMENTS

This book has been in the making for a long time. Researching and writing it bear much similarity to undertaking a journey. That is to say, without the support and encouragement of many people in many locations this book would not have been possible.

This study began as a Ph.D. dissertation in the Department of Sociology at the State University of New York at Binghamton. It is difficult to find enough words to express my gratitude to Giovanni Arrighi for his intellectual guidance, critical spirit, and human warmth, not to mention unwavering confidence in my professional goals over the years. I owe a special debt of thanks to Immanuel Wallerstein, Director of the Fernand Braudel Center, for enabling me to get this study off the ground by welcoming me into the Research Working Group on Households, Labor Force Formation and the World-Economy, and supporting my interest in immigrant women's waged and nonwaged labor. Anna Davin worked tirelessly to provide extensive comments on each draft; her encouragement, compassion, and inspiration sustained me throughout the process. Her wisdom and gentle passion continues to be the ideal I strive for in my research and teaching. Evelyn Nakano Glenn and Bat-Ami Bar On took time out from their busy schedules and provided careful readings and valuable comments at various stages of research and writing.

The professional staffs at the Morris Raphael Cohen Library, City College of New York; the Rare Book and Manuscript Library, Columbia University; the Labor-Management Documentation Center, Martin P. Catherwood Library of the New York State School of Industrial and Labor Relations, Cornell University; and the Robert F. Wagner Labor Archives of the Tamiment Institute Library, New York University, were very helpful in locating key materials and documents used in the book.

Colleagues in the Liberal Studies Program at the University of Washington-Tacoma have fashioned a community that is not only conducive to the work of teacher-scholars, but is one that nourishes the creative spirit. I am grateful to my colleagues for their enthusiasm and helpful suggestions. I am particularly indebted to Janet Primomo and Marcy Stein for sharing their family photographs and stories with me. I owe a special debt of thanks to the Faculty Affairs Committee for subsidizing the cost of many of the photographs included in this book.

Many friends, students, and colleagues have contributed to the development of my ideas and have read and commented upon various parts of the manuscript. I am deeply appreciative of them all. Torry Dickinson, Shirley Yee, Rachel May, Yolanda Prieto, Sue Hammons-Bryner, Donna Gabaccia, and Suzanne Sinke provided valuable feedback and words of encouragement on various chapters. Paula Shields and Purnima Mankekar patiently listened as I explored "half-baked ideas" with them, and eased the loneliness of the journey. My students in both "Migration in the Modern World" and "Women in the Global Economy" were enthusiastic "sounding boards" for ideas in progress; I am grateful for their spirited cooperation and generous feedback.

My parents, Harold and Harriet Friedman, provided loving support and the opportunity to know my eastern European grandparents, first through years of visits, then through stories and photographs. Jay and Lisa Friedman, Münip and Kerime Senyücel, Muzaffer Kasaba, and my nieces and nephews provided many joyful distractions, and with them, a sense of proportion to the task.

I owe the greatest debt of gratitude to my husband, Reşat Kasaba, who gently nourished the person who evolved alongside the book. His everyday love and faith sustained me; his humor uplifted me. He has lived with this book as long as I have, listened to and commented upon every possible version with wise and supportive suggestions. Delighted that this particular road is now traveled, he reminds me, in good humor, that migration is, at the least, a lifelong process.

INTRODUCTION

Starting from Home

Make an effort to remember. Or failing that, invent.
—Monique Wittig[1]

My eastern European grandmothers showed me how to prepare *palacsintas* (Hungarian crepes) and "Popeye salad" (hard boiled eggs surrounded by spinach). I learned how to sew a dress out of old muslin bedsheets first in order to avoid spoiling expensive fabric, as well as how a "proper" 1940s American-Jewish nuclear family ought to be organized.

Although I was fortunate to witness the dailiness of my grandmothers' lives into my twenties, I knew precious little of their feelings and thoughts on immigrating to the United States in the early twentieth century. How had migrating changed their lives? For the better or for the worse? Had they alternatives to migration? Would immigration have been their choice, in retrospect? Did they have regrets about leaving close-knit families and religiously observant ethnic communities for the chaos of American pluralism?

Growing up in post-Holocaust suburban Detroit, a social climate dominated by a musical play about pogroms—*Fiddler on the Roof*—race riots, and anti-Vietnam War protests, I looked in part to my grandmothers for help in sorting out my proper place in the world.[2] Regina always seemed to me to be a bit melancholy, as if she were worn down by life in America. Edith appeared to me to be always in control, as if she had made her will power into fuel for crossing the Atlantic. Yet, the silence of both implied resignation, and I interpreted their unspoken words then as code for "America was something that happened to me" or "Had I

1

remained in Europe I would have perished in the Holocaust." Would this be all that I would ever know about the meanings of migration?

The unspoken dialogue between my grandmothers and myself was the original catalyst for this study. Although I have never found answers to the questions I still have about my own grandmothers, the search opened the door to the world of migration studies in which I have now immersed myself for many years.

SCOPE OF THE BOOK

This book explores migrating women's struggles to remake and redefine themselves in a world that constrained them. It examines and contrasts the experiences of Russian-Jewish and Italian women who immigrated to New York City, from the last third of the nineteenth century to the closing of the immigration door in 1924. My primary aim in comparing these two groups of immigrant women was to analyze how each, in relation to the other, experienced and tried to negotiate both the potentially empowering and corrosive aspects of transnational migration. To what extent did women's migration experiences provide the conditions under which they could free themselves from preexisting social constraints? What meanings of migration did women construct to make sense of and to evaluate their changing geographical and social locations? I undertook this study because I wanted to understand the relationship between international migration and women's social position, and because I wanted to find out whether one or another group of migrating women was somehow better positioned to improve their status in America, and if so, why.

Women constituted an overall minority of those who departed European ports and entered the United States during these years. Yet, when viewed through a lens focused on ethnicity and nationality, the relative numbers of women migrating varied considerably from one group to another. Between 1881 and 1924 the United States received, from all origins, over 26 million new immigrant arrivals; little more than one-third were women (U.S. Census, His. Stat., 1960:62). Approximately 2 million eastern European Jews entered the United States between 1881 and 1914 (Kahan 1978:236; Wischnitzer 1948:98–99). Yet, nearly half of the flow over the years from 1889 through 1924 was composed of women (Hersch 1969:483). During the same general period, 1876–1914, approximately 14 million Italians left their homeland for a variety of destinations; of these only 4 million entered the United States (Foerster 1919:8; Martellone 1984:391). Among Italian arrivals in the United States between 1881 and 1920, women averaged only one-fourth, gradually increasing their share to 40 percent in the 1930s (Furio 1979:10; Martellone 1984:405).

The dynamics of development and change within the late nineteenth-century modern world-system had created the possibility for a diversity of subjugated peoples to leave their homelands and remake their lives in a so-called new world. These turn-of-the-century mass migrations from eastern and southern European peripheries represented a collective response to the increasing coerciveness of both market and nonmarket discipline that accompanied capitalist expansion and transformation. But, the study of migration as a selective group reaction to global structural pressures has too often been divorced from examination of the personal meanings of migration for individuals. Much less have studies conducted at these different levels of analysis addressed migration as a gendered phenomenon, and fewer still as a process that has differentiating outcomes among women, with regard to their age, generation, social class, or nationality/race/ethnicity. Moreover, the diversity of women's migration experiences has yet to be fully analyzed within the context of a developing world-system. It is my hope that this book can contribute to the ongoing but still fragmented efforts at reinterpreting immigrant women's experiences, and thereby assist in making the sociology of migration more receptive to the ideas of multidimensional, interdisciplinary, and comparative research on migrating women.[3]

ORGANIZATION OF THE BOOK

This study analyzes and contrasts the migration experiences of Russian-Jewish and Italian women in order to determine whether, and to what extent, migration to the United States altered their social position. Chapter 1 begins by situating the study within the multidisciplinary literatures of contrasting and polarized theories about international migration and adaptation; feminist scholarship on gender inequality; and analyses of ethnicity, race, and the racialization process. This chapter suggests implementing an alternative framework in order to overcome some of the unproductive polarizations that have impeded understanding of immigrant women's experiences.

Chapters 2 and 3 discuss the interaction of micro- and macro-structural forces in organizing women's European departures and migration to the United States. These chapters highlight women's responses (collective and personal) to changing core-periphery and interstate relations within the modern world-system, as well as their participation in the shifting gender, nationality/ethnicity, and class relations of nineteenth-century Russia and Italy, respectively.

Chapter 4 examines and contrasts the experiences of Russian-Jewish and Italian women who were married and/or mothers at the time of their incorporation into the United States. The chapter focuses on the particular ways racial nativism affected migrating women and differentiated among them, and on how immigrant women's relationships with Americanizing institutions, organized both by dominant racial/ethnics and coethnics, shaped their respective social positions in the United States.

Chapter 5 focuses on the reception of young single immigrant women in America, contrasts the experiences of young Italian women with young Russian-Jewish women, and compares the outcomes of their migration with that of older women, who migrated as wives or mothers. Both chapters 4 and 5 emphasize the potential value, but ambiguous nature, of coethnic community networks in improving immigrant women's social positions against a tide of racial nativism.

Chapter 6, the concluding chapter, differentiates among the outcomes of migration for Italian and Russian-Jewish immigrant women, older married women and younger single women, and isolates the factors most responsible for the improvement, deterioration, or transformation in women's social position. Women from the European periphery were neither uniformly nor unambiguously empowered by migrating to the United States at the turn of the century. The extent to which their lives were transformed rested upon their interactions with state migration policies, private Americanization efforts, coethnic communities, and household income-producing opportunities. Despite sharing both gender status and origin in underdeveloped regions of the world-economy, Russian-Jewish and Italian women faced distinctly different contexts of departure and incorporation in the United

Figure 1.
Regina Haimowitz (center) poses with her seamstress apprentices in Austria-Hungary shortly before she migrated to America after World War I. Collection of the author.

States. This chapter returns to the initial research questions, to the rethinking of theory and method in migration research, and suggests the broader implications of this study.

Over the years of studying immigrant women, I have had the opportunity to rethink and remember fragments of past conversations with my grandmothers. Some family members also recall these stories, others do not. Some remember variations, or entirely different truths. Regina remembered herself as a competent young woman in Austria-Hungary who stood up to her mother one day and declared that she was no longer content to grow and peddle radishes in order to support what remained of the household after her father had migrated to America. No, she was going to study dressmaking, open a shop of her own with the assistance of apprentices, and use her income to improve her life further by migrating to America. Edith, as a young girl, accompanied her mother and sisters on their journey from Russia to America, where they rejoined her father, the undisputed head of the household. That was until the day arrived when, in order to keep the office job and salary that she had studied and worked so hard to obtain, Edith stood up to her father and against his orders began to earn wages on the Sabbath, or Saturday, in America.

Regardless of whether I, or my grandmothers, remembered these events or recollections accurately, or improvised upon memories of migration in order to tell "a good story," these moments of autonomy have disrupted and displaced any linear interpretation of their experiences as ones of resignation or even of simple empowerment. What remains, however, is to develop an understanding and interpretation of the *whole* story, which requires a wide lens, focused as much upon large-scale and long-term global processes as on community and family relationships and the personal experiences of individual immigrant women. It is the development of that lens to which I turn next.

CHAPTER 1

Women and International Migration: Moving Beyond Unproductive Polarizations

No description can even begin to lead to a valid explanation if it does not effectively encompass the whole world.
—Fernand Braudel[1]

Neither the life of an individual nor the history of a society can be understood without understanding both . . . No study that does not come back to the problems of biography, of history, and of their intersections within society has completed its intellectual journey.
—C. Wright Mills[2]

Our collective goal ought to be to advance a theoretical framework to our scholarship that transcends the victim/heroine, domination/ resistance dualism and incorporates the varied experiences of women. We need . . . work that insists on presenting the complexity of the sources of power and weakness in women's lives.
—Linda Gordon[3]

Migrating women at the turn of the century found themselves living a paradox. On the one hand, migration to the United States promised the fulfillment of "old world" dreams in a new land or, at least, a degree of emancipation from old world hierarchies and greater self-determination. At the same time, however, migration had the potential to intensify existing subordination, as well as to subject women to new forms of control and domination.

Rosa Cavalleri, who emigrated from Italy to the United States in 1884, cooked and cleaned over forty years for the female social reformers of the Chicago Commons Settlement House. "How can I not love America," she proclaimed to a resident settlement worker, "an angel woman," taking down her life story (for which she was never paid). "I hope I do my work so good so I never have to leave this place! . . . Even if they didn't pay me I would not want to stop working in the Commons" (Ets 1970:221). Writing about the same time, Russian-Jewish immigrant Anzia Yezierska, expressed a contrasting view of immigrant women's experiences in America. In her autobiographical short story, "The Free Vacation House," Yezierska sharply criticized Americanizing reformers of the "Social Betterment Society." "For why do they make it so hard for us," an immigrant mother implores. "When a mother needs a vacation, why must they tear the insides out from her first . . . why do they boss the life out of us? (Seller 1981:194).

Migration, like "city air," might make women "free," but the paradox of this metaphor of modernity was that women, like men, seldom migrated and resettled under conditions of their own choosing. Whether or not, the conservative reaction to large-scale social change, or the collective resistance to it, mass migration posed a potential threat to the personal and group identities of all who made the journey, transforming the initially hopeful into the most recent wave of the dispossessed.

Recently, Salman Rushdie in his novel, *Satanic Verses* (1989), portrayed the assault on his immigrant protagonists' identities by the gatekeepers of the dominant nationality. "They have the power of description," he wrote, "and we succumb to the pictures they construct." Nearly a century before, a young Russian-Jewish immigrant, Mary Antin, offered her own terse characterization of this particular dimension of displacement. In the preface to her autobiography, *The Promised Land*, she wrote: "I was born, I have lived, and I have been made over" ([1911] 1969:x). Russian-Jewish novelist, Anzia Yezierska, struggled "to become a person," as she put it, an active agent in control of her own life. During the same period, Leonard Coviello's teacher took it upon himself to change the young Italian immigrant's name to Covello, claiming it was easier to pronounce. Upon discovering this, Coviello's father exploded in anger; his mother, in an attempt to mediate the conflict between cultural and generational authorities, internal and external change, explained to the boy: "A person's life and honor is in his name. A name is not a shirt or a piece of underwear" (Covello 1958:23). The road to potentially wider opportunities and empowerment for both individuals and social groups was often strewn with new forms of domination and control.

My goal in this study was to analyze how Italian and Russian-Jewish immigrant women experienced and tried to negotiate both the potentially empowering and the coercive dimensions inherent in the process of international migration. To what extent did migration provide women the conditions under which they could free themselves from preexisting social constraints? How did Russian-Jewish and Italian immigrant women compare with regard to the extent of their empowerment or subordination in America? What meanings of migration did these women construct to make sense of and to evaluate their changing geographic and social locations?

TRANSNATIONAL MIGRATION: THE REMAKING OF SOCIAL RELATIONS AND SOCIAL CONCEPTS

A variety of social relationships systematically structured women's migration experiences and outcomes. The various modes of adaptation, accommodation, collaboration, negotiation, reconciliation, and resistance through which migrating women responded to change and transformed themselves and their environments, were shaped by their multiple, linked, and often contradictory positions in social relationships. More specifically, the class, nationality/ethnic/race, and gender relations of the world-system all intersected to shape the timing and organization of women's European departures and their patterns of settlement in the United States. Thus, in order to understand if the position of women improved as a consequence of migration, it is not only necessary to explore the historically changing meanings of gender relations, but also those of race/ethnicity/nationality, and social class in a developing world-system. One task of this project has been to develop a framework for interpreting and evaluating the extent of changes in immigrant women's social position, or status, by connecting it to the forces of proletarianization, sexism, and racism/nativism embedded within the developmental processes of the modern world-system.[4] While the focus of this study is migrating women, considerable attention then is given to the overarching, but historically specific, social institutions and social relationships that constrained their options and aspirations, or alternatively served as their points of leverage in subverting, manipulating, or resisting the multiple and intersecting dominations they faced.

Historical and comparative analyses of transnational migration have a unique potential to illuminate both the rigidity and the flexibility inherent in categories of group identification. In migrating, women both challenged and reflected changes in what are traditionally assumed to be "authentic" social group boundaries and differences, not only between "feminine" and "masculine" behaviors, but between a number of socially constructed and paired opposites, including "alien" and "native," "race" and "ethnicity," "child" and "adult." Geographic and political relocation exposes the extent to which these categories of identification do not have some "authentic" essence or universally fixed content. The multiple contexts and conflicts that give meaning to categories of nationality, race, ethnicity, gender, age, and social class are reorganized in the course of migration. Thus, one aim of this study has been to explore how a comparative and historically contextualized analysis of migrating women's shifting personal and collective identities might unsettle and rearrange traditional understandings of international migration.

The Multiple Dimensions of Immigrant Women's Position

Before discussing the implications of various traditional migration and resettlement theories for understanding immigrant women's experiences and outcomes, it is necessary to make explicit which dimensions of women's lives are examined in this study. Feminist scholarship in the humanities and social sciences has shown that *gender*—the socially constructed and historically situated relationships and practices patterned around perceived differences between the sexes—is a significant organizing principle of overall social life, one which shapes women's opportunities and life chances, as it does men's.[4] Gender is, thus, "a set of social relations which organize immigration patterns," in much the same way as other social institutions and practices are organized through gender relations, such as the economy and work, the family and mothering, ethnic communities and social networks. In her application of gender analysis to the study of Mexican undocumented migration and settlement in the U.S., sociologist Pierrette Hondagneu-Sotelo reminds us that "the task is, then, not simply . . . to ask the same questions of immigrant women that are asked of immigrant men, but to begin with an examination of how gender relations facilitate or constrain," in this case, eastern and southern European immigrant women's opportunities for greater self-determination (Hondagneu-Sotelo 1994:3).

My use of the terms *social position* and *status* are meant to convey the multifaceted nature of immigrant women's experiences, collectively and personally, within a range of gendered social relationships, and to draw attention to both the possibilities of an improvement in their material well being, as well as in their sense of increased empowerment, or greater relative control over their lives. This study foregrounds immigrant women's interactions with state migration policies, private Americanization efforts, coethnic community networks, and income-producing opportunities. Within these sets of social relations, women came to exercise varying levels of authority or autonomy as "foreigners," as workers, and as family, household, and community members.

Immigrant women also evidenced a range of experiences as participants in the determination of their individual identities. One of the tasks of this study was to explore what I took as Anzia Yezierska's sense of personhood, the more subjective side of self-determination. I looked at the extent to which immigrant women demonstrated greater personal autonomy in terms of developing and pursuing more self-defined identities, outside the range of gender, ethnic/nationality/race, and social-class-defined roles traditionally open to them. In other words, I examined the extent to which women, in the course of migrating and resettling, imagined, defined, or identified themselves as somehow apart from the larger collectivities into which others had defined them. The capacity to develop more self-defined identities may have been indicative of a sense of empowerment that transcended the individual and reflected a more general expansion in the content and meaning of social categories.

Over the past decade many scholars, feminist scholars of color in particular, have commented critically upon notions of gender inequality which implied a universal "sisterhood" formed by and through common subordination to a male patriarchy, without regard to historical or cultural context or to relations of domination-subordination between women.[6] For feminist philosopher, Sandra Harding, "[In] cultures stratified by both gender and race, gender is always a racial category and race a gender category" (Harding 1986:18). This study considers the hierarchal relations of gender, nationality/ethnicity/race, and class to be tightly interwoven within each set of interactions between immigrant women and state migration policies, private Americanization efforts, coethnic community networks, and income-producing opportunities. What was prescribed for, forbidden to, or experienced by working-class Italian immigrant women, single and married, as compared to working-class Russian-Jewish immigrant women, single and married—rather than by *all immigrant women in general*—is precisely the objective of this study.

European Immigrants, Racialization, and Not-Yet-White Ethnics

My use of the terms *race, racialization,* and *racial nativism,* in the context of a study about European immigrant ("white ethnic") women requires some clarification. My overriding concern has been to distance this analysis from those framed within assimilation and cultural pluralist perspectives that claim to seek, but more often to justify, why some different, but equivalent, ethnic groups (white) became more economically successful than others (nonwhite). Assimilation theorists have actually had very little to say about "race." African-Americans, like Irish-Americans, Italian-Americans, and Jewish-Americans were all perceived as recently arriving immigrant (i.e., ethnic) groups in northern U.S. cities by the classic assimilationists (Wirth 1928; Park 1950). Mistakenly, the assimilation/ethnicity perspective equates the durability of prejudice and discrimination against people of color with the comparatively ephemeral and fluid nature of coercive Americanization policies directed against not-yet-white ethnics.[7] Neither assimilationists nor cultural pluralists have analyzed the differences and hierarchical ranking systems between ethnic groups or within any particular ethnic group designation, for instance among Jews or Italians in America.

My use of racial terminology is meant to signal the removal of this study from the assimilationist and cultural pluralist paradigms. In contrast, I place the interpretation of southern Italian and Russian-Jewish immigrant women's experiences within the developing literature on the social construction of whiteness as a racial category and social identity.[8] More specifically, I examine how processes of national/regional/ethnic stratification within eastern and southern Europe shaped the migration of particular social groups, as opposed to others, and how those groups were constructed during the period under examination as "not-yet-white ethnics."

Racialization refers to "the extension of racial meaning to a previously racially unclassified relationship, social practice, or group" (Omi and Winant 1986:64). Racism is defined here as "those social practices which (explicitly or implicitly) attribute merits or allocate values to members of racially categorized groups solely because of their 'race'"(Omi and Winant 1986:145). Racial nativism is racism modified by distinctiveness based on citizenship status. Racism and racialization are simultaneously ideological, economic, and political processes. They are historically and contextually specific. In particular, the meanings attached to *white, nonwhite, American, Hebrew,* and *Southern Italian* are historically contingent ones. The boundaries, the boundary-setting processes, and the identification of similarities and differences between groups that emerge, develop, and change are only analyzable within clearly demarcated sets of historical and social relationships (Wallerstein 1987). The same nominal group classification (e.g., southern Italian or Russian-Jewish) may, in the context of one set of historically specific hierarchical relations, be understood as a "nationality" (attributing a political dimension to peoplehood). In another entirely different set of social relations, the same name may be descriptive of a "race," (attributing a physical distinctiveness to peoplehood) or possibly, an "ethnicity" (attributing a cultural distinctiveness to peoplehood).

It seems clear from contemporary sources that the "new immigration" from southern and eastern Europe in the late nineteenth century was, to some extent, racialized and depicted in terms of specific "scientifically derived racial traits" based on the so-called immutable laws of nature.[9] But the rationale for interpreting southern and eastern European immigration within a paradigm based on race can be strengthened if we consider that turn-of-the-century understandings of the relation between biology, race, and culture differed from those developed in the mid- to late twentieth century. The predominant nineteenth-century understanding of race, which informed political and economic activity, defined race on the basis of *both* biological and cultural distinctiveness. Moreover, the characteristics of biology and culture were assumed to be equally heritable across generations, as well as equally subject to modification or disappearance in the course of historical development (Paul 1981).[10] Race, racialization, and racism understood in the nineteenth-century conceptualization of the terms, thus encompassed for a limited time the identities and experiences of southern Italian and eastern European Jewish immigrants in the United States.

While one aim of this book is to analyze the process by which "not-yet-white ethnic" women were differentiated from each other, as well as in relation to "white" and "white ethnic" women, the study does not attempt to examine the specific ways in which "not-yet" and "not-quite" white ethnics, to paraphrase historian David Roediger (1994), eventually became white Americans. As Roediger aptly points out, "in the process of Americanizing European immigrants acquired a sense of whiteness and of white supremacy" (Roediger 1994:187). He goes on to suggest that "immigrants often were moved to struggle to equate whiteness with Americanism in order to turn arguments over immigration from the question of who was foreign to the question of who was white" (Roediger 1994:189). At some point, possibly by the 1920s, not-yet-white ethnic women emerged simultaneously as both the subordinate gender and as part of the dominant race in the U.S. This study addresses the preconditions for white ethnic women's contradictory experiences of dominance and subordination.

In the section that follows I situate immigrant women's experiences within a multidisciplinary literature of contrasting theories about international migration and adaptation, and discuss its implications for understanding the relationship between migration and changes in women's social position.

CONTRASTING PERSPECTIVES
ON WOMEN AND MIGRATION:
TRANSCENDING INVISIBILITY, PASSIVITY,
AND REDUCTIONISM

Following two decades of research in women's studies and ethnic studies, it would seem appropriate that a study of this nature begin with a focus centered clearly on women's premigration lives in their nineteenth-century European regions of origin. But, as historian Donna Gabaccia has aptly pointed out, "the very proliferation of specialties that allowed ethnic and women's studies to develop as multidisciplinary fields has also helped institutionalize the conflicting categories, methods, and modes of analysis that contribute to the marginality of scholarship on immigrant women" (Gabaccia 1991:74). In other words, one legacy of the lively outpouring of multidisciplinary research on women has been misunderstanding, polarization, and the lack of any common ground, language, or research agenda. Neglect of the relationship between women and migration by many researchers and conflict over mode and unit of analysis by others suggests that a critical examination of the various theoretical frameworks and their implications for this study is much needed before proceeding. The need to draw explicit connections between migrating womens' personal and social origins, destinations, and destinies exists in the first instance and is made all the more complicated by a combination of omissions, misrepresentations, and false dichotomies in much of the migration literature.

Three fundamentally problematic trends have tended to characterize research on the role of women in the migration process, historically, as well as in contemporary international migrations. The sources of these analytical difficulties can be traced to certain, until recently unchallenged premises within general theories of international migration, starting with the central stereotyped assumption that the prototypical migrant was and continues to be a male breadwinner. Still problematic although no longer the dominant tendency, the role of women in international migration was sociologically invisible; women were excluded both from general theories of migration and historical-empirical research.[11] Of course, it is no longer the case that women are completely overlooked in the migration process. Rather, the analytical difficulties have increasingly become those which developed in the varying stages of their becoming visible. The second trend in research concerning women and migration was to recognize the category of "woman" simply as synonym for unproductive dependent, to consider women only within the framework of the family and, as with children, to acknowledge them merely as passive followers of "the real migrant," the male labor migrant or political exile. Finally, from the mid-1970s onwards, social scientists increasingly turned their attention to women. In an effort to redress past stereotypes, researchers, for the first time, discovered migrating women as important persons in their own right and produced a literature that centered on migrating women's wage labor. Some have even claimed that "the massive increase in the female labor force throughout the world is to a large extent the result of female migration" (Brettell and Simon 1986:4). While there has been widespread agreement on the importance of studying migrant women's purposive behavior, it seems legitimate to ask, following Morokvasic, "why [are] only the economically active women migrants . . . 'sociologisable' [considered worthy of sociological analysis]?" (Morokvasic 1983:14). In the otherwise praiseworthy attempt to correct previous omissions, migrating women have been reduced to genderless, cultureless units of labor power, as researchers liberated them from kinship, household, community and all other nonmarket relationships.

The source of women's invisibility, passivity, and reduction in the literature on migration is rooted in fundamental premises of widely held theoretical explanations for the dynamics and consequences of international migration, as well as in the nature and organization of the historical evidence. In particular, the invisibility of women's participation in population movements, termed "the world of our father's perspective," by historian Laura Anker Schwartz (1983:102), is as much a matter of the nature of the available evidence as it is of biased research questions. The concentration on evidence collected by the receiving state, particularly U.S. Immigration Commission records and census data, reveals little about the emigration process as one of gender selection. As a consequence, studies based on this evidence were unable to acknowledge or explain population movements dominated or pioneered by women, as in the cases of Irish women's migration to New York in the mid-nineteenth century, or Jamaican women's in the mid-twentieth (see Diner 1983; Rudd 1988; Foner 1985).

The roles and experiences of women left behind after the migration of fathers, husbands, and sons have similarly been overlooked until fairly recently. Rather than "left out" of migration, these women were simply located at one end of a global process. Some became temporary, even permanent, heads of households in their countries of origin. Although they worked at maintaining family property and status, thereby enabling the movement of men and, indirectly subsidizing the low and unsteady wages paid to the male members of their transnational households, their contributions have only recently been acknowledged in the migration literature. But other women left behind just as easily found themselves bound more firmly as subordinates in their own families of origin or in their missing husbands' families.[12]

Reliance on U.S. census and immigration records have similarly underestimated or excluded entirely much of immigrant women's paid work. In immigrant communities women's earnings in the home, whether in the form of wages from industrial homework or profits from small informal sector/family enterprises, were seldom reported to government investigators. Moreover, the existence, let aside the importance, of women's nonwaged domestic labor, whether performed in the country of origin or destination, whether combined with paid work or not, has been systematically neglected in U.S. government investigations of migration.

Thus, the areas where women's involvement in the migration process might have been discovered were precisely those omitted from government data collection, whose reports have traditionally served as the primary source of information about U.S. immigration history. At bottom, however, it has been the underanalyzed theoretical assumptions that bear most responsibility for guiding researchers to the particular bodies of evidence that have depicted migration as a flow of adult male breadwinners, and immigrant communities as primarily collectivities of fathers and sons.[13]

Migrating Women, Modernization, and Assimilation

The most widely held theoretical perspective on the dynamics of international migration, the push-pull/modernization model, together with complementary human capital and assimilationist approaches to immigrant outcomes, have contributed to and justified the study of migration from the vantage point of the receiving state. A central premise underlying these approaches holds that migration is primarily a matter of individual choice and a movement of unencumbered individuals. The individual, as the unit of analysis and source of the decision to move, is distanced from any constraining or facilitating social relationships, just as conditions in the sending country are analytically separated from those in the receiving society. Thus, the mass movement from eastern and southern Europe to the United States in the late nineteenth century is explained by means of a compilation of economic, political, and social disadvantages that prompted individuals to leave their homelands, and a separate calculation of advantages that pulled these individuals toward the United States (e.g., Thomas 1954). The social origins of immigrants are acknowledged only insofar as they appear, from time to time, as justifications for their subsequent "successes" or "failures" in the receiving society. In this case, origins or backgrounds are, in the language of the human capital model, translated as attributes of individuals, (i.e., Western male middle-class individuals) such as years of schooling, knowledge of English, or industrial experience. Sociologist Janet Abu-Lughod has described the push-pull model as follows: "Human beings, like iron filings, were impelled by forces beyond their conscious control and like atoms stripped of their cultural and temporal diversity, were denied creative capacity to innovate and shape the worlds from which and into which they moved" (Bach and Schraml 1982:323). Largely as a consequence of working within this framework, researchers had not seen it necessary to question or to rethink their reliance on evidence gathered nearly exclusively beside "the golden door" to the United States.

A popular variant of the push-pull migration model suggests that only those individuals who had been exposed to "modern Western values" and who thus could project themselves into the role of "Western man," had the ability to uproot themselves and migrate.[14] When this view is combined with the stereotyped assumptions of men as goal-directed risk takers and women as guardians of traditional culture and mothers of the future generation, the consequence was the near invisibility of women in population movements and their exclusion from analytic frameworks.

Once migrating women emerged from scholarly invisibility, analysis of their adaptation experiences quickly became entangled in the polarized debate between proponents of models based on cultural destruction, or uprooting, in contrast to those based on cultural continuity, or transplanting. Premised upon a traditional-modernity continuum and an assimilationist perspective, the model of cultural destruction posited that migration was accompanied by the breakdown of preindustrial values, cultural practices, and social structures. Because the ethos of individualism was more in keeping with the needs of a modern urban-industrial society, proponents of this view argued that most new immigrants eventually abandoned their old-world kinship and community loyalties.[15]

Advocates of the cultural uprooting thesis have had some difficulties, however, reconciling traditional gender stereotypes with women's migration patterns. When migrating women first emerged from scholarly invisibility the most widely held perspective explained their presence away as the dependent wife, mother, sister, and/or daughter of the prototypical breadwinning male migrant. Portrayed as passively following the decision maker out of the sending country, migrating women were not yet analyzed as individuals motivated by the same "modern" ambitions as men. Although many southern Italian and eastern European Jewish women did migrate as part of families, and this approach does recognize them, it fails by continuing to depict women as if they had been somehow untouched by modern social change prior to emigration.

Migrating women's lives have been typically analyzed only from the moment they entered the new world. They are assumed to have entered modern history just as they emerged from the hold of a ship with traditional values and practices unshaken; in other words, from point zero of individual subjectivity or group acculturation. Where it has become necessary for proponents of a push-pull/modernization approach to survey immigrant women's old-world backgrounds and identify those attributes that either promoted or retarded assimilation, contradictory stereotypes of race, gender, and class collude. The representation of immigrant women as passive accessories to an overarching process in which they were not fully engaged both reflects and contributes to their continued depiction as "victims" by researchers, as well as policymakers. Immigrant women have, on the one hand, been portrayed as dependent, saintly, sacrificing, secluded from the outside world, and subjugated completely to the will of a traditional male patriarch for whom they must bear untold numbers of children. At the same time, social reformers have defined immigrant women as "social problems" and "social projects." They have been alternatively characterized as unproductive, ignorant, crude, brash, and miserly matriarchs who struggled for total control over their households.[16]

Most frequently, immigrant women have been blamed for delaying Americanization and thus retarding the upward mobility of their families and ethnic communities. Although this approach no longer predominates as such, it has reemerged in a subtly assimilationist version of contemporary feminism, which promotes and measures immigrant women's empowerment by extent of paid employment, number of children, and method of child rearing. In one of the more recent attempts at writing a general history of immigrant women in America, *Foreign and Female*

(1986), Doris Weatherford begins her book with the following unfortunate claim:

> The word that most fittingly describes the immigrant woman's attitude toward her body, her life, and her world was *fatalism*. It was a European attitude, developed from long centuries of a class structure that wiped out the peasant who showed any signs of assertion. It was a woman's attitude, formed by aeons of submission to the men who controlled her life—and her body. The direct result was fecundity far greater than that of the average American woman. (Weatherford 1986:2)

In this example, the author has extracted migrating women from history and reconstructed their social origins on the basis of gender, race, and class stereotypes. An ideal typical immigrant woman is thus constructed and then represented as a complete tabula rasa upon arrival in the new world. The fact that a Russian-Jewish or southern Italian woman may have been a productive, responsible, and knowledgeable person in Europe for whom emigration was only one chapter in a broader and longer-term process of personal and social change cannot be acknowledged from within this theoretical model. Within the evolutionary schema of push-pull/modernization theory, the point of reference for evaluating the consequences of migration in women's lives is a static, unitary, and oppressive traditional society that stands in marked opposition to a modern, progressive, and enlightened new world. When viewed solely from within this perspective, how can migration be interpreted as anything other than liberating for women?

A variation of the "uprooting" thesis depicts the migration of women in the same individualistic or psycho-culturalist terms as modernization/assimilation theorists claimed for migrating men (Morokvasic 1983:14). In other words, the dynamics of women's migration is interpreted simply as the response of the so-called best individual women attempting to better themselves. In the otherwise praiseworthy effort to correct the passive "victim" and "social problem" bias and portray women as other than simply members of larger kin and family units, some studies have erred in another direction; in these, researchers have liberated migrating women nearly entirely from the nineteenth-century political, national/cultural, class, and kinship relations in which their lives were embedded. These studies stress the pursuit of self-interest in explaining women's migration. In so doing, the social relationships and networks that directly or indirectly prohibited, pro-moted, and/or organized gender-selective population movements have been disregarded.

For instance, in their introduction to *Jewish Grandmothers*, Sydelle Kramer and Jenny Masur discuss the immigrant women whose life histories they included in their book:

> They are not passive. None of the women in this book was con-tent to stay at home and do nothing. They pursued either educa-tion or a career and, by doing so, broke out of the ghetto of pas-sive domesticity for women. (1976:xv)

In recovering immigrant women's voices and acknowledging individual immigrant women as economically active protago-nists, the authors redressed a serious imbalance in the literature at that time and introduced important new methods. However, their interpretation of women's mass migration is still framed in terms of economically calculating individuals or atypically adven-turous women. Their possibly unavoidable error was to position and evaluate turn-of-the-century immigrant women's experiences in accordance with the cultural values and class interests of femi-nist scholars of the 1970s.[17]

In marked contrast to the cultural destruction model of immi-grant adaptation, proponents of cultural continuity attempted to counter the depiction of international migration as a process even-tuating always and for everyone in assimilation/Americanization and individualization/atomization. Revisionist social and labor his-torians argued that it was women in particular who preserved premigration cultural values and social structures, rather than allow them to fall victim to the disaggregating pressures of urban-industrial capitalism (e.g., Gutman 1976; Yans-McLaughlin 1977). Immigrant women were placed at the forefront of social change, in flexibly maintaining extended kinship networks and household economies from destruction by the dominant culture (Ewen 1985; Deutsch 1987; Weinberg 1988). In case after case, historians doc-umented the crucial role of kinship networks in the migration and settlement process and in the provision of housing, jobs, and other assistance in times of crisis. Some scholars also explored the link between the resilience of immigrant kinship systems and labor pro-test.[18]

Although the cultural persistence thesis is valuable insofar as it recovered the history of popular cultural autonomy and the nature of resistance to anonymous social and economic pressures, certain underanalyzed assumptions and dichotomies detract from its potential usefulness in explaining immigrant women's experiences. First, although advocates of this perspective acknowledge women as productive members of immigrant communities, the source of their resistance to disruptive social change is nevertheless based on an uncritical acceptance of a set of primordial oppositions between maleness and femaleness. These are presumed not only to have existed in preindustrial, "traditional," southern and eastern European societies, but to have been transported and transplanted fairly intact in urban-ethnic settings in the United States as well.

Particularly disturbing is the appearance here of the well-worn universal assumption that women's identity and behavior, unlike men's, is rooted in a sense of family obligation and loyalty. One analytic problem that arises from this is that the very same preindustrial value of family cooperation is called upon to do double duty as both explanation for a woman's entry into the wage-earning labor force and for her retention in the home as a nonwaged worker in the service of her family.[19] Alternative conceptualizations of mothering and women's roles in families as dynamic social constructions, formed and transformed by individuals interacting and negotiating with each other and with broader political and economic forces in historically specific contexts, still needs to be made part of this theoretical approach.[20]

Some proponents of the cultural continuity model have explained the presence of "familial consciousness" among immigrants by emphasizing traits supposedly natural to women (Cornelisen 1976:155). Other perspectives focus on the attributes of a static preindustrial culture, in which women are more visibly embedded than men (Banfield 1958). Patricia Pessar, in an early article quite uncharacteristic of her later work, inadvertently managed to combine both problems. In an otherwise useful analysis on "The Role of Gender in Dominican Settlement in the United States," Pessar stated:

> By contrast [to men], women's identity is firmly rooted in the household. Even as a "bird of passage," the woman may be metaphorically compared to an actual bird which carries in its genetic make-up the capacity and proclivity to construct a nest wherever it goes. As part of her cultural programming the Dominican woman transports the values and roles associated with the home wherever she settles. (1986:276)

The link between femaleness and familial consciousness appears to have survived the transition from one theoretical framework to another, rather than becoming itself a subject for sociological and historical inquiry.

A second source of difficulty with the way the cultural continuity model has depicted women's part in international migration concerns its tendency to romanticize immigrant preindustrial practices and structures (e.g., Bodnar 1985). Overemphasis on the resourcefulness and inventiveness of new immigrants in adapting old-world kinship, household, and cultural patterns to new-world settings has obscured the extent to which these same "family survival strategies" could impose severe limitations on the ability of migrating women to "become persons," subjects of their own lives. Immigrant families and households may have survived the journey to industrial capitalism, and their preindustrial cultural values may have aided in this and even, at times, served as an instrument of resistance, but often only at very great cost to individual family members. The resilience or, more likely, the reconstitution of ethnic and kinship solidarities could facilitate employment and upward mobility for some individuals, but it could more than likely subject the less-powerful members of the same family or community to high degrees of exploitation, as in the "ethnic economy."[21] Women, in particular, were often the ones to forfeit opportunities for schooling and meaningful employment; they frequently delayed marriages, gave up the chance for a free-choice marriage, or conversely were coerced into marriages against their will when kinship obligations and cultural loyalties left few or no alternatives. Late twentieth-century desires for a more "collective consciousness" should not be permitted to invent a past that obscures the systematic power inequalities that were a part of so many pre- and postmigration practices. Women's own varied understandings of their migration and settlement experiences have needed to be included and analyzed as part of the historical record.

A third analytical difficulty with the direction taken by advocates of cultural continuity in immigrant history became cause, in part, for the emergence of an alternative theoretical framework. Critics of "the new social history" charged it with "photographing the positive aspects of the culture of the oppressed with a focus too close to show the framework: the prison bars" (Gordon 1986b:24).

Migrating Women and the
Global Development of Capitalism

Many social scientists in the 1970s and 1980s began to situate the study of international migration within research on the global development of capitalism, in response to both the excessive individualism of the push-pull/human capital/assimilation perspectives and the overemphasis on "agency," "resistance," and "cultural autonomy" in the preindustrial continuity model. Writing about women in the migration process at this time, Anthony Leeds argued that "the emphasis on the individual and internalized norms and personal motivations . . . tends to obscure socially determined strategies . . . in individual and group action within social-structural contexts" (1976:69). Henceforth, the central unit of analysis in an emerging alternative macroframework for migration research was shifted upward from the individual (and the aggregate of his/her decisions) to the social structures and processes of an overarching global economic system. More precisely, proponents of a historical-structural, or world-systems approach, conceptualized "migration as part of the routine activities of a single unified economic system" (Portes and Walton 1981:59). Rather than a one-way transfer of individuals between separate and unevenly developed nation states, world-systems theory recast international migration as part of the ongoing circulation of resources, both capital and labor, within the boundaries of a single global division of labor, that is between a dominant core and a dependent periphery (Sassen-Koob 1980b, 1981, 1988). Advocates of this approach placed emphasis on the exploitative nature of the relationship between sending and receiving countries in international migration.

From this perspective, scholars committed themselves to the task of analyzing the structural origins of constraints that faced members of laboring classes in peripheral societies, as potential migrants. Utilizing the conceptual language of "political economy," researchers linked migration to large-scale social structures and long-term processes in the global accumulation of capital, for example, development and underdevelopment, international division of labor, world labor market, split or dual labor markets, reserve army of labor, class formation.[22]

The most important distinguishing feature of international migration "since the advent of capitalism and especially during the last 150 years" is, according to this approach, its identification as a "migration of *labor*," that is of individuals whose purpose in moving is to sell their work capacity in the receiving areas. For Portes and Walton, as for other proponents of this perspective, "the historical function of immigration has been to provide a source of cheap labor" (1981:21, 56).

A historical-structural or world-systems approach to international migration has, however, been applied predominantly to the analysis of post–World War II population flows from Third World peripheries and semiperipheries to core regions of the world-economy. Very little work within this general perspective has been directed toward historical analysis of the turn-of-the-century mass migrations from eastern and southern Europe to the Americas.[23]

A world-systems perspective considerably broadened the conventional limits of migration scholarship by focusing on longer-term larger-scale social change. Where migration was typically looked at from the viewpoint and interests of an individual receiving society in the push-pull and assimilationist perspectives, the historical-structural approach observed the process through a lens singularly focused on the functions of geographically circulating labor for the developing capitalist world-economy. Viewing the large-scale upsurge of transnational migration at the end of the nineteenth century from the vantage point of the modern world-system dramatically highlighted the expansion of the capitalist world-economy and the increased pressures for the further commodification and proletarianization of labor. It also revealed the reorganization of the global division of labor, as the United States, in the process of becoming a core zone, drew nearly 26.5 million new immigrant arrivals between 1880 and 1924 (U.S. Census, His. Stat., 1960:62).

By interpreting population flows as part of long-term economic transformations within a single interdependent global division of labor, rather than as a transfer between two distinct and unrelated political units, the world-systems approach managed to circumvent some of the more tenacious conceptual polarizations that traditionally characterized the study of immigration. By making the mode of incorporation into the world-economy of migrant-sending regions a central question of research, this perspective drew attention to migration as both a reflection of and a response to earlier and ongoing transformations in the nature of global economic, social, and political relations. But most important of all, it made it possible to analyze the backgrounds or social origins of migrants as dynamic and flexible arrangements within a broader context of social relations and social change.

In the context of a discussion on post–World War II Mexican and Cuban migration to the United States, Portes and Bach offered a succinct description of a historical-structural approach:

> Large-scale migrations always reflect the internal structure and political and economic dynamics of the sending nations. Such internal processes do not occur in isolation, however, but are themselves influenced by the position of the country in an over-arching world system. Both the internal origins of migrations and the countries to which they are directed are deeply conditioned by such global relations. Chances of individual economic success are similarly dependent on the migrants' correct assessment of these relations as they determine changing modes of reception in the host societies. (1985:74–75)

But, if a historical-structural perspective enlarged the scope of explanation, corrected some stereotypes, and avoided certain conceptual difficulties, it may have inadvertently reproduced some of the problems of previous models, insofar as women's part in migration is concerned. First, this approach has, with few exceptions, failed to include the perspective of migrating women themselves, either as a group or as individuals attempting to understand and respond to the changing circumstances of their lives.[24] Given the origin of the historical-structural alternative in a context of opposition to the individualism of human capital, push-pull, and assimilation theories, it is perhaps understandable, if not predictable, that the individual by definition would be disregarded.

But, as Bach and Schraml pointed out in an effort to both critique and build upon a world-systems analysis of migration, the polarization between individual agency and global structure has been a major obstacle to reconceptualizing the migration process.

> No longer metal pieces, migrants are now treated more like empty grocery carts, wheeled back and forth between origin and destination under the hungry intentions of world capital. The migrants themselves engage in very little action. Rather, they are mere "agents" of social change, carrying the necessary attributes of labor to satisfy the abstract requirements of "the general law of capitalist accumulation." (1982:324)

In short, the historical-structural alternative may only have successfully countered the conventional, but inaccurate, depiction of the individual migrant as some sort of unimpeded free trader in labor power on the world market, by replacing it with an equally unsatisfactory portrayal of the migrant as an empty bottle tossed by the hand of capital into the migration stream and left to bob from shore to shore. Without connecting broader structural relationships—viewed both as opportunities and constraints—with the collective and individual agency of migrants, there is little chance of understanding how migration is organized, by whom, for whom, or what its varied consequences are for *all* those involved.

Women's presence in the migration process was first recognized by historical-structural and world-systems theorists within the context of efforts to redress the unproductive polarization between individual agency and structural determinism (Wood 1982; Pessar 1982). While still relying on structural analyses for their capacity to delineate the overarching international and national arrangements that led to patterned population movements from one region to another, many researchers started to search for "more refined explanations of the nature of migration," and to identify the "mediating social units between structural factors and individual decision making" that made migration possible (Pessar 1982). For sociologist Patricia Pessar, "immigration is foremost a household initiative . . . a strategy whereby household members seek to establish a fit between the material and social resources at the group's disposal . . . , the consumption needs of its members, and the alternatives for productive activity" (1985:1203). This model predicted migration only "when the household is unable to maintain the desired level of income despite the strategies adopted, or when viable alternatives to improve its condition exist elsewhere (net of the cost of migration)" (Wood 1982:314).

Initially, researchers interested in the significance of households in the migration process borrowed heavily from the stereotypical association between women and this domain. Yet, at the same time however, they also responded to the outpouring of feminist challenges to traditional family sociology, and to the discovery of women's nonwaged contributions to the social reproduction of working-class families. Against this background, it is in some sense understandable that when women became visible in a world-systems approach to migration, they were reduced to the role of working contributors of mostly nonwaged but also low-waged labor to a "household income pooling unit," or "collective income fund" (Smith, Wallerstein, and Evers, eds. 1984; Friedman 1984; Pessar 1982, 1985, 1986).

From the standpoint of understanding women's part in migration, the literature on the relationship between household structures and migration has tended to reproduce more of the same analytical problems. First, historical-structural approaches, and world-systems theory in particular, have tended to reduce women's part in migration to their economic functions, generally as producers of nonwage income, renewing or reproducing the low-waged labor of the prototypical male migrant. Second, the impact of unequal power relations, hierarchical gender relations, and unstable interdependencies *within* households on women's experiences of migration has been analytically neglected. Finally, households have rarely been linked to other key social relationships involving women that help to organize migration, such as friendships, ethnic communities, and local political networks.[25]

However essential a global perspective is to understanding the relation between migration and women's status, reductionist interpretations that analyze migration only as an economic phenomenon, or depict immigrant women's experiences only with regard to their role in social reproduction, or discount systemic hierarchical relations based on nationality/race/ethnicity and gender merely repeat the unproductive polarizations of previously discussed approaches.

Although historical-structural and world-systems theorists have acknowledged that a global perspective must include ideological, cultural, social, and political dimensions, most work of this nature remains highly abstract and little has been done on migration directly.[26] In particular, the comprehension of race, nationality, and ethnicity as analytically distinct and flexible constructions of "peoplehood," or status-groups, embedded in the development of historical capitalism but not reducible to class, can be especially useful to the study of transnational migration. Rethinking such as this has the potential to provide crucial insight into the global forces that have shaped the meanings and expectations by which immigrant women oriented themselves in the world and related to others. However, analysis of women's international migration requires more historically grounded investigation into the ways in which the discourses and practices of gender, nationality/race/ethnicity, and class *together* structured population movements and recomposed individual and collective identities in a global system.

CONCLUSION:
GENDER AND NATIONALITY/RACE/ETHNICITY
TRAVEL TOGETHER

The study of turn-of-the-century migration of southern and eastern European women to the United States can be a window on how the expansion of the capitalist world-economy and the industrial development of a core region was accomplished through the interacting processes of proletarianization, racialization, and the social construction of gender. But, the primary objective of this book is to analyze the meanings and outcomes that migration and resettlement held for eastern European Jewish and southern Italian women. How did immigrant women explain and respond to the contradictions of expanded possibilities, to the promise of autonomy and freedom from constraints in a new world, on the one hand, and on the other hand, to the pressures to (re)constitute them as subordinates in family and household systems, ethnic communities, the labor market, and American society at large? What were the attitudes and actions directed towards migrating women by political authorities in both sending and receiving states, by kin and other household members, by coethnics, by employers, and by social reformers? What were the patterns of immigrant women's responses to the disruptions, opportunities, and ambiguities of social change?

To discover the meanings migration held for women it is as necessary to view them as historical agents and reflective thinkers as it is to contextualize their experiences within hierarchically organized households, communities, and broader global structures and processes. As this chapter has demonstrated, accomplishing these tasks demands cognizance of the analytical difficulties and unproductive polarizations of previous theoretical frameworks. But it also requires borrowing from their insights and, at the same time, moving beyond them.

Understanding women's experiences of migration means transcending the exclusive focus on *either* cultural *or* economic explanations, and *either* individual/micro *or* structural/macro levels of analysis. This means avoiding the ahistorical individualism and "psychoculturalism" of the push-pull and assimilation approaches. The development of an alternative framework for interpreting migration requires moving beyond the aridity of an unpeopled political economy of migration and restoring a sense of analytical holism, multidimensionality, and ambiguity that has been ignored in much research on transnational population movements.

It is not simply a matter of adding additional variables to the mix or, more precisely, gender, race, nationality, and ethnicity to gender-free and race-blind models of migration. What is required is to reconceptualize migration and to construct a framework that recognizes the multiple, coexisting, often contradictory, and shifting social relationships that join an individual to households, to communities, and to workforces.

It is vitally important to develop a way of understanding sociologically the meaning of migration within individual women's lives and the impact of human agency in making migration history without caricaturing the immigrant as either heroine or victim. If immigrant women were limited by macrostructural constraints and pressures, by their given social circumstances, by the relations, institutions, and ideas of their time, they were simultaneously part of the world; and whether through acquiescence, accommodation, subversion, or resistance their beliefs and behaviors surely changed it.

An analysis of the processes, outcomes, and meanings of transnational migration in the late nineteenth and early twentieth centuries needs to be wide enough in vision and multidimensional enough in scope to weave these distinctive themes, levels of analysis, and points of view together in a more productive relationship.

The extent and nature of empowerment that migrating women experienced depended largely on their changing places in the global reconfiguration of gender, class, and national/racial/ethnic relations occurring at the turn of the century. Thus, their status in the United States was not simply shaped by their individual ambitions and skills nor their degree of malleability but rather in accord with their treatment by and responses to historically gendered, classed, and racialized contexts of departure and reception. I turn next to developing an understanding of the context of departure for Russian-Jewish women and how it shaped the patterns of their migration and their experiences and outcomes in the United States.

CHAPTER 2

"Why Did We Have to Leave?":
The Shifting Patterns
of Jewish Women's Lives in Russia
at the Turn of the Century

People in my village—the Jews, not the peasants—started to talk
about immigrating around 1910 . . . Sometimes I'm sorry we ever
left that village. I say to myself, "Why did we have to leave such a
heavenly place?" I forget what happened in the middle, and all the
reasons. All I see is the beautiful forests, the river, and when we were
running around, and all the good things, all the food that we had.
                                                            —Minnie Fisher[1]

"I know there was poverty in the shtetl, Mama." My voice speaks
these words calmly as if they were facts. "I know that I can't easily
explain the nostalgia I feel for that vanished world" . . . "What we—
my generation—long for, grew up in the shtetl in spite of hunger and
dust; a sacred dimension to daily life, which held its own alongside
the terror and violence." For a moment, she says nothing. I have the
curious sensation that I have spoken in some strange tongue that is
incomprehensible to her. But then, clearing her throat, she says,
"This is a different shtetl than the one I knew. Or maybe," she whis-
pers, and a look of great weariness comes into her eyes, "maybe I
have forgotten."
                                                            —Kim Chernin[2]

Migration disrupts the meaning attached to *home*, both for the
immigrant generation and for us, their descendents. Each, then,
struggles to reinvest the home with meaning, the home in the
present, and the home in memory.

We pictured them as the persecuted mothers of "huddled
masses," as the bearers of too many children, as appendages of
their fathers and husbands, as victims of their patriarchal and

stagnant homelands. We learned of them, in contrast, as prostitutes "imported for immoral purposes," as rebellious factory girls, as social problems for the country that received them. As their children and grandchildren, some of us embraced them nostalgically with the warm images and symbols of an idealized family, protectively embedded in an organic ethnic community, breaking bread together at a traditional feast. But hardly did we know them as competent and sturdy young women who worked responsibly to transform their environment into a place in which they and others might feel comfortable and safe; or as once-abandoned wives, mothers, and daughters of whom some not only made do, but did well, as skilled artisans, operators of small businesses, social activists, storytellers, and writers. Hardly did we consider those who became materially and emotionally impoverished as a consequence of absorbing the pressures of prejudice and discrimination. Rarely, and this is the root of the problem, have we thought of them as individual participants in a changing world-system, interpreting and improvising their lives against shifting economic, political, and social contexts.

How do we make sense of this variegated portrayal of immigrant women's lives? Which parts of it are true? If it is accurate, as is commonly believed, that the great emigration of Jews out of eastern Europe was the unambiguous result of religious persecution (pogroms) and the accompanying economic devastation, how then are Minnie Fisher's warm memories of a life of plenty to be explained? Can Kim Chernin's present-day longings be satisfied by projecting them onto "that vanished world"? Daydreaming aloud, Chernin imagines herself walking through muddy streets in a Russian shtetl of the early twentieth century: "I carry heavy books beneath my arm; around the corner is a study house." Abruptly, her immigrant mother interrupts her (re)vision of the old world. "You are a woman. Don't you understand? In that world, you think you would have become a scholar?" (Chernin 1983:28). Who exactly were the women and girls that peopled the shtetl landscape, some of whom eventually migrated to America? What was the nature of their backgrounds, the structure of their households and communities, their experiences of work, family, gender, and ethnicity in Europe? Which parts of Russia did they leave, and why? How was it that they came to settle in the United States?

Figure 2.
The Kaufman family poses for a photo in the village of Vasalevitch in Minsk, Russia, 1910, seven years before Sadie, age 17, and her father migrated to America. Courtesy of the Stein family.

WOMEN'S PREMIGRATION BACKGROUNDS:
MISSING PIECES

Understanding women's experiences of migration and establishing the ways that migration to America affected their status requires exploration into specific aspects of their identities and backgrounds in Europe. The questions posed previously help identify the contexts, relations, and characteristics that lay at the source of women's migration and that bear a significant degree of responsibility for their subsequent destinies as immigrants in the United States. This chapter explores the ways that Russian-Jewish women's immigration experiences were shaped, not merely by the American contexts in which they resumed their lives, but in important ways by both an overarching world-system and by the European contexts and social relations in which their lives were deeply embedded.

Which were the particular contexts and social relationships in migrating women's European backgrounds likely to be most influential for their subsequent fates as immigrants in the United States? To fully answer this question it is necessary to briefly reencounter and reformulate certain assumptions of the two dominant frameworks of immigrant adaptation: first, those rooted within an assimilation perspective and, second, those based on a historical-structural approach.

With a focus on individual abilities and motivations, or human capital "resources," researchers working within the assimilationist traditions in general argue that the degree and/or rapidity of immigrant social and economic adaptation is dependent primarily upon the quality of the resources the individual or group arrives with or acquires in the process of resettlement. The assumption is that immigrants who receive less than equal socioeconomic outcomes, with respect to an established native-born majority, have entered the host society with inferior skills and qualifications.

The attributes or resources that assimilationists generally consider most fundamental are Western or "modern" cultural orientations, occupational skills and labor force experience, and education and knowledge of English. Their expectations are for a gradual but linear diffusion of modern values and attributes that will eventuate in a merging of identities and social positions between immigrants and natives. That is to say, assimilationist models would predict an ultimately positive relationship between migration and women's status; migrating women can expect to experience more, rather than less, self-determination and economic leverage in the receiving country. Interestingly, the dominance of the assimilationist model among researchers has been so great that even its sharpest critics suggest that while it fails at analyzing the experiences of colonized or racial minorities in the U.S., it more or less accurately describes and explains the historical experience of all European immigrants in the United States, including presumably Russian Jews and Italians (Glenn 1986:12–13; Omi and Winant 1986:14–24).

The strongest challenges of the assimilationist frameworks have emerged from the historical-structural schools of thought (e.g., internal colonialism, split or segmented labor market, dual economy theories). These groups of researchers generally deemphasize the role of immigrant origins/backgrounds in shaping life chances, whether in the form of national or regional origins or in terms of individual attributes. Instead, they prefer to focus upon the structure of unequal economic opportunities open to immigrants and their hostile reception by the institutions of dominant groups in the host society. The origin and social composition of particular migrant flows, as well as the experiences and socioeconomic consequences for immigrants are thus explained, most of all, by the dynamics of labor market forces and relations in the receiving country, the United States, rather than in the sending region. The expectation that follows from this position is that of continued subordination, if not greater exploitation, of immigrant women who were pulled out of Europe by the demand for cheap labor in the United States.

This book, based on a synthesis of feminist and historical-structural theories, published and unpublished documents, historical studies, immigrant memoirs, letters, and autobiographical fiction, makes the contrasting claim that it is rather the interplay between immigrant women's personal and social backgrounds and the political, economic, and cultural structures of the host society that is key to understanding women's subsequent experiences in the United States. Both the assimilation and historical-structural schools of thought are seriously limited by a tendency for each to see only a singular sequence of immigrant adaptation; this tunnel vision has precluded giving due attention to the full diversity of paths and outcomes followed by immigrants. The full variety of migration patterns can be illuminated only if we start to focus on and reinterpret neglected aspects of immigrants' backgrounds; that is, the specific political, economic, and social conditions under which a particular immigrant group leaves its country of origin, and the interplay between the class, racial/ethnic, and gender dimensions of the specific immigrant flows. At the same time, we must be attentive to the varying nature of the reception that confronts new immigrants, that is, the stances of the host government, major employers, the dominant population, and the preexisting coethnic community.

Chapters 2 and 3 begin examination of the relation between women's migration and status by developing and employing an alternative framework through which the importance and meaning of personal and social origins may be demonstrated. Without a clear understanding of how migrating women's personal and social origins have been woven into their American destinations, we would be unable to evaluate the extent to which continuity and/or change, subordination and/or empowerment characterized women's immigration experiences. In short, I begin by redefining and relocating the backgrounds of immigrant women and girls in economic, political, and social relationships that sometimes transcended not only their individual capacities but also the respective boundaries of sending and receiving states in a world-system. This analytical step constitutes one of the necessary preconditions for connecting women's European backgrounds to their life chances and self-identities in the United States.

Women's migration from Russia and Italy to the United States was structured within the context of three intersecting sets of hierarchical relationships. It is within the context of these stratified yet by no means static relations that women's personal and social backgrounds are reexamined and redefined.

First, migrating women are located within the context of changing economic relationships in the nineteenth-century world-economy, as they affected Russia and Italy. Processes of economic development in these regions and their changing connections to the world-economy reshaped the material resources and economic opportunities available across classes and social groups and gave rise to migrant flows with distinctive social compositions. That is to say, the gender composition of particular migrant flows, the age, marital status, life-cycle stage, ethnicity, as well as the occupational and social-class distribution of migrants, can all be linked, at some point, to economic transformations, which predisposed women to certain patterned outcomes as immigrants in the United States. To take this analytical step, however, necessitates transforming those background attributes that have traditionally indicated economic position—social class and occupation—into categories that have real meaning for the experiences of turn-of-the-century women and girls in eastern and southern Europe. Economic change is thus reformulated to encompass also the transformations in unpaid work that bound women as individuals to families, households, and ethnic communities. Similarly, changes in other important but traditional indicators of economic position, such as education, literacy, and skill, are broadened to include the socially undervalued and invisible training girls received since early childhood, often from female kin, in skills appropriate to culturally specific communities.

The second set of stratifying forces that encompassed and structured migrating women's backgrounds consisted of a variety of political relationships. The politics of emigration (attitudes and policies) in Russia and Italy at the end of the nineteenth century reflected not only changing domestic relations but, to a great extent, the changing framework of interstate relations in a world-economy. Russian and Italian emigration policies directly determined which social groups (primarily by class, ethnicity, and nationality) were forbidden, allowed, or even pressured to leave. Similarly, U.S. immigration policies directly shaped the social composition of newcomers, by means of the criteria through which individuals were grouped, categorized, and then selectively allowed or denied entry. Indirectly, political decisions made in Russia and Italy, but deeply conditioned by each country's position in an overarching world-economy, concerning land reform, industrialization, and so forth, promoted migration for particular social groups by constraining their local income-producing opportunities.

The third and most important, but most problematic, set of stratifying relationships that organized women's migration to the United States was comprised of the multitude of social and cultural ties that bound women to communities, families, households, kinship and ethnic groups. These social ties are examined from two angles. First, emerging and evolving as part of the exigencies of the migration process, migrants commonly developed and/or relied on various forms of transnational social support mechanisms. Numerous studies on household income pooling, chain migration, social networks, and ethnic economies have demonstrated the significance of these social and cultural linkages in providing not only resources for the early survival of immigrants but also, in some cases, facilitating considerable, if not rapid, economic mobility for the group in the receiving country.[3] From the angle of social support mechanisms, these linkages have been of great value in explaining the social composition of any particular flow, its direction, duration, and patterns of return migration.

But, until fairly recently, a blindspot has persisted in most analyses of immigrant social and economic networks. Both assimilationists and historical-structuralists, in their respective discussions of "cultural orientations" and "ethnic economies," had neglected to question the extent to which these social networks may have originated in and were sustained by intragroup class, gender, and ethnic hierarachies. This analytic gap is, in part, related to the tendency in both schools of thought to see ethnic solidarities or cultural ideologies in essentialist terms, that is as internally homogeneous and fixed traits rooted in primordial group affinities rather than as fragmented, dynamic, fluid, and reactive social relations among group members and in relation to others.[4] Such assumptions have lent themselves too easily to celebrating or blaming unified and universal "Jewish" or "Italian" ideas about women, men, and families for the outcome of migration.

To move beyond simple racial/ethnic and gender contrasts in accounting for women's experiences of migration, we need to change some of the questions we have been asking. The blindspot created by the invisibility of social conflict and intragroup divisions in thinking about cultural orientations and ethnic connections has only lately been acknowledged in research on contemporary immigrant communities. In a recent study of Vietnamese-American families, sociologist Nazli Kibria critiques the tendency "to ignore or downplay the internal fissures of immigrant life"; she asks "do all members participate and benefit in the same way from immigrant institutions?" (Kibria 1993:21). Parminder Bhachu takes this critique of the imagined immigrant/ethnic community a step further in her research on South Asian women in Britain. For Bhachu, the blindspot in scholarship has been the inability to see immigrant women as "active negotiators of the cultural values that they choose to accept," or as "cultural entrepreneurs who are actively engaging with their cultural frameworks, whilst continuously transforming them" (Bhachu 1993:101). What remains is to apply these recent insights in research to the historical and comparative study of migrating women. As a start, scholars might cease asking, for example, how Jewish or Italian cultural values and practices affected the outcome of migration for women. In contrast to such questions, I suggest we ask more pointedly how the interplay of racial/ethnic, gender, and class ideologies and hierarchies were implicated in the very formation and structure of the networks that may have enabled or sometimes obstructed the migration of women. Only then can a question comparing outcomes between and among Italian and Jewish women's experiences of these cultural networks be asked. Cultural affinity, as the basis for forming and transforming migration networks of support and exchange, is thus reframed here to cast a critical spotlight on its own development within class-, ethnic-, and gender-stratified regions of immigrant origin.

The ideas and practices of turn-of-the-century social inequalities intersected and influenced the treatment of women and girls in both sending and receiving countries and shaped their behaviors and self-definitions. Certainly, in one sense, the personal destinies of immigrant women like Minnie Fisher and Rose Chernin (Kim Chernin's mother) evolved out of their own individual responses to the push and shove of immediate exigencies and the family relations in which they were enmeshed. But, in a broader sense, their fates as individuals derived from their responses to their positions within social collectivities like nation states, classes, households, racial/ethnic and gender groups. These statuses fundamentally shaped their social identities and life chances. It was, furthermore, these social relationships and interdependencies that joined them to an overarching world-system.

The position of Russia, Italy, and the United States in the global division of labor and interstate rivalries of the mid- to late nineteenth century set the broad historical parameters within which women's migration occurred. Changes in these global hierarchical relationships had reverberating effects on the internal dynamics of sending states, communities, and households, the social units that ultimately released some women and girls from their preexisting obligations and responsibilities and influenced their selection of destination. In other words, it was the interplay between global economic and political pressures and local social networks that translated a propensity for many to emigrate from the peripheries of Europe into actual immigration to the United States for only some. This chapter initiates discussion on the extent to which and on the ways women's involvement in these economic, political, and social relationships ultimately preserved, diminished, and/or transformed their status as immigrants in the United States. This reconceptualization of Russian-Jewish and Italian immigrant women's backgrounds, including discussion of their own perceptions, represents the context for the further analysis of their life chances in the United States.

BEING JEWISH AND FEMALE
IN THE PALE OF SETTLEMENT

Subjects within a World-System

Until the successive partitions of Poland (1772, 1793, 1795) relatively few Jews lived within the Russian Empire. But by 1897, according to the Russian Census, Jews in the Empire numbered more than five million. Although they constituted half of world Jewry at the time, they amounted to but little more than 4 percent of Russia's population. Yet, late nineteenth-century Russia seemed preoccupied, if not consumed, with the fate of its national minorities. Russian policy confined most Jews to the "Pale," and except for certain classes, prohibited Jews from entering the interior of the country. The territory of the Pale included the fifteen western districts of Russia and the ten districts of Russian Poland; in other words, less than 20 percent of European Russia, or about 4 percent of the entire Russian Empire. Although 94 percent of all Russian Jews lived in the Pale, even within this restricted territory, they comprised only 11.6 percent, or about one-ninth of the entire population (Rubinow [1907] 1975:488,490–91).[5]

Jewish women's emigration was neither outside of nor marginal to the trajectory of Russian history, but was embedded in the principle economic and political transformations of the Empire. For Jewish women, as for Jewish men, migration to America represented opportunities to solve problems that had become increasingly insoluble at home, such as avoiding an iminent but unsatisfactory marriage or making an acceptable marriage or contributing more towards the support of a household, rather than any invidious economic comparisons between the two countries. And yet, while the immediate problems they faced may have, on the surface, seemed generated by processes internal to Russia, in reality, many had been induced by the gradual expansion of a global economic system. The initial point of departure, then, for an investigation into the historical-structural processes that disrupted Jewish women's lives and led so many out of the Pale of Settlement, must be with the economic and political impact of the western European core states on their eastern European peripheries during "the long nineteenth century," that is, from the 1780s through 1917 (Berend and Ranki 1982:7).

The relationship of these large-scale and long-term stratifying processes to the mass migration of Russian Jews, and of Jewish women in particular, seems often abstract and indirect. However, Russian-Jewish women experienced quite tangibly the ramifications of these forces through three interacting domains: in the increasingly restrictive Russian state policies concerning ethnic and national minorities on the western borderlands; in the acceleration of class differentiation and conflict among Russian Jews and between Jews and peasants; and in the shifting obligations and responsibilities of Jewish women and men in households and workplaces. The intersection of these trends significantly influenced the timing, composition, and motivations constituting Jewish women's migration to the United States.

Poland, between the sixteenth and seventeenth centuries, had been incorporated as a periphery in the ongoing global divisioning of labor, but Russia remained external to these stratifying relations until the world-economy expanded again in the mid-nineteenth century. By 1850 Russia had been effectively incorporated and peripheralized (Wallerstein 1989:134, 184). The consequence, according to economic historians, Berend and Ranki, of these long-term large-scale processes, incorporation and peripheralization, was "not only a division of labor that tended to confirm these countries in their subordinate position as backward economies, but also the development of economic ties which necessarily initiated also processes promoting capitalist transformation" (Berend and Ranki 1982:18).[6]

After 1750, the trade of rapidly industrializing Britain and France, the two major centers of the world-economy at the time, expanded significantly in volume and velocity into eastern Europe (Wallerstein 1989:138). With an insatiable hunger, western Europe drew to itself whatever food and raw materials eastern

Europe could produce. Not only did Russia's trade with western Europe dramatically increase in volume but it changed in composition as well; primary products constituted 95 percent of its exports by 1850, with hemp and flax in especially high demand by British and French manufacturing industries (Wallerstein 1989: 141–42). As of 1860, 89 percent of Russia's work force was engaged in agriculture and only 7 percent in industry (Berend and Ranki 1982:17). When Britain's technological innovations led to the decline of Russia's small iron export industry early in the nineteenth century, Russia, already in the grip of the world-economy, responded to the steady rise in world market prices for wheat; wheat thus replaced iron (Wallerstein 1989:142; Grossman 1973:488). By 1910 the peasantries of the eastern European peripheries were providing about one-fifth of the world export of foodstuffs and raw materials; most was directed to markets in western Europe but also to the United States and Scotland (Morawska 1989:240; Wallerstein 1989:142).

Western Europe's increased demand for agricultural products went hand in hand with its growing interest in eastern Europe as a market for its rapidly expanding industrial exports and as a locale for capital investment (Berend and Ranki 1982:25). Russia was not a disinterested partner in this exchange. Desirous of modern industrial and transportation materials and techniques as a means of shoring up its position among the Great Powers, especially after its humiliating defeat in the Crimean War (1854–55), the Imperial government opened its doors ever wider to foreign trade and investment in the 1860s and 1870s (Berend and Ranki 1982:27, 40, 70).

During the final decade of the nineteenth century, Russia embarked on an even more ambitious crash industrialization program. The implementation of this "state-guided industrialization" strategy involved heavy government financing for railroads, subsidies to private industrialists, high protective tariffs for Russian heavy industries and mines, increased exports, and increased encouragement to foreign investors (Skocpol 1979:91). Between 1870 and World War I roughly one-fifth of all western European capital investments found their way to the eastern European periphery (Morawska 1989:239). Among the chief capital exporters to Imperial Russia were France, leading with 33 percent of the total, followed by Britain with 23 percent, and Belgium, with 20 percent (Grossman 1973:492). Foreign investments were especially concentrated in the construction of a railway transportation network, the production of iron and steel, and mining (Berend and Ranki 1982:79–86; Morawska 1989:240). This industrial program may be considered a qualified success; during the 1890s industrial growth in Russia averaged 8 percent per year, and 6 percent per year between 1906 and 1913 (Skocpol 1979:91). Between 1860 and 1910 the gross national product of the Russian Empire grew threefold, and by 1913 industrial production comprised 28 percent of its national income, due in large part to the significant foreign investment (Morawska 1989:240).

The industrial growth and economic development taking place in Russia during this period was, however, linked to and dependent on the requirements of the western European core powers; it was, in other words, the growth of a peripheral zone in the world-economy. To help finance expenditures and investments, above and beyond the massive foreign investments, the Imperial government depended on a combination of increased taxes and foreign loans brokered in Germany, England, and France. By 1913, Russia was the second largest debtor nation in the world, but first in amount of payments per year to service the debt (Skocpol 1979:93).

Agricultural productivity, meanwhile, stagnated and international prices for grain dropped. Famines were widespread in the country in 1891. Russian economic development was so closely tied to foreign finance that when, in 1899–1900, the western European money markets contracted, Russian industry immediately plunged into a far deeper crisis than the recession in western European industry (Skocpol 1979:91, 93). At the start of the nineteenth century, the per capita GNP of eastern Europe was 65 percent of that produced in the West, by 1860 it had dropped to 61 percent, and by 1910, to 58 percent (Morawska 1989:241; Berend and Ranki 1982:15–16; Skocpol 1979:94). As eastern Europe began to shift to the rhythms of the world-economy, the inequities between it and the core states of western Europe intensified.

If Russia was developing as a periphery during these years, then Russian-Poland, as a major part of the Pale, was becoming "a politically subordinate semiperiphery of the periphery" (Morawska 1989:244). Although, when compared to the rest of the Russian Empire, Russian Poland was considerably more urbanized and industrialized, it was heavily dependent on both western European capital and Russian political interests. At the turn of the century, these foreign investors owned 40 percent of all industrial capital, 25 percent of all factories, and 60 percent of the value of gross industrial production and total assets of major Polish banks. The dominant industry, textile manufacturing, was dependent on Russia both for its supply of cotton and its markets. Yet, it continued to face stiff transportation and customs tariffs as a result of Russia's attempts to protect its own industries in the interior. But perhaps Russian-Poland's greatest utility for the Empire came to be "primarily as an advanced strategic bulwark to delay foreign invasion (the Tsars' constant fear)" (Morawska 1989:245). The unification and rapid industrialization of Germany in the 1870s threatened Russia's interests especially in the Balkans, as Germany gradually came to ally itself with Austria. Russia found itself pushed toward an alliance with its western European creditors, Britain and France, in order to secure its multiethnic western borderlands (Skocpol 1979:93–94).

During the second half of the nineteenth century, Russian governmental policy toward the Jews came to express the defensiveness of a peripheralized state. It attempted to strengthen itself, in part, by securing vulnerable frontiers, which in the state's view were peopled, at best, by uncertain and, at worst, by hostile ethnic and national minorities.

After its suppression of the Polish Rebellion of 1863, for example, the government decided to secure Russian-Poland by strengthening Russian peasant landownership in the area as a counterweight to the Polish nobility. Jews and Poles were barred from using tax exemptions and government financial assistance to purchase land there; neither were they allowed, at first, to lease, manage, buy or inherit these lands, although Jews were permitted to continue to operate distilleries and taverns on them. By late 1867, however, the Committee of Ministers loosened restrictions on leaseholding because "Russian estate owners found Jewish experience and capital as indispensable for the running of mills, distilleries, sugar beet refineries and other works as had their Polish predecessors" (Rogger 1976:15–16). Ambivalence, often mixed with violence toward the Jews in the southwest provinces, continued to define Russian governmental policy for so long as it remained preoccupied with the question of adversaries on its borderlands.

Russian policy on migration until the emancipation of the serfs in the 1860s was dominated by the net inflow of immigrants, mostly German settlers. Emigration had been severely restricted.

But gradually, over the last quarter of the nineteenth century, state emigration policy shifted from a general prohibition to the selective release of certain national minority and ethnic groups.

Since the 1870s, German industrialization had been drawing Russian-Polish peasant workers across the border to its agricultural estates, mines, and factories in back-and-forth cycles of seasonal labor migrations. Although it had a politically enforced seasonal character to it, Polish labor migrations to Germany (from the three partitions) rose steadily from about 60,000 in 1895 to 150,000 in 1900 to over 600,000 in 1913 (Morawska 1989:251).

The regulated migration of Russian-Poles was one more attempt at defending an unruly and vulnerable multiethnic frontier. But, more generally, state migration policy was used as one of several means to strengthen "the state" by redefining it as "a nation." The state policy of increased "Russification" vacillated over the remainder of the century between an easing of the restrictions on Jewish domicile and occupational rights, in order to assimilate them into the nation, and the indirect promotion of their exodus, as non-Russians, through a variety of means (Aronson 1977; Lowenstein 1984; Pearson 1983; Rogger 1976).

The differential rate of emigration between the various national minorities ultimately was a combined product of an individual ethnic group's sense of historical persecution or disadvantage and of intensifying discriminatory imperial policy as earlier edicts on minority "privileges" were revoked. In the 1880s and 1890s, Jews almost monopolized emigration from the Empire, reaching 91.6 percent of the total in the peak year of 1891. Between 1899 and 1901, the Jewish proportion of the total outflow averaged nearly 44 percent, compared to the Polish, at 27 percent, and the Russian, at 4.4 percent. One historian refers to these figures as "an index of discrimination within the Romanov territories" (Pearson 1983:101).

Imperial Russia's strategies for achieving industrial growth and military and political parity in the world-system involved, in part, the defining and selective targeting of particular ethnic/national and regional groups for "elimination." Whether through the liberalization of emigration policies for national minorities only, the restriction of residential and occupational rights, the sanctioning of pogroms, or other forms of Russification (linguistic, cultural, etc.), Russian Jews were created as a politically disempowered ethnic group prior to their arrival at New York port.

JEWISH GIRLHOOD IN RUSSIA:
THE POLITICS OF GENDER, ETHNICITY,
AND GEOGRAPHY

What was the relationship of the peripheral/semiperipheral incorporation of Russia into the world-system to the mass migration of Russian Jews to America, or to Russian-Jewish women in particular? How were their daily lives and future expectations shifting during the last quarter of the twentieth century? Further, how did individual women and girls perceive and interpret the social transformations which confronted them during these years? What was the range of their options and responses? In order to understand more fully how and when migration to the United States became a viable alternative for Russian-Jewish women, we need to begin to see the changing world through their eyes.

Some of the conditions surrounding Jewish women in the Pale are illustrated by the experiences and words of Mary Antin (Mashke, as she was known to Yiddish speakers, or Marya to Russian speakers). Mary was born in 1881 in the small Russian-Polish town of Polotzk in the Pale, the year the "relatively liberal" tsar, Alexander II, was assassinated. She was one year old when the legal, social, and economic position of the Jews began to deteriorate seriously with the issuance of the notorious "May Laws." When she was between eight and ten years old, Mary's father, a downwardly mobile trader, succumbed to "emigration fever," then at its height in Polotzk, and left the family "to begin life all over again" in America (Antin [1911] 1969:78). Torn between feelings of excitement, curiosity, confusion, apprehension, and pain at her father's departure from her family and community, Mary painted her ambivalence in words:

> Then came the parting; for it was impossible for the whole family to go at once . . . It struck me as rather interesting to stand on the platform before the train, with a crowd of friends weeping in sympathy with us, and father waving his hat for our special benefit, and saying—the last words we heard him speak as the train moved off—"Good-bye, Plotzk (sic), forever!" Then followed three long years of hope and doubt for father in America and us in Russia. (Antin [1899] 1970:12)

At thirteen, with her mother, two sisters (one younger, and one older), and younger brother, Mary joined her father in the United

States. When she was not quite thirty, feeling "bound to unravel . . . the tangle of events, outer and inner" that shaped her adaptation to America, Mary published her autobiography, *The Promised Land* ([1911] 1969:181).

Mary's father was not prompted to emigrate by a rare or singular event. The expulsion of 20,000 Jews from Moscow by a 1891 government edict, which coincided with his decision, served as the culmination of a century-long series of restrictions on Jewish domicile and occupational rights (Antin [1911] 1969:140; Greenberg [1944] 1976:44). Although Mary's early family life in Polotzk was circumscribed by the intersection of her gender, class, and ethnic identities, it was dominated, above all, by her experience of Russian governmental national minority policies, or ethnic intergroup relations.

More specifically, under the rule of Alexander II (1855–1881), some Jews enjoyed expanded educational opportunities, permission to live outside the Pale, and the beginnings of upward economic mobility. The number of Jews who learned Russian, identified with Russian culture, and became involved in Russian politics increased enormously. In 1862 Jews in Russian-Poland were permitted to acquire land on former manorial estates in the rural districts of Pale, to practice trades and crafts without special taxes, and to settle wherever they liked. Following the Polish insurrection of 1863, however, the government formally retracted both Jewish and Polish land claims, and the rights of all national minorities suffered serious setbacks. (Lowenstein 1984:314; Greenberg [1944] 1976:73–100; Dubnow 1918:154–205).

> The assassination of Alexander II in 1881 put an end to the hopes of some Jews for easy amalgamation into Russian society . . . the tsars were no longer encouraging Jews to become part of Russian society . . . The fear of revolution and the association by some of the Jews with the revolutionary forces, caused the government to try to retain and even increase the isolation of the Jews. The pogroms (whether instigated by the government or not), the expulsion of Jews from St. Petersburg and Moscow back into the Pale, and the institutions of quotas in secondary and higher education, all served notice on Russian Jews that even Russified Jews were unacceptable. (Lowenstein 1984:314)

"Officially sanctioned bigotry and open religious and ethnic chauvinism" characterized the period from 1881 until the revolution of 1917. No less than 650 special statutes restricting Jews were issued during these years (Morawska 1987:36). The serious deterioration of Jewish legal rights was preceded, however, by a wave of pogrom violence beginning in Odessa in 1871. The pogrom in Kiev in May 1881 initiated a second round of violence (1881–1884), followed by a third wave in 1903–1906. Most of the violent riots against the Jews occurred in the southwest provinces in the Ukraine, but also in Lithuania, Bieylorussia, and sporadically in Russian-Poland.[7] Following the Kiev pogrom, some of the rioters were brought to trial in the local Military Court. The chilling proposal of the public prosecutor, Strelnikov, has an eerie ring to it, in retrospect: "If the Eastern frontier is closed to the Jews, the Western frontier is open to them; why don't they take advantage of it?" (Dubnow 1918:265).

Although most of the pogroms originated in towns, the government response to them centered on protecting peasants in the countryside from alleged Jewish economic exploitation. In the so-called May Laws of 1882, Jews were forbidden from settling in rural districts in the Pale and from owning or managing real estate or farms outside cities in the Pale. These laws were followed by a long series of restrictions on domicile and occupational rights: restriction of movement from one village to another; limitations on the numbers of Jewish students in secondary schools and universities; denial of the right of Jews to practice law, and so forth. Many small towns in the Pale were suddenly declared to be rural villages and thus closed to new Jewish residents; others were suddenly declared to be outside the Pale and thus barred to Jews. If a young Jewish military recruit failed to report for duty, his entire family could be fined and their household goods auctioned off. The small group of privileged Jews (first-guild merchants, university graduates, artisans, and their employees) who had been permitted since 1865 to live outside the Pale, in Kiev, Moscow, and St. Petersburg, were increasingly harassed and subject to periodic expulsions (Dubnow 1918:243–323, 335–413). The governor of Kiev forbade the wives of Jewish artisans to sell food in the market on the grounds that under the letter of the law artisans could trade only their own manufactures (Dubnow 1918:385). A governmental edict in March 1891 finally expelled two-thirds of the Jews of Moscow—about 20,000 individuals, mostly artisans, merchants, and their families. Only the highly educated, the most wealthy merchants, and the children of soldiers who had served under

Nicholas I were formally permitted to remain (Greenberg [1944]
1976:44).

Given these transformations in ethnic intergroup relations, it
is not at all surprising that Mary initially weaves the story of her
unfolding personal identity around the ethnic geography of Russia. For Mary, ethnic identity and personal development were
fused. Both entered her consciousness in geographical terms; both
were alternatively constrained or transcended in geographical
terms.

> When I was a little girl, the world was divided into two parts;
> namely Polotzk, the place where I lived, and a strange land called
> Russia. All the little girls I knew lived in Polotzk, with their fathers
> and mothers and friends. Russia was the place where one's father
> went on business. It was so far off, and so many bad things hap-
> pened there, that one's mother and grandmother and grown-up
> aunts cried at the railroad station, and one was expected to be
> sad and quiet for the rest of the day, when the father departed
> for Russia. After awhile there came to my knowledge the existence
> of another division, a region intermediate between Polotzk and
> Russia . . . Vitebsk . . . Vilna . . . Riga . . . From those places
> came photographs of uncles and cousins . . . These uncles were
> just like people in Polotzk; the people in Russia, one understood,
> were very different . . . Vitebsk was not so different, only bigger
> and brighter and more crowded . . . Polotzk and Vitebsk were
> now bound together by the continuity of the earth, but between
> them and Russia a formidable barrier still interposed. I learned,
> as I grew older, that much as Polotzk disliked to go to Russia,
> even more did Russia object to letting Polotzk come . . . (Antin
> [1911] 1969:1, 3)

Inscribed within the multiethnic landscape of Russia, with
which Mary/Mashké/Marya was becoming acquainted as a very
young girl, were the lessons of identity, collective group identity
and self-identity. Who was similar to her and her family? Who was
different from them? What was she to make of her position in relation to others around her?

> I do not know when I became old enough to understand. The
> truth was borne in on me a dozen times a day, from the time I
> began to distinguish words from empty noises. My grandmother
> told me about it, when she put me to bed at night. My parents
> told me about it, when they gave me presents on holidays. My
> playmates told me, when they drew me back into a corner of the

gateway, to let a policeman pass. Vanka, the little white-haired boy, told me all about it, when he ran out of his mother's laundry on purpose to throw mud after me when I happened to pass . . . There was no time in my life when I did not hear and see and feel the truth—the reason why Polotzk was cut off from the rest of Russia. It was the first lesson *a little girl* in Polotzk had to learn . . . We must not be found outside the Pale, because we were Jews. So there was a fence around Polotzk, after all. The world was divided into Jews and Gentiles. This knowledge came so gradually that it could not shock me. It trickled into my consciousness drop by drop. By the time I fully understood that I was a prisoner, the shackles had grown familiar to my flesh. (Antin [1911] 1969:4–5; my emphasis)

As an intrinsic part of her developing ethnic and gender identity, as a Russian-Jewish girl, Mary describes how she, more painfully, learned of her subordinate status, and how she was taught by her mother to cope with it.

The first time Vanka threw mud at me, I ran home and complained to my mother, who brushed off my dress and said, quite resignedly, "How can I help you, my poor child? Vanka is a Gentile. The Gentiles do as they like with us Jews." The next time Vanka abused me, I did not cry, but ran for shelter, saying to myself, "Vanka is a Gentile." The third time, when Vanka spat on me, I wiped my face and thought nothing at all. I accepted ill-usage from the Gentiles as one accepts the weather. The world was made a certain way, and I had to live in it. (Antin [1911] 1969:5)

Later, painfully aware and articulate about the "marks [left] upon [her] flesh and spirit" by episodes such as this, Mary adds, "I knew how to dodge and cringe and dissemble before I knew the names of the seasons" (Antin [1911] 1969:26).

Looking back on her adolescence in a shtetl in the Ukraine at the turn of the century, Sophie Saroff confirmed the tight relationship among ethnic identity and personal development, geography and migration, but to this she added the element most critical to her, the social class of her household. Given a none-too-successful traveling blacksmith for a father and a mother occupied in selling milk and geese and "always figuring out ways of earning money," Sophie recognized the constraints of her family's class position upon her (Saroff 1983:3).

Figure 3.
Jewish women buy and sell in the Demblin marketplace, Lublin, Poland.
YIVO Institute for Jewish Research.

My horizons were not that wide—at least when I was young . . .
I knew there was a world outside of Brusilov, but I was given to
understand that it wasn't attainable for me. For instance, when
I got through the Russian state school, the next thing would
have been to go to Kiev or a different big city and continue, but
we weren't rich enough and, as Jews we couldn't go there. You
could go, but you couldn't live there. You could only if you had
special permission. You either had to be a rich merchant and get
those kind of rights, or be an outstanding artisan who was given
the rights. But the average Jew couldn't go and live there. It was
at that particular time when thoughts about America first came.
(Saroff 1983:8–9)

By even considering migration, Sophie gradually and quietly
begins to resist the resignation to her subordinate status, which
earlier Mary revealed was taught to Russian-Jewish girls as a survival strategy in childhood. She starts to unravel the tangled knot
of subordinated femininity, ethnicity, personal aspirations, and
geography by acknowledging for herself "the American option."

RUSSIAN-JEWISH WOMEN AND
THE PROLETARIANIZATION
OF RUSSIAN-JEWISH HOUSEHOLDS

Although a politically or legally disempowered ethnic group, all
Jews were not equally impoverished as the Russian Empire
became incorporated into the capitalist world-system. The crash
program of industrialization, induced by global interstate rivalries
and economic pressures, and undertaken by the Russian state during the second half of the nineteenth century, restructured Jewish
economic life and intensified class differentiation among Jewish
households. More specifically, the economic repercussions of ethnic discrimination were differentially distributed by region, by
occupation, by gender, and by age. As the Russian government
periodically tightened or loosened restrictions on Jewish entitlements to practice particular livelihoods in given localities, both the
characteristics of the providers of income and the types of income
to Jewish households shifted. Although it is impossible to understand Jewish emigration from Russia only as a response to economic pressures, the shifting economic fortunes and gender and
age divisions of labor among and within Jewish households helps

to explain why some Jews left and others stayed on, either temporarily or permanently.

On the one hand, the relative liberalization of government policies under Alexander II, at first, further advantaged a small minority of Russian Jews. During the first half of the nineteenth century a small number of Jews made large fortunes in alcohol distilling and in foreign trade along Russia's western borders. The capital they accumulated was invested primarily in railroad construction, sugar refining, and later in manufacturing industries, particularly in the production of consumer goods for the domestic market, like woolen and cotton textiles (Rubinow [1907] 1975:537–39; Kahan 1986:3–4, 20–21, 87). By 1897 the Russian Census counted some 82,000, or 1.6 percent of the Jewish population, as an economic elite, comprised of nobles, honorary citizens, and first-guild merchants. This group, presumably, would have been included in the 4 percent of Russian Jews still permitted to live and work outside the Pale, in the interior cities of European Russia (Kuznets 1975:78–79).

On the other hand, the emancipation of the serfs and the extension of railroads throughout the countryside gradually displaced the vast majority of Jews in the Empire from their long-held position as a "middleman minority," or economic intermediaries in the manorial system (Kugelmass 1980; Bonacich 1973). At the beginning of the nineteenth century, some 60 percent of Russian Jews were occupied in commercial pursuits (as innkeepers, leaseholders, traders, and brokers); only 15 percent were artisans involved in handicraft production (Rogger 1976:22; Mendelsohn 1970:2–3). By the end of the century, the shift in Jewish livelihoods was apparent. The proportion of Jews occupied in manufacturing industry rose to 40 percent by 1897, although at least half of all Jews in the Pale still followed various commercial pursuits (Rubinow [1907] 1975:501).

The shift towards manufacturing among Jews was unevenly distributed between regions in the Pale and was accompanied by some noticeable changes in the age, gender, and ethnic composition of the labor force, as well as in the conditions of work. The combination of legal restrictions on Jewish residential rights and the loss of former livelihoods increased the numbers of rural or village Jews who were compelled to resettle in larger urban areas and find alternative ways to make a living. Some of the remaining *yishuvniks*, Jews who resided in peasant villages, continued to rent land and work the fields and fruit orchards; others made their living from stores, inns, and petty trade. In the village of Volovike, Y. Kaplans's mother ran an inn, while his father sewed and mended furs for the peasants. After they were forced into town by the new regulations, his mother continued to be the main breadwinner, now decorating fabric in bright colors for sale to peasant women (Kugelmass 1986:213).

Typically, the plots of land Jews worked were too small to completely support a household. Women and children generally worked the land, while men found work in town. With competition from the rural cooperatives at the end of the nineteenth century however, the domestic production of foodstuffs became important in a new sense, as additional sources of nonwaged income for the households of both displaced Jewish shopkeepers and of more urbanized artisans. A craftsman, a storeowner, or a peddler, who had managed to put together a deposit for a lease, might move his household to a fruit orchard for several months a year. The tasks of the women and children of the household were to guard the fruit until harvest time, pick it, and pack it for sale in the town market. About 90 percent of orchard lessees were town craftsmen who were occupied with other work a day or two a week (Kugelmass 1986:212–13, 238–240, 263).

After a disappointing three-month stay in America, Fannie Shapiro's father returned to Russia and moved the family to a village estate, which he managed. Fanny's description of this period makes clear the importance that access to the land had in her family's standard of living:

> We lived very good, comparing with other poor people. You came to the town, and saw the way the poor people lived there, and I used to come back and tell my mother . . . The house was actually in the orchard, right at the end. We had nuts growing there, and grapes and strawberries. And there was a lake where we could catch fresh fish. All during the week, we'd have all kinds of butter and cheese, and everything you get from the cow . . . and then sometimes my mother would cook some fish, and for the weekend, then we had chicken . . . Oh we ate, we ate good. Maybe this is why I'm still around, 'cause I had a hard life here. (Kramer and Masur, eds. 1976:3)

By 1898, nearly 80 percent of the Jewish population of the Pale—including the former *yishuvniks* as well as factory owners, small-scale merchants, traders, peddlers, artisans, craftsmen, and homeworkers—had become urban dwellers (Rubinow [1907] 1975:493). Some large cities grew rapidly much larger and became major centers of industrial employment, such as Odessa in the south, as a center of shoe production, and Warsaw and Lodz in Poland, for textiles and shoes.

The greatest population congestion and most rapid shift from commerce into manufacturing occupations, however, developed in the northwest provinces of the Pale. There, most of the urbanized Jewish population still lived in *mestechkos*, or *shtetls*, small towns of fewer than 10,000 inhabitants. Shtetls served as commercial and industrial centers for the surrounding rural population (Rubinow [1907] 1975:493, 495; Kahan 1986:29, 91; Obolensky-Ossinsky [1931] 1969:540–41; Kugelmass 1986:24). It was the shtetls of the northwest Pale that produced both the strongest labor movement and, at first, most of the overseas emigrants. Rubinow reports that by the turn of the century, "scarcely a Jewish family can be found in Lithuania that has not some members in the New World" ([1907] 1975:495, 502). The comparatively higher-waged southern provinces also attracted a sizable adult male migration from the northwest Pale, but sent relatively few migrants overseas until the 1905–1906 pogroms (Rubinow [1907] 1975:492, 530).

In Lithuania and Bieylorussia in the northwest, manufacturing industry captured 44 and 42 percent, respectively, of the recorded Jewish working population, as opposed to 24 and 27 percent occupied in commerce (Rubinow [1907] 1975:502). Although these figures may represent the overall trend, they obscure the fact that practically all the commercial activity in the northwest, almost 90 percent, remained in the hands of Russian Jews. In Lithuania, for example, Jews comprised more than 90 percent of all dealers in grain, building material and fuel, dry goods and clothing; they were 93 percent of all peddlers (Rubinow [1907] 1975:554, 556).

Fierce and intensifying competition came to characterize the relationship among Jewish small traders who attempted to buy up the agricultural products of the local peasantry, a consequence of the crowding of Jews into the Pale and the denial of any legal right to travel from one town to another. The influx of non-Jewish traders and the spread of producer and marketing cooperatives throughout the countryside further undermined the position of the Jewish trader. The income of the typical small merchant dropped to the level of the average artisan without capital or the average factory worker (Rubinow [1907] 1975:559; Kahan 1986:23–25). Some larger merchants, however, continued to prosper by increasing the hours of work and cutting the pay of their employees, whose wages had become a supplement to the unpaid labor and nonwaged income of other household members (Rubinow [1907] 1975:562).

As the commercial labor market became ever more saturated throughout the Pale, and particularly in the northwest, Jewish household members, in order to make ends meet, were compelled to take up alternative and auxiliary occupations and otherwise augment their incomes. As the older generation became more impoverished the younger generation increasingly shifted into handicraft and factory production (Kahan 1986:25). By 1898, almost one-fifth of the total Jewish population of the Pale was receiving some type of charitable assistance (a 28 percent increase since 1894), and in Lithuania, 22 percent of families required charity in order to observe the Passover holiday (Rubinow [1907] 1975:571–72).

Perhaps because of their poverty, as well as familiarity with seasonal or short-term migrations, Jewish entreprenuers and traders tended more often, or at least initially, to migrate to the southern provinces, rather than overseas (Kahan 1986:25). Prior to migrating to the U.S., Mary Antin's father abandoned the family for nearly three years as he worked in petty commercial positions in the south and east of Russia. He returned only to help his wife run the business she inherited from her father. A series of illnesses bankrupted the family and ruined the business. Finally, the pogroms, expulsions, and the consequent overcrowding of the Pale labor market persuaded Mary's father to start life anew, in the United States (Antin [1911] 1969: 66, 71, 141). The nature of his exit and that of the remaining family members was fairly characteristic. He traveled with borrowed money to a German port, and from there was transported to Boston along with many others at the expense of a Jewish emigrant aid society. Borrowed money was the source of the tickets he sent to Mary's mother and the children to join him in the U.S. later (Antin [1911] 1969:141, 162). Emigration was just as often the catalyst for the formation of resource-sharing and income-pooling networks among family, friends, and community, as it was the outcome of utilizing preexisting relationships. The networks that facilitated the mass migration of eastern European Jews not only changed over time, but seem to have operated differently for women and men. While borrowed money and organizational assistance characterized the help extended to the earliest waves of men and "middle-class families" in the 1880s, most migrating women, in contrast, had few alternatives but to wait for "family help," prepaid tickets from husbands or fathers, or finance their own way on savings from work (Glanz 1976:11–12, 154–55). This suggests an additional reason for the uneven gender composition of early Russian-Jewish emigration.

Despite the lower social status of most artisans in Russian-Jewish society, especially when compared to traders and merchants, craft occupations increased noticeably prior to World War I, as Jews, men and women both, were driven to take up these livelihoods under the twin impact of industrialization and selective expulsion. By the end of the century, artisans comprised between 30 and 44 percent of the recorded Jewish labor force (Rubinow [1907] 1925:520). It was said that there were enough Jewish tailors "to supply clothing for half the urban population of the Russian Empire" (Mendelsohn 1970:14). Although the lowest status work, that of producing clothing and shoes, offered the most numerous opportunities, Mary Antin pointed out that the costs of accepting such degraded labor were great, extending beyond the prestige of the individual to the future life chances of other household members. "A shoemaker's daughter could not hope to marry the son of a shopkeeper, unless she brought an extra large dowry; and she had to make up her mind to be snubbed by the sisters-in-law and cousins-in-law"(Antin [1911] 1969:36–37; Kahan 1986:25, 59).

In the small towns, or shtetls, of the Pale, and particularly in the northwest, the typical artisan shop was located in the home of an adult male master artisan, who worked alongside his unpaid wife, sons, and daughters, and perhaps a few hired journeymen or young apprentices, male and/or female. Squeezed by competition, however, from the larger-scale Jewish handicraft shops in big cities and the more capital-intensive factories owned predominantly by non-Jews, master artisans increasingly lost their independence and journeymen were forced to give up their future expectations of self-employment. Artisan households were gradually transformed into cottage industries; members worked for a merchant or jobber, who provided the raw materials and collected the finished product (Kahan 1986:26). In Vitebsk, in the northwest Pale, tailors' households worked mainly for the dealers in ready-made clothing, just as they would continue to do for the sweatshop contractors on New York City's Lower East Side following emigration (Rubinow [1907] 1975:525). Jewish journeymen found degraded employment as pieceworkers in large-scale relatively nonmechanized Jewish-owned shops. There, they saw their work day lengthen to between fifteen and eighteen hours, that is when there was work to be had (Mendelsohn 1970:11–13).

Of the 46,313 Jewish industrial workers counted by the Jewish Colonization Association in 1898–99, 43,240 were employed by Jewish capital (Kahan 1986:60–61; Peled and Shafir 1987:1441). But, if adult male Jewish wage earners looked nearly exclusively to Jewish employers for work, Jewish employers looked increasingly to alternative sources of labor. As factory mechanization spread eastward from Poland, Jewish adult male skilled artisans were increasingly displaced by three groups of recent entrants to the waged labor force: recently urbanized non-Jewish peasant workers, adult female Jewish homeworkers, and young Jewish apprentices, both male and female. (Kahan 1986:41; Peled and Shafir 1987; Mendelsohn 1970). What accounts for this unexpected response of Jewish employers to Jewish workers? What explains this unlikely transformation of the Jewish work force? First, despite evidence of overall declining wages and living standards for artisans and industrial wage earners over this period, Jewish industrial workers nevertheless remained higher waged than their non-Jewish, Polish, Lithuanian, and Russian competitors (Peled and Shafir 1987:1448). This was, in part, an unintended consequence of Russian state restrictions on Jewish land holding. In contrast to its policy toward Jews, the Russian government did not deny non-Jewish households access to village subsistence. Thus, non-Jewish workers were not made nearly so dependent on wages or cash income to cover their survival needs as were urbanized adult male Jewish industrial workers. This allowed them to successfully undercut higher-priced Jewish workers. Second, recently proletarianized Jewish workers, in disgruntled acknowledgment of their new, more permanent wage-earning status, increasingly mounted strikes for higher wages and better working conditions that were often fairly successful. Peled and Shafir argue convincingly that these very "successes" may have created the incentive for Jewish employers to locate alternative sources of labor (1987:1450). Channeled into a dead-end sector

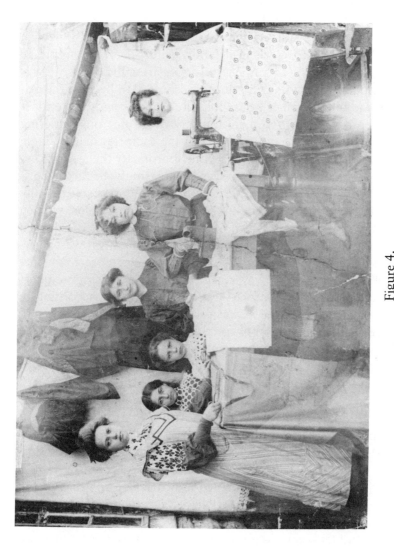

Figure 4.
Jewish seamstresses pose for a photograph in a shtetl garment factory, Ziezmariai, Lithuania in the Pale of Settlement. YIVO Institute for Jewish Research.

of the Pale labor market and faced with a bleak economic future, many young adult male Jewish artisans took the option of emigration to the United States. By the 1890s, adult male Jewish industrial wage earners were reported migrating overseas in large numbers from Kovno, Bobruisk, and Bialystok in the northwest Pale (Mendelsohn 1970:15, 23).

It was not considered unusual, at the time, for a Jewish woman in Russia to work in a family enterprise after marriage with her husband or to run the business after his death. It was commonplace for a wife of a "fulltime scholar" to become the primary breadwinner in her household. But, by the end of the nineteenth century, Jewish women and girls were not only entering petty commerce, the hand trades, and the factories in very large numbers—as much-needed cash contributors to their shrinking household income funds—but were increasingly becoming primary breadwinners in a variety of household types (Rubinow [1907] 1975:523). According to the 1897 Russian census, women comprised more than one-fifth of the economically active Jewish population of the entire Pale; in the deteriorating northwest provinces, women's share in the labor force rose to more than one-quarter. These figures however neglected the increasing numbers of cottage industry producers—more than 100,000 according to Kahan—which brings the actual proportion of women closer to 28 percent of the Jewish labor force (1986:6, 51, 64). In the 1880s in Vilna Province, Jewish women by the hundreds attempted to augment their household's income by manufacturing hosiery at home, under the control of middlemen (Mendelsohn 1970:23). Among the 500,000 Jewish artisans in the Pale, women comprised more than 15 percent and, in the northwest, nearly 18 percent (Rubinow [1907] 1975:524). By the end of the century, women and girls came to supply well over one-third of all Jewish industrial wage labor in factories in the northwest (Rubinow [1907] 1975:546). The only Jewish-owned industries of any real size to employ Jewish wage labor in the Pale—cigarette and match factories—hired predominantly women and young children. Six-year-old boys and ten-year-old girls could be found working sixteen to eighteen hours at a stretch in almost every major city in the northwest Pale. In the production of matches, cigarette wrappers, and tobacco, Jewish women and children constituted, respectively, 70 percent, 85 percent, and 62 percent of all employees. For Mendelsohn "the cigarette and match factory workers comprised the only real 'factory proletariat' among the Jewish population of Belorussia-Lithuania" (Mendelsohn 1970:24–26; Peled and Shafir 1987: 1441–42).

Young people of both genders, aged ten through nineteen, were also increasingly compelled to join the waged work force. By the turn of the century nearly 30 percent were employed as apprentices to artisans and large-scale industry, and were thus wage contributors to their households (Kahan 1986:6,64). In the northwest, girls constituted nearly 6 percent of all apprentices to the trades, and boys, 16 percent (Rubinow [1907] 1975:524). But inside factories, young girls were nearly 9 percent of all Jewish wage earners, compared to 7 percent of boys (Rubinow [1907] 1975:546).

CONCLUSION

From the mid- to late nineteenth century, Jewish women in Russia were gradually creating new household and work patterns. Rather than withdrawing from the paid work force at the age of marriage as was the tradition, many married women were compelled to continue supplementing their nonwaged domestic labor or subsistence income with monetary income derived from factory production, as well as peddling and petty commerce. Single women increasingly sought after paid jobs, often as a means of contributing to the viability or advancement of their parent's household but equally often as a means of eventually escaping it's obligations and expectations.

The traditional path for a young Russian-Jewish woman to empower herself and "become a person" involved marriage and starting one's own household. But in order to marry, one required a dowry. If a single theme predominates in the memoirs, life stories, and novels of Russian-Jewish immigrants, it is the lament of a poor father unable to marry his daughter(s) well for lack of a dowry; and the parallel terror of his daughter(s) over the bargain bridegroom a father may select. For many young Jewish women of near-marriageable age, migration emerged as a nontraditional means of satisfying a traditional rite of "passage" into female adulthood. For them, saving for a ticket to America was synonymous with accumulating a dowry, but, in this case, migration offered the possibility of making a more satisfactory free-choice marriage, as the distance between fathers and daughters widened.[8] But for many others, the process of becoming an earner in pursuit of passage to the new world, was itself transformative and thus constituitive of empowerment or of "becoming a person." America offered these women some previously unimaginable choices and unpredictable outcomes.

CHAPTER 3

"Take Me to America":
The Origins of Italian Women's
Migration to the United States
at the Turn of the Century

It was really miserable in Italy. But in America, when you worked, you earned money and could eat and drink what you wanted. And there was freedom, no war, no soldiers. So as I said, I was sort of a rebel. I hated ugly and brutal things. I hate injustice and prejudice. So I said to myself, when I get old enough to marry, I'm going to marry the first man who promises to take me to America.

—Clementina Todesco[1]

Back in the old country, a white beaver coat
Would be presumptuous, even in a dream;
I'd dress in black or in a cotton print
And bless the Lord for a warm shawl
On Sunday. In the evening, I'd sit
By the fire, knitting caps and sweaters,
Listening to the scratch of pens
Over notepaper as the children add up
Their days, conjugate the past in two
Neat columns, and dream of the future.
Back in that other world, I might have been
A country girl, singing my mornings
To the fountain's tune, carrying a pail
Of water effortlessly on my head.
In my father's village, shabby urchins
Stare at me and young girls smile
As if they knew me. Among my people,
In my own place, I feel secure—as though
I had not come on a visit from afar
In a magnificent white beaver coat,
An American with a familiar kind of face
And a nostalgic look around the eyes.

—Anne Paolucci[2]

Accounts of Italian women's migration to the United States have customarily been prefaced by two discouraging qualifications. First, readers were cautioned about the virtual impossibility of calculating the numbers of immigrating Italians, male or female, given massive repatriations, or return migrations to Italy.[3] Second, we were informed that Italian migration flows were composed overwhelmingly of labor migrants, the vast majority of whom were male. These two factors have been held, in large part, to account for the differing rates and extent of acculturation and economic mobility between Italian and Russian-Jewish immigrants.[4] Most important, these two qualifications have contributed to making the presence and participation of Italian women in migration and resettlement invisible.

After, however, nearly two decades of new research in history, sociology, anthropology, women's studies, ethnic studies, and development studies, much of it produced by the descendents of migrants, this much qualified introduction to the study of Italian immigrant women can be revised. The lives of Italian immigrant women are no longer unexplored territory.[5] Yet, as historian Donna Gabaccia (1991) has made clear, due to the lack of interdisciplinary communication between these relatively autonomous fields, the contributions of new research to correcting flawed assumptions, revising analytical categories, and altering explanatory frameworks about migrating women, and Italian immigrant women in particular, has been minimal. This chapter integrates classic studies of Italian migration with recent research on Italian immigrant women, but attempts to go beyond disciplinary particularisms. It suggests a more inclusive framework, one that makes the interaction of gender, ethnic/race/nationality, and class relations in a world-system the prism through which the full diversity of Italian women's migration is viewed, and only then compared with Russian-Jewish women's experiences.

Although no single woman can represent the diverse group of Italian women differentiated by regional background, class, age, and marital status who migrated between 1870 and 1930, Clementina Todesco's story, quoted in part at the start of the chapter, suggests one of several distinctive patterns to Italian women's migration. Todesco, who in 1930 left her rural village in northeastern Italy (in the Dolomite region) for the United States, gave voice to a paradoxical thread that runs through and connects disparate immigrant women's lives, both Italian and Russian-Jewish.

Clementina remembered and identified herself as "sort of a rebel," with definite ideas, beliefs, and objectives of her own. This characterization certainly runs counter to the gendered and racialized stereotype of the silent and sacrificing, passive and powerless Italian woman. Yet, what were Todesco's objectives? In contrast to the expectations of some students of women's migration, Clementina did not see the irony or inherent contradiction in using marriage as the means of realizing her individual ambitions. For her, planning marriage to a man going to America was a strategic decision, a moment of personal initiative in an otherwise indeterminate process of empowerment.[6]

Anne Paolucci, a much more recent immigrant to America, casts a different light on Italian women's experience of migration in her poem, "Back in the Old Country," published when she was Chair of the English Department at St. John's University in New York. Paolucci's protagonist, the Americanized daughter of an Italian immigrant, finds it unthinkable that an impoverished and powerless village woman would dare to dream of improving her life chances. It was not only unfathomable for an Italian mother to covet a beaver coat, but a transgression against gender and family norms. The white beaver coat represents the frivolous desires of an independent modern woman, against the obligations of a poor peasant mother to her children. No, imagining herself a mother "back in the old country," she would not have dared to dream beyond the borders of maternal respectability, compelled instead to sleepwalk within the constraints of her village household. And as a young girl she would have sung out of gratitude for bare survival, while performing daily household tasks. Yet, this modern and emancipated American-Italian daughter, wrapped in American images of Italy and a white beaver coat, returns to her imaginary homeland and only there feels comfortable, safe, and accepted among familiar faces, faces similar to her own.

The memories of Clementina Todesco, the poetic reflections of Anne Paolucci—to what extent do these constitute distinct, mutually exclusive patterns and outcomes of migrating Italian women's lives and experiences? Did Italian women transform customary gender expectations into strategies for personal empowerment and autonomy through migration? Or, were they dragged unwillingly behind patriarchal fathers and husbands to the new world? What were the costs of migration for mothers and daughters? What did they give up for promises of future material and personal empowerment? Was migration, for Italian women, just another sacrifice in the name of household survival and family stability? What factors can explain the seemingly divergent experiences and sentiments expressed by Paolucci and Todesco?

Italian women's immigration experiences were shaped not only by the American contexts in which they continued their lives but in important ways by both an overarching world-economy and the southern European contexts and social relations in which their lives were deeply embedded. This chapter explores these issues and responds to the preceding questions by situating migrating Italian women's personal and social backgrounds within the context of three intersecting sets of hierarchical yet dynamic relationships in the world-system. Italian women's participation in these sets of social relations bears an important part of the burden of responsibility for their subsequent destinies as immigrants in the United States.

Migrating women were, first, situated within the context of the principal economic transformations in nineteenth-century Italy, as its changing connection to the capitalist world-economy reshaped the material resources and opportunities available across regions, social groups, and classes. New challenges to making a living and changing class relations gave rise to migrant flows with distinct social compositions. These factors predisposed some Italian women to certain patterned outcomes later as immigrants in the United States.

The second set of stratifying processes that encompassed and structured Italian women's backgrounds consisted of various political relationships. In particular, Italian emigration policies and United States immigration policies encouraged population flows with distinct social characteristics corresponding to the economic development strategies taken in each state. Additionally, political decisions made in Italy but shaped by its position in the world-system, concerning land reform and agricultural policies, industrialization, and so forth, indirectly promoted migration for particular social groups by constraining their local income-producing alternatives.

Third, a variety of social, cultural, and ideological ties that bound Italian women to household and kinship groups shaped their migration possibilities and outcomes in complex ways. On the one hand, kin and community networks made migration materially possible for some women by providing important resources

Figure 5.
Italian immigrant mother and her children search for their baggage, Ellis
Island, 1905. George Eastman House.

and information. These networks, to an important extent, facilitated and organized migration flows, determined their social composition, duration, and direction. On the other hand, the sexual
and household divisions of labor, regional culture, and class
assumptions regarding appropriate feminine and masculine
behavior more directly determined the nature of Italian women's
involvement in these "networks of opportunity" and their subsequent status in immigrant communities.[7]

The positions of Italy and the United States in the world-system only set the broad parameters within which Italian women's
migration took place. But, changes in global hierarchical relationships had reverberating effects on the internal dynamics of sending
states, communities, and households, the social units that ultimately constrained or released women and girls into migration
streams. This chapter continues the discussion on the extent to
which the changing interplay between global economic and political pressures and local social and cultural relationships, in which
migration was situated, preserved, diminished, or transformed
immigrant women's status. Did migration intensify, decompose,
or recreate Italian women's subordination in a new location? The
reconceptualization of Italian immigrant women's social and personal backgrounds in this chapter, including discussion of their
own perceptions, provides the necessary context for the further
analysis of their life chances in the United States in the first quarter
of the twentieth century.

WOMEN AND SOCIAL CHANGE IN NINETEENTH-CENTURY ITALY: "IN THE OLD DAYS THERE WERE MORE MIRACLES"[8]

Italian emigration has been studied for some time as the unre-
strained and unconditional escape from timeless poverty by mil-
lions of peasants, pushed out of their homeland by economic
forces they could neither control nor understand.[9] More recently,
students of Italian migration have attempted to avoid such sweep-
ing generalizations by redirecting their attention to a regional
focus, and in many of these studies, to the active participation of
emigrants (nearly always male) in planning their own departures.[10] These studies acknowledge that while waves of migration
roughly followed national and international economic cycles,

flows from each region, and even distinct sections of the same region, often differed from one another and followed their own logic or trajectory, often based on local class relations and household practices, notwithstanding broader economic trends.

Yet, what has still been missing from these revised accounts is an integrative framework that joins capitalist world-systemic pressures to the dynamics of regional social relationships, and in particular, to the agency of individuals, especially women. Early misapprehensions of womens' roles in society and in migration still persist to a surprising degree for Italian women. As an aggregate, Italian women are still portrayed as "women of the shadows," standing on the margins of world history and economic development, outside of time.[11]

> The one thing . . . a[n] [Italian] woman must not do was change. Since everyone leaned on her for support, she was supposed to be permanently accessible and permanently unchanging. She could not exist as an individual with autonomous needs and wishes, for that would have undermined the common good. (Barolini 1985:10–11)

Nonetheless, despite a paucity of woman-centered research, this idealized image of Italian womanhood, as embedded within a static culture based on female self-nullification, ought not to substitute for historical analysis. Such an analysis would necessitate questioning whether, how, and to what extent Italian women complied with or contested these role prescriptions, which may themselves have contained contradictory ideals.[12]

Italian women—northern, southern, and Sicilian—all participated in the principal economic, political, and social transformations of the nineteenth century in their households and communities. While many women may not have joined the paid or formal labor force outside their homes, from early childhood on all made regular contributions of unpaid labor and goods to the household income fund. Most common, though, was for women and girls to earn wages at home, informally, in a family enterprise (Odencrantz 1919:27–28). Allthough few women and girls, in contrast to their male kin, undertook seasonal labor migrations to other parts of Italy and Europe, these migrations gradually and increasingly unsettled their working lives and future prospects as well. Historian Miriam Cohen speculates that by disrupting the local sex ratio, the process of male outmigration may have presssured women themselves into moving in search of husbands, perhaps even increasing their freedom of choice over prospective mates (Cohen 1992:26). But, before their motives and movements can become more understandable, migrating Italian women must be situated analytically in the fluid and shifting relations of the regions and households they ultimately left.

Long before the mid- to late nineteenth-century mass migrations of Italians to the Americas, internal seasonal migrations and temporary migrations to western Europe and North Africa had become well-established patterns among many Italian provinces. Each of the four provinces that showed the highest rates of transatlantic migrations between the 1880s and the 1920s—Genoa in the northwest, Lucca in the central west, Cosenza in the south, and Palermo in Sicily—also experienced long histories of seasonal migrations within Europe.[13] Records from Genoa indicate a consistent seasonal movement of population since at least the seventeenth century. In 1823 a local governmental official from the town of Savignano in Genoa observed that: "It has become a custom for families which need to balance their budget or for people who want to buy land to emigrate for one or several seasons to set aside the cash they need." At the same time, the mayor articulated quite clearly the meaning these migrations held for the town: "Without the money arriving in this community through the seasonal migrants, this commune could not survive" (Cinel 1982b: 50). By the mid-1860s young men from Genoa—at first merchants, sailors, and political refugees, later day laborers and small landowners—had extended their temporary emigrations to Latin America and the United States.

In Lucca, by the beginning of the eighteenth century, seasonal migrations had become commonplace, and by the 1850s, three destinations predominated—the islands of Sardinia and Corsica, Marseilles in southern France, and Pisa, in the Tuscany region. Interestingly, the little evidence that is available on women in these seasonal movements indicates that the migrations to Marseilles were initiated by women, specifically wet nurses, who then were followed by agricultural day laborers and small landowners (Cinel 1982b:52).

Seasonal migrants from Cosenza had, by the early 1860s, established routes to the large estates of Sicily, as well as to Algeria and Tunisia. According to the prefetto of the province in the early 1870s:

Seasonal migrants to Sicily return in the spring with savings of from three to four hundred lire, with which they pay their debts and rent some land. In the fall they are ready to depart again, leaving wives and children to take care of the land until the following spring. Their hope is to rent enough land not to have to go to Sicily every winter.[14] (Cinel 1982b:55)

Meanwhile in Palermo, Sicilian migrants continued their long tradition of temporary migrations to Cairo, Barcelona, and Marseilles (Cinel 1982b:55).

The evidence clearly demonstrates that long before the time of the mass overseas migrations northern and southern Italians were far from the stereotypical timeless peasants of a traditional and static society, untouched by social change.[15] Moreover, women's early participation in these seasonal migrations is revealed to take two distinct and coexisting forms, both important to understanding their subsequent involvement in migration to the United States. First, evidence from Lucca shows that women were among the earliest of temporary migrants. Second, information from Cosenza illustrates that without the work of women and children in maintaining the family's small holdings, the migrations of men and/or oldest sons would have been pointless, thus constituting an important pattern of women's early involvement in migrations (Cinel 1982a:50; Furio 1979:7–8).

Although certainly not all seasonal migrations to regions within Europe and North Africa developed into transatlantic migrations, for a time they did share some important features. First, insofar as objectives were concerned, migrants, both women and men, viewed these moves as necessary in order to solve economic problems at home. Or as one peasant observed at the turn of the century: "If America did not exist, we would have to invent it for the sake of our survival" (Cinel 1982a:41). Second, in both these migrations, small landowners seemed to predominate at first; the poorest did not migrate. In 1881 the provincial prefetto in Lucca observed that:

Those who leave are not the poorest people, but those who can afford to leave their families behind, with the assurance that their families can survive without their help for a few months. In general, it is the head of the family or the oldest son who emigrates. (Cinel 1982b:52)

Figure 6.
William Olimpio Primomo and Maria Domenica Martelli Primomo
pose for a photograph soon after their marriage in Mozzagrogna,
Abruzzi, and just before William departs for work in New York, 1919.
Courtesy of the Primomo family.

One of the most persistent patterns in areas of high temporary emigration, despite a virtually endless variety of regional adaptations, was the increasing distribution of property rights (after 1860) and the growing expectation by both the landless and small holders of eventually finding the means to purchase more land. As the customary paths for earning enough to rent or purchase land narrowed, many looked across the Atlantic for the means to realize their hopes. A member of the Cosenza Chamber of Commerce explained in 1887: "The peasants who relied on internal migration in the past are now forced to go abroad to make the extra money they need" (Cinel 1982a:68). Ironically, the increased supply of money kept inflating land prices, at a time when the prices of agricultural commodities were deteriorating. Seasonal migrants from some regions then lengthened the period of their stay abroad and/or made multiple trips (Barton 1975:38–40; Cinel 1982a:59–64).[16] Carlo Toti, a thirty-four-year-old peasant from Calabria had been in the U.S. twice by 1909. Although he had managed to buy some land, he explained: "I do not have enough to make a living out of it. To make ends meet I have to hire myself out, exactly as I did before going to the United States. This is not what I expected" (Cinel 1982a:276).

"AMERICA HAS BECOME A DISEASE, BUT OUT OF NECESSITY"[17]

By the end of the nineteenth century, the seasonal migrations of Italians had increased in magnitude and also changed direction— towards the Americas, and the United States in particular. At first, during the last quarter of the nineteenth century, the majority of Italian emigrants originated in northern Italy. More than 2.2 million of these left for European countries, compared to 1.1 million who crossed the Atlantic. Of southern Italians and Sicilians, 1.3 million went to European destinations, while only 182,000 headed across the ocean. Until the turn of the century Italian migration to Argentina and Brazil overshadowed the flow to the U.S., but from 1900–1914, the United States received about two-thirds of all Italian emigrants to the Americas, mostly from southern Italy and Sicily (Caroli 1973:39; Martellone 1984:389, 399; Ratti [1931] 1969).[18]

During this time, Italian women's involvement in both migration streams intensified. Between the turn of the century and the restrictions on southern European migration to the United States in the 1920s, an average of 30 percent of all emigrating Italians were female (Furio 1979:44). The percentage of females among Italian immigrants to the United States, however, increased markedly over the period. Between 1881 and 1890, 21.1 percent were female; from 1891 to 1900, 22.8; from 1901 to 1910, 22.9; from 1911 to 1920, 30.6; and from 1921 to 1930, 39.4 (Furio 1979:47). Miriam Cohen characterizes southern Italian women's migration to the United States as a "delayed migration," where women arrived, on average, one year and two months after the men (Cohen 1992:39). While many migrating women were wives and mothers who reunited with their husbands and set up nuclear family households, many others were single women whose journeys carried them to parents, siblings, aunts, uncles, and fiances with whom they resided (Cohen 1992:41).

Those women who had not yet emigrated, or who would not, increasingly bore the sole responsiblity for making family decisons and providing for the needs of their households for months and sometimes years at a time. As one observer noted in 1908:

> I saw many a field with long rows of women toilers, the overseer, the only man in sight . . . Near Tivoli, I met a sunburned peasant woman coming down the steep stony path, carrying on her head a basket in which slept a little child. And often the poor woman has besides the basket cradle on her head, her "zappa," her black bread and water jug, a cord tied about her waist by which draws an unyielding pig or sheep to pasture." (Mangano 1908:22)

The gradual increase of Italian emigration to the United States between 1880 and 1900 and its swift growth up to the eve of World War I are linked to Italian political and economic dynamics, which are themselves connected to the impact of global economic cycles and Italy's changing position in the world-system. However, despite Italy's increased integration into the rhythms of the capitalist world-system, at local levels the particular social structures and relations of production varied profoundly. For Bell (1979:116), by 1800, rural Italy was a semiperipheral sector within a capitalist world-system. Arrighi and Piselli (1987) discovered, however, the existence of three distinct social formations in

Figure 7.
Maria Domenica Martelli Primomo poses with her son, Giovanni, in
Mozzagrogna, Abruzzi, 1921. Her husband has migrated to New York
for work. Courtesy of the Primomo family.

their analysis of the peripheralization of Calabria, in southern Italy, in the nineteenth century. And, concerning Sicily, Gabaccia (1988a:17) asserts that "in the nineteenth century, visitors from northern Europe hesitated to call Sicily part of Europe, as if they knew when they had crossed the border separating core from periphery." Thus, the prolonged agricultural depression at the end of the nineteenth century and the increased mechanization of industry would have different effects on the social composition of the population flows from each region (Martellone 1984; Bell 1979:199–200).

In Lombardy, one of the major sources of northern Italian immigration to the U.S., a greater diversity of local income-generating opportunities existed for both men and women than, for example, in southern Italy or Sicily. There, cattle raising, the production of dairy products, the cultivation of wheat and corn on a share-crop or money-rental system coexisted with linen production, mulberry growing, silkworm rearing, and an expanding silk industry in the nineteenth century. Silk industries in northern Italy, especially Piedmont and Lombardy, produced both raw and spun silk thread for the spinning and weaving mills of France, Great Britain, Germany, Switzerland, and North America. By the middle of the nineteenth century, silk reeling and throwing gave employment to some 150,000 people in Piedmont and Lombardy. Among these semi-proletarian peasant workers were many young women who worked seasonally and mostly on hand looms in small mills scattered throughout the countryside. Investment in the mechanization of silk weaving spurred increased productivity before the war, and exports of woven silk (as a percentage of total silk exports) moved from 6 percent in 1885 to 17 percent by 1913 (Ets 1970:viii; Cafagna 1973: 279–80, 306; Martellone 1984:393–94). Although northern Italian regions had long been sending seasonal migrants to other European countries, emigration to the Americas only began around 1890 when peasants and day laborers were driven off lands by crop failures and the threat of lowered living standards. Changes in the world market demand for silk added to the pressure to intensify migration in new directions, as prices for Italian silk began to fall in the context of increased mechanization and competition from India, China, and Japan (Cinel 1982a:97; Martellone 1984:396).

In southern Italy and Sicily the intensive cultivation of cereals on large and medium-sized estates, owned by absentee landlords and managed by major tenants, dominated agricultural produc-

tion. Wheat continued to be the most important export after uni-
fication in the 1860s, raised by peasants both on the older large
estates and the newer smaller holdings of the *civili*, a new rural
elite. Until the late nineteenth-century agricultural crisis, Sicily
successfully traded its sulfur, wine, and citrus fruits with the
United States, France, and England. In the Nicosia district, in the
early 1880s, at least 80 percent of family heads owned some land,
but less than one in seven owned enough to be classified as even a
smallholder. Tenant farmers in Nissoria (part of Nicosia) were
twice as numerous as sharecroppers, and among men, agricultural
wage laborers outnumbered those with longer-term contracts. In
such tenuous economic circumstances, the cultural opposition to
women's agricultural wage labor did not seem to keep many
women away from it. Nearly one-third of all recorded agricultural
laborers were women by 1910 (Bell 1979:123–24).

Poor wheat harvests in the 1880s and 1890s were exacerbated
by the invasion of U.S. grain on the world market, depressing
prices. Around 1900, Florida oranges began to compete successfully with Sicilian and southern Italian citrus fruits on the U.S.
market. New techniques allowed the United States to produce sulfur from indigenous sources, reducing their dependence on Sicilian mines. The phylloxera epidemic hurt Sicilian grape vines, just
as France's wine industry recovered from an earlier epidemic, and
just as France shut its doors to Italian wines in response to Italy's
new (from 1887) protective tariffs. By the turn of the century, Italian exporters were reporting crises in all primary products. Earlier,
small-scale artisan and industrial enterprises, which had been left
unprotected during a period of free trade (1867–1887), lost their
local markets to outside producers of cloth and other goods
(Gabaccia 1988a:19–20; Cafagna 1973:288).

Scholars commonly link mass migration to the United States
to these economic trends of the late nineteenth and early twentieth
centuries, as changing world market relations disrupted older
habits of production and exchange in Italy. But before the links in
the chain of migration can be fastened, several more pieces must
be added to the Italian side of the equation. In particular, the role
of the Italian state in encouraging temporary labor migration to
the Americas requires some examination.

Unified only nominally in 1861, the new Italian nation state
issued warnings against the abuses of emigration agencies and forbade the departure of young men subject to military service. How-

ever, given the relative weakness of the state, the longstanding and widespread tradition of seasonal migrations, and the increased importance of migrant earnings, not only for household subsistence,[19] but in expectation of purchasing more land, measures to discourage the outflow had little effect. On the contrary, state policy served to indirectly promote and regulate emigration, *but only if it were temporary*, as well as to protect against the worst abuses, especially when faced with the mounting criticism of receiving countries like the United States. For example, knowing of the many attempts of the U.S. Congress to pass a literacy test requirement for entry, the Italian Commisariat of Emigration (established in 1901) discussed how to raise literacy rates in areas of high emigration. And in response to mounting U.S. criticism before World War I concerning the crowding of Italians on the eastern seaboard, the Commisariat recommended the establishment of employment offices for Italian emigrants in New York. "Only in this way can we both ward off new threats of restrictive legislation and also assure a better situation for our emigrants in the United States" (Caroli 1973:57). Not until the borders were shut de facto by the war did the Italian government use its power to refuse permission to emigrate. The encouragement of temporary migration was clearly tied to the earnings emigrants remitted to their households *and* to Italian banks.[20] In a speech before Parliament in 1910, Senator Eduardo Pantano argued that

> the great current of returning emigrants represents an economic force of the first order for us. It will be an enormous benefit for us if we can increase this flow of force in and out of our country . . . if we can increase this temporary migration. (Caroli 1973:72)

As one scholar of Italian migration history has explained,

> Temporary emigration was their own solution, they said, to economic problems which they faced as individuals. They seemed unaware of the actions of the Italian government to facilitate their return to Italy by reducing costs of parts of the return journey, by subsidizing agencies in America which fostered ties between Italians abroad and their native land and by making resumption of Italian citizenship easier. (Caroli 1973:v)

In this way, profits made from state-protected shipping[21] and emigrant remittances together not only helped to solve Italy's unfavorable balance of trade during the 1900–1914 period when its exports never equalled its imports, but additionally spurred northern industrialization (Caroli 1973:96; Ratti:466–69; Cafagna 1973:303, 318, 325). Gino Speranza, Secretary of the Society for the Protection of Italian Immigrants during this period, claimed that "it was quite possible that 'Little Italy' in New York contributes more to the tax roll of Italy than some of the poorer provinces in Sicily or Calabria" (Speranza [1906] 1974:309–10).[22]

THE PATHS OF EMIGRATION AND THE POLITICS OF GENDER, CLASS, AND REGION IN TURN-OF-THE-CENTURY ITALY

What was the impact of the agricultural depression and the decline of home textile production in southern Italy and Sicily on the position of women and, in particular, on their participation in the mass migration movements?[23] What did the increased mechanization of silk manufacturing in northern Italy have to do with women's migration? Italian women's migration was embedded within the principal economic and political transformations of the period. Yet, these large-scale and long-term processes affected individuals only indirectly, as impersonal forces. In order to understand more fully how and why migration to the United States became a viable option for Italian women, we need to explore how the patterns of their daily lives and their expectations were changing during the last quarter of the nineteenth century and the first quarter of the twentieth. What impact did these social changes have on the immediate social environment in which girls' and womens' lives were embedded, on the towns and village communities, households, and families from which women emigrated most directly? How did individual women and girls interpret the social transformations confronting them during these years? In 1909, a Calabrian observed: "In this region the man who has not been brave enough to cross the ocean at least once is not considered a free man. As a matter of fact, those who have never migrated have a hard time finding a wife" (Cinel 1982a:87). Did women and girls share these assumptions? In short, what is needed is to begin to see in their eyes, as much as is possible from available information, how their world changed.

Figure 8.
Maria Domenica Martelli Primomo poses with her two sons, Giovanni
and Luigi, and her father-in-law Pietro Primomo in Mozzagrogna,
Abruzzi, 1926. Her husband is a labor-migrant in New York. Courtesy
of the Primomo family.

When migrating women's lives are examined collectively or individually, the nonrandom or self-selective nature of migration becomes startingly clear. If the primary cause of migration was the lure of America, then we should expect to see struggling people from all corners of the world entering the U.S. in roughly equal numbers with similar intentions and backgrounds. However, only a small minority of Europeans left their homelands in the nineteenth century, and men were more likely to leave than women. Migration rates varied between and within regions, with changes in class and occupational status, in household organization, and in gender relations (Gabaccia 1988a:78–79; Bodnar 1985:2–4, 52).

Economic and political change in Italy in the late nineteenth century intensified some customary household economic strategies, such as seasonal labor migrations, which ultimately unsettled the relations between class, generational, and gender groups. In both northern and southern Italy and in Sicily, peasants, artisans, and laborers who had maintained their households by combining income from a variety of different sources, came under heightened pressure to add more or new sources of nonagricultural income. However, with Italian agricultural products less competitive on the world market as well as the declining availability of work for artisans due to foreign imports and the mechanization of industry, the actual means of adding to the household income fund was gradually diminishing (Smith 1985:26, 32–33).

In turn-of-the-century Sicily some families still combined work in their own fields with agricultural day labor and craft production for the market. They raised crops and produce to eat, and on slack days the children picked fruits and vegetables on neighboring farms for a minimal wage while their mothers wove cloth to wear and to sell. Frequently, during harvest seasons, all household members worked in the fields. Women combined these activities with their domestic labor (cooking, cleaning, child rearing), and often marketed surplus produce as well (Smith 1985:26–27).

But, from the 1880s, as home textile production declined and Sicily's main export crops suffered severe reversals on the world market, the division of labor and the distribution of household income contributions between men, women, and children changed. Men increasingly monopolized what wage-earning opportunities were still available on the large wheat estates, while formerly waged female agricultural workers found themselves unemployed and "domesticated." Although Sicilian men's wages were simply not high enough to cover necessary cash expenditures in many cases, they were not as free to migrate alone as were men elsewhere; this would have meant the abandonment of remaining female family members without any income-generating possiblities in many parts of Sicily during the men's sojourn abroad. For these reasons, Sicilian women tended to migrate more than other Italian women (Gabaccia 1987:172–74). But in regions like Turin and Abruzzi-Molise, where women had continued access to subsistence on the land after the decline of the rural textile industry, even if unwaged, they were able to support themselves and their children while the men of their households migrated for wages abroad (Gabaccia 1987:173–74).

Parents trained their children, boys and girls, at a young age to work for their households; learning to contribute to the household income fund was a central part of childhood. By 1911, nearly 50 percent of Italy's children, aged ten to fifteen, were recorded as gainfully employed.

> Girls [1901–1910] learned sewing and, in country places, weaving and spinning even before their small hands could properly handle the necessary tools. They shared in household tasks, joined their mothers in field work, and even aided in herding smaller animals in sight of home. In fisherman's families, women and girls did much of the work connected with the making and repairing of lines and nets . . . Little girls usually had to give up playing games at an earlier age than boys . . . Even the small amount accomplished by quite young children was frequently so necessary an addition to the family's efforts that they were kept from school for these purposes. (Williams 1938:20–21)

Mrs. D., born into a gardener's household in the farming town of Spinoza, in the province of Potenza, immigrated to New York City in 1914, when she was eighteen. After a second grade education, she stayed at home to help her mother. Mrs. D. remembered how she made rag dolls to amuse herself and her friends when she was very young. This was a common way for young girls to first learn how to hold a needle and to sew. As she grew older, Mrs. D. and one of her three sisters were sent to the town dressmaker to get patterns for dresses. Afterwards, she sewed all of her own clothes (Furio 1979:397–98).

Most Italian peasant women did not make their own clothes entirely, no matter how poor, but always arranged for a trained

Figure 9.
James Girolomo Bolognino and Carmela Figliomeni Bolognino and
their two sons (1925) pose in their best clothes to demonstrate to their
parents in Calabria how they have prospered since migrating to New
York. Courtesy of the Primomo family.

woman to, at least, lay out the work for them. In the poorest families, in order to minimize the cost of such services, parents often arranged for one daughter to learn the dressmaking trade, even if only for the service of her own family (Williams 1938:26–27, 68–69). This was also the case in Mrs. L.'s family. Mrs. L. was born in 1892 in Palermo, Sicily, and immigrated to New York City as a young woman. Her father owned a small grocery store, a *bottega*, in which her mother worked also. After grade four, Mrs. L. was sent to the home of a *sarta*, or dressmaker, in the city, where she was taught along with other girls how to design, cut, and sew dresses, blouses, and coats. As she learned, she helped the dressmaker fill custom orders for wealthy women. Finally, when she was fourteen, after apprenticing for five years, Mrs. L. began to stay at home and train her own girls to be dressmakers. It was at this time, she recalled proudly, that she began to earn some money for the family (Furio 1979:409–10).

Both Mrs. D. and Mrs. L. faced many of the typical expectations of daughters at the time, but with the added burden of intensifying economic constraints. Most sources indicate that the number of women gainfully employed in agriculture was lowest in rural towns, where generally men treked to distant fields to work for a week or so while women and children stayed in town until the harvest. In these towns, women and girls, like Mrs. D. and Mrs. L., performed unpaid domestic labor in and near their households, worked as skilled artisans, dressmakers, tailoresses, and midwives, and also engaged in paid market work as small traders.[24] Living in households increasingly pressed for cash in the agricultural depression of the late nineteenth century, poor women in southern Italy and Sicily sold spoons, eggs, fans, and ran errand services for wealthy women. They delivered letters, sold garden produce, spun, wove, and manufactured handicrafts (Williams 1938:28–29). Increasingly, however, the poorest women, those in households without regular income contributions of male relatives, itself a result of high male outmigration, hired themselves out as seasonal or day agricultural laborers. These women earned only about half of what men earned (USIC 1911, 4:160; Noether 1978:3–12; Gabaccia 1988a:41–43).[25]

Of course, the degree to which women entered the agricultural labor force varied enormously from region to region. By the early 1880s, women in the Sicilian town of Sambuca comprised 40 percent of the agricultural laborers of the region. Many had been spinners and weavers until the liberal trade policies following uni-fication. Later, however, falling wheat prices and poor harvests in this agrotown resulted in women's displacement nearly completely by peasant men between 1881 and 1901.[26] Historian Donna Gabaccia has suggested that the term *casalinga*, or housewife, was first used in the 1890 census, probably to refer to these under- and later unemployed peasant women. By 1901 the average Sicilian peasant household contained one fewer worker than it had twenty years earlier (Gabaccia 1988a:43). But taxes still had to be paid and daughters still required dowries. It was women who were responsible for saving enough monetary income to pay the annual taxes, and many women publicly protested being told that they should take jobs as servants if they were unable to pay (Gabaccia 1988a:57–58). Although conventional wisdom has it that south-ern Italian and Sicilian women were constrained during these years from taking domestic service jobs and thereby dishonoring their families, waged domestic service nonetheless emerged as the largest single female occupation outside of agriculture in Sicily. According to Italian government data for 1905–1907, 34 percent of all women recorded as employed in Sicily were domestic ser-vants, 23.5 percent were so employed in Basilicata, 18.9 percent in Campania, but only 9.2 percent in Calabria. In northern Italy, by contrast, the percentages of women employed in domestic ser-vice were lower: only 16 percent in Piedmont and 12.5 percent in Lombardy (Cohen 1992:20–21).[27]

A primary motive for emigration on the part of many young women and their parents was the increasing difficulty of providing daughters with a dowry (Odencrantz 1919:26; Furio 1979:27). Wives and mothers in southern Italian families, to a considerable degree, managed the household budget, made decisions as to the disbursement of funds for daily expenses, and thus implicitly con-trolled the amount to be saved for a child's dowry or inheritance (Cohen 1992:30). Most Sicilian agrotown households, like those in Sambuca, strove to provide their children with property—houses, land, and/or household furnishings—at the time of their marriages. Although the distribution of these items between sons and daughters varied widely from town to town, the fact that it was the children's earnings that made these provisions possible remained the common denominator. Where daughters faced diminished income options and the household lacked sufficient male earners, the motivation to emigrate was very powerful.

Many parents in Sambuca failed to acquire houses for their children between 1881 and 1901, thus encouraging their migration (Gabaccia 1984a:21–23). Mrs. R., who was born in Naples in 1904 and immigrated to New York City in 1909, typified this pattern. Her father ran a business of trucks and horses in this southern Italian city, but their household consisted also of her mother, nine sisters, and two brothers. Her mother, she recalled, insisted on immigrating to the U.S. in order to avoid the economic disaster of attempting to provide each daughter with a dowry (Furio 1979:399–401).

Mrs. D., living in a town in Potenza, composed primarily of *contadini* (peasants) and no factories, became interested in migration to the United States, like so many others, after seeing the well-dressed Italian returnees and hearing stories of the great wealth they had accumulated. Mrs. D. recalled immigrating alone; that is, not with her immediate family but with a friend of the family who promised to help set her up in business. In 1914, at the age of eighteen, she migrated to New York and stayed at the house of a relative in Greenwich Village (Furio 1979:397–98).[28]

Mrs. M., born in Siena in 1903, followed an alternative path of migration to New York City, the one from which most generalizations have emerged. For a long time people in her town had difficulty in finding employment locally. She remembered her brother working in Germany for part of the year, and her father working in France; that was until he migrated by himself to the United States. These were common patterns of the time in Siena. Following her mother's death, her grandparents cared for her, but when she was five her father finally established himself and sent for the rest of the family to join him in America (Furio 1979:402–5).

Family status and changes in family life were important factors in migration decisions. Abandoned children and children of unmarried mothers evidenced a great propensity to emigrate, from both northern and southern Italy. In Sambuca, at least three-quarters of the illegitimate children born after 1871 migrated to the United States (Gabaccia 1988a:79–80). Rosa Cavalleri[29] (nee Inez), who migrated to the U.S. from Bugiarno, a silk-making village in Lombardy (northern Italy) was born in such circumstances. Taken from a foundling hospital in Milan by a poor woman from Bugiarno who earned income as a wet nurse, she was subsequently moved from home to home, as a foster child. At age three, Rosa joined the household of Maddalena Mateo (Mamma Lena), a former silk mill worker. It was at this early age that she first started to contribute her share of the household income by gathering sticks and dead pieces of wood from the ground for firewood (Ets 1970:34). At age four, Mama Lena taught Rosa two skills, common in the socialization of little girls in this region. Both storytelling and knitting would prove to be of some practical and economic value in Rosa's future.

> I would sit there beside her and listen and listen [to Mamma Lena's stories and prayers]. I had to sit there anyway because she was making me learn to knit. I would knit little pieces of string on some wooden needles Papa L. had made for me. (Ets 1970:27–28)

By age five, Rosa had already begun work in the silk worm camps, and by the time she was six she was put to work, like all the other little girls of the poor in Bugiarno, in the *filatoio*, the silk factories of Negrina.

> In the filatoio we were winding the silk from one spool to another. Each little girl had about seventeen spools to watch and when the thread to one of those spools broke we had to quick catch the ends and tie a knot. We had to stand there between the big belts that turned the wheels and watch. There was one spool above that was so big it took my arms to reach around it . . . One woman used to go back and forth behind us to watch and if we didn't tie fast enough she would hit us. (Ets 1970:75)

Rosa's graphic descriptions of work as a little girl in the various stages of silk manufacturing illuminate the extent to which her evolving identification as a worker was tightly interwoven with her socialization as a northern Italian female. Rosa took on more complex and physically arduous tasks as a measure of her bodily development and growth into adolescence and young womanhood. These experiences provided an important reference point for her later evaluation of life in the United States as an immigrant woman. Rosa's detailed accounts of the silk production process also shed light on the degree to which the industry was as of yet incompletely mechanized and still dependent on the skilled, but exploited, labor of women and girls.

At age seven, Rosa was sent to work in the *filanda*, "the real silk mill," where "big girls and women unwind the silk from the cocoons":

Those women used to sit four in a square—two facing two—and at each corner of the square was a big wheel to turn the reel. But there were no belts and no machines to turn those wheels. The machines were us little girls. All day we had to stand there by our wheel, turning and turning and watching the thread as it unwound from the cocoons. (Ets 1970:77)

Boys in Rosa's town never worked with the silk; instead they migrated to another village to work in the cloth mills. Only when the silk mills closed down during the time of the worm camps was Rosa permitted to earn income of a different sort, working in the rice fields. In lieu of wages, Rosa's mother received a bag of rice from the harvest (Ets 1970:79). When Rosa was ten and starting to physically mature, Mamma Lena threw her into an institution for orphan girls.[30] The girls received room and board and took classes in exchange for working at the local silk mill on Lago Maggiore near Canaletto. Rosa took pride in her years of experience in the silk industry compared to the other girls, but noted with some ambivalence:

Here in Canaletto we didn't have a little girl to turn the wheel for us. We had something new—a foot pedal. With the foot pedal you could turn the reel yourself as fast as you wanted it to go . . . But everyday my hands got more sore. You can't make the silk without getting sore hands. (Ets 1970:112)

Nevertheless, thinking back, Rosa recalled how fortunate she had been to be contracted to the mill for three years. "In a way I was glad. I wouldn't be getting any more of those terrible beatings from Mamma Lena" (Ets 1970:88).

During these years Rosa began to contrast her own life with what she imagined life to be like in America. For Rosa, life in Bugiarno was shrouded in fear. "The poor people didn't dare look in the faces of the high people . . . All the poor people knew they got from each other . . . And they were always afraid" (Ets 1970:41). Sitting in the courtyard of the mill one day sharing stories with the other women workers, Rosa heard about a recent returnee from America who challenged a landlord in court and won. "'That's what America does for the poor!' the woman said. And I began wishing that I could go to America too" (Ets 1970:120).

Rosa did leave for America several years later, but not under the conditions she had hoped for. Against her will, Mamma Lena married Rosa off when she turned fifteen to Santino, an older man who beat her. After a short while, Rosa's husband left her to join a work gang headed for the Missouri iron mines. After reimbursing the mining company for his own ticket, Santino eventually sent a ticket to Rosa and demanded that she join him. His work gang needed women to cook and wash for them. Once again, bullied by Mamma Lena, Rosa had little alternative but to join her husband in America. "But Rosa, don't be so sad!" She remembered her friends' words. "It is wonderful to go to America even if you don't want to go to Santino. You will get smart in America. And in America you will not be so poor" (Ets 1970:162).

CONCLUSION

Rosa Cavalleri followed one of the several alternative paths open to the Italian women and girls who migrated to the United States at the turn of the century. Their numbers and the mode of their departure depended upon the interaction of many elements: family composition and household arrangements, gender norms, age and marital status, the location of their region of origin in the world-economy, and finally the migration policies of a weakly unified Italian state.

Some women left as dutiful wives without options, imagined or real, but with years of experience in supporting a household alone or in close-knit communities with the assistance of other women. Some came as mothers with dreams of possibilities for their children. Some arrived as daughters in search of dowries and husbands and better options. Some entered the United States as hopeful young women with agricultural training and artisan skills but with experiences of collective action and protest also.

This chapter has demonstrated that it was not the case that migrating Italian women turned their backs on traditional roles as silent and passive females of a premodern society, and encountered social change and capitalism for the first time in American cities. Italian women left regions in varying degrees of social, cultural, economic, and political transformation. They had encountered processes of peripheralization within a global capitalist economy long before departing. By the turn of the century they were entering a part of the world equally integrated into the rhythms of the world-system. However, unlike the Italian male labor migrants so often disparagingly referred to as "birds of passage," Italian women increasingly immigrated permanently (Caroli 1973:43, 48–49). They were not sacrificing lives that had met their needs, their hopes, or those of their households in order to recreate like images elsewhere. In contrast, I have suggested that Italian women and girls migrated in order to continue the process of "becoming persons," in what they hoped would be a more agreeable climate.

CHAPTER 4

"So, We Have Crossed Half the World for This?": The Incorporation of Immigrant Wives and Mothers in New York, 1870–1924

All my memories of that kitchen are dominated by the nearness of my mother sitting all day long at her sewing machine, by the clacking of the treadle against the linoleum floor . . . the kitchen was her life. Year by year, as I began to take in her fantastic capacity for labor and her anxious zeal, I realized it was ourselves she kept stitching together.

—Alfred Kazin[1]

My brother who became head of the family had to take orders from her [the mother]. But that was only in our home. On the street he tried to impress everybody that he was the boss of the family . . . also, as I remember, I could never make out why my mother would tell untrue things to other women in the street. She would always complain how strict our older brother was. She would say . . . "Oh, no, I must first ask Rocco" . . . And she said these things while we knew perfectly well that the big bully Rocco would probably at the same time complain to my uncle saying how unreasonable, how impossibly crazy my mother was, and "Oh, if only I had the power, what I wouldn't do."

—South Calabrian immigrant male in New York City[2]

Immigrant mothers are, as one might expect, remembered by their sons with an abundance of nostalgia. Not surprisingly, they are most often recalled in connection with the intimacy of family life. In memory, their lives have merged into the singular life of the household, in which they typically have not been granted individual identities. Reminiscences of immigrant mothers have emphasized their heroic self-sacrifices and subservience in the name of collective family survival.

At the same time, immigrant mothers have been depicted as neither fully gendered nor fully human beings, but rather as wielders of enormous power and authority as "bosses" of their families. One of anthropologist Robert Orsi's informants spoke of his mother as a powerfully strong, in fact, overpowering woman, "'all three hundred and fifty pounds of her' going about the chores on the streets of Italian Harlem" (Orsi 1985:135). In his memoirs, *Jews Without Money*, Michael Gold remembered his "funny little East Side mother" as someone who "would have stolen or killed for us. She would have let a railroad train run over her body if it could have helped us. She loved us all with the fierce painful love of a mother-wolf, and scolded us continually like a magpie" (Gold 1930:158).

These paradoxical recollections of immigrant mothers suggest, perhaps, the larger-than-life-size expectations and obligations their sons assigned to them in the "new world." They also evoke the exaggeratedly powerful role Americanizers attributed to immigrant mothers. But, most importantly, they illuminate the persistent ambiguities and questions surrounding the fate of first-generation immigrant wives and mothers in the United States. To what extent could they wield meaningful power and authority in an unfamiliar world? In which domains did immigrant mothers exercise most control? Could they be considered so strong as to have constituted important obstacles blocking the path to their families' assimilation and adaptation? Indeed, was the magnitude of their power enough to resist or subvert the intentions of Americanizers? Or, ought the type of power immigrant mothers exercised be construed as "a cage," constraining them to abide by patriarchal gender ideals, family expectations, and household obligations?[3] Did the pressure to be a "good mother" prevent them from imagining or realizing more self-determined needs in America? Were social reformers correct in their assessment that immigrant mothers required their guidance, if not rescue? This chapter explores these questions in the context of analyzing the extent to which migration intensified women's existing subordination, diminished it, or alternatively subjected immigrant wives and mothers to new forms of control and domination in the United States.

As traditionally expressed, migration to developed regions of the world-economy from underdeveloped or peripheral areas improves women's life chances and emancipates women in all dimensions of their lives. As women pass through "the golden door," or so the story goes, they leave behind their acquiescence (a product of coercion and/or ignorance) to the demands of traditional patriarchal households and communities.

The liberating effect of immigration for women, according to assimilation and modernization theorists, occurred primarily through the uprooting of old world beliefs and values by exposure to new world ideas, especially to middle-class American standards of homemaking and child raising. In contrast, most feminist scholars and political economists have viewed immigrant women's opportunities for greater self-determination as primarily dependent upon their entry into the labor force. Presumably, an individual wage confers on a woman an increased level of consciousness in her interests, a significantly higher degree of control over her economic circumstances, and an enhanced status in her household and community.

Preceding chapters explored and highlighted both the commonalities and variations among migrating women in terms of their social, economic, and political backgrounds, as well as the diversity in their paths of emigration. This chapter revises the assumption that European women were, in one way or another, uniformly and unambiguously empowered by migrating to the United States at the turn of the century. Immigrant wives, and especially mothers, faced distinctly different and far more negative experiences of immigration than did unmarried women. But the divergence in migration experiences between married Russian-Jewish and Italian women was even more striking. Despite shared gender and life-cycle statuses, and shared origin as emigrants from underdeveloped regions of the late nineteenth-century world-economy, Russian-Jewish and Italian women were channeled towards different (although related) positions in the U.S. social structure. The nature and extent of their empowerment depended primarily on their place in the global reconfiguration of gender, class, and racial/ethnic/nationality relations occurring at the turn of the century. Their status in the United States was shaped not simply by their individual ambitions and skills, nor their degree of malleability, but rather in accord with their treatment by and responses to historically gendered, classed, and racialized "contexts of reception" (Portes and Rumbaut 1990:85–93). More precisely, the extent to which immigrant women's lives were transformed rested upon their interactions with state migration policies, private Americanization efforts, coethnic organizations and communities, and household income-producing opportunities.

This chapter focuses on three themes, or organizing questions, which illuminate the principal factors differentiating immigrant women's experiences and outcomes. The first centers on the surge of racial nativist ideas and practices in all sectors of American life at the end of the nineteenth century. What did the expression of racial nativism mean for an emerging core region of the world-system? How did it shape the reception of peoples from underdeveloped areas? To what extent did the discourse about the imputed characteristics of the so-called new immigration differentiate between U.S.-born and immigrant mothers, or between Italian and Russian-Jewish women?

The second question addresses an ongoing historical policy debate about the effect of Americanization organizations on newly arrived immigrants. In a climate of pervasive racial nativism, to what extent did the relations established between immigrant mothers and middle-class Anglo-American social reformers provide the means by which immigrant women could empower themselves? In other words, in what ways did the process of Americanization create conditions by which racial/ethnic, gender, and class hierarchies were reproduced, resisted, and/or transformed?

The third concern of this chapter is with immigrant women's mode of incorporation into coethnic communities in New York. To what extent were Russian-Jewish and Italian wives and mothers received similarly into communities of coethnics? In what ways did the establishment of coethnic economic relationships reproduce, transform, or contribute to the erosion of their subordination? When examined in the nexus of their household and ethnic community relationships, to what degree was immigrant women's work and income production empowering?

SIFTING THE WHEAT FROM THE CHAFF; OR, CROSSING THE RACIAL/ETHNIC DIVISION OF LABOR IN THE CAPITALIST WORLD-SYSTEM

It cannot be gainsaid that immigration in the past has been an important factor in the development and growth of this Republic . . . [But] the time has now come to draw the line, to

select the good from the bad, and to sift the wheat from the
chaff. (Congressional Record 1899:999, quoted in Calavita
1984:69)

Turn-of-the-century commentators and policy makers expressed
more than a little ambivalence about the capacity of the United
States, as an emerging core region of the world-system to absorb
a flood of newcomers. Varying in intensity with economic upturns
and downturns, racial nativist protest against unlimited immigration had nonetheless persisted from at least the early 1830s. Yet,
at the same time, leading industrialists and public officials widely
acknowledged the crucial role that foreign-born labor played in
America's ascent in the world-economy.[4] In recognition of the
unrivaled position of the U.S. in mechanized production world-
wide, the U.S. Industrial Commission of 1901 observed: "The fact
that machinery and the division of labor opens a place for the
unskilled immigrants makes it possible not only to get the advantages of machinery, but also to get the advantages of cheap labor"
(quoted in Calavita 1984:49).[5] Thus, the first effective numerical
restriction on European immigration—the Emergency Quota
Law—was passed by Congress only in 1921.

In this context, the ideology of racial nativism, operating in
tandem with a relatively open door to immigrants, contributed
significantly to the surge of industrial expansion in the U.S. by
reinforcing the social vulnerability of eastern and southern European immigrants. The more central immigrant labor became to
economic expansion, the more racial nativism became incorporated into particular labor force structures and the more it regulated immigrants' lives outside of employment. Racial nativism
provided the answer to Theodore Roosevelt's call for "some system by which undesirable immigrants shall be kept out entirely,
while desirable immigrants are properly distributed throughout
the country" (quoted in Davis 1920:88). Historian of American
immigration, John Higham, characterized the ideology of racial
nativism as "the intersection of racial attitudes with nationalistic
ones—in other words, the extension to European nationalities of
that sense of absolute difference which already divided white
Americans from people of other colors" (Higham 1955:132).[6]

However, before the newest immigrant additions could seem
to be "a fundamentally different order" of people, "sharp physical
differences between native Americans and European immigrants

[that] were not readily apparent . . . had to be manufactured" (Higham 1955: 133). The principle that immigrants of a particular nationality could be "racialized," categorized as unfit for U.S. society, and thus targeted for exclusion had been firmly established with the Chinese Exclusion Act of 1882 (Conk 1985:39). The categorization of eastern and southern Europeans together as "the new immigration,"[7] in contradistinction to "the old immigration," was but one effort to construct a new composite identity for peoples from the late nineteenth-century periphery. By 1899 the U.S. Bureau of Immigration had begun to classify immigrant arrivals according to race or people; until that time statistics concerning the foreign-born population in the U.S. had been recorded only by country of birth (USIC 1911 V:1).

Public discussion of eastern and southern European immigrants expressed ambivalent and contradictory sentiments, paralleling the movement for selective immigration restriction. As President Theodore Roosevelt argued in his 1905 message to Congress:

> We cannot have too much immigration of the right sort [but] there should be an increase in the stringency of the laws to keep out the insane . . . pauper immigrants . . . anarchist tendencies . . . all people of bad character, the incompetent, the lazy, the vicious, the physically unfit, defective, or degenerate, should be kept out (quoted in Calavita 1984:89–90).

Comments such as these shaped as well as reflected anxieties about what this "new immigration" meant for the development of an "American identity" and what it boded for the maintenance of "national strength."

Characteristic of the myopia of an emerging core power, the U.S. pictured itself as a magnet drawing in the poor of the world. It overlooked that the majority of the world's population had not migrated and, of those who had, most arrived in destinations outside of the United States. From New York and other major ports of entry, the U.S. seemed entirely dominated by immigration. Between 1880 and 1924 over 26 million immigrants entered the country. The city's population grew from 1.5 to 5 million, between 1870 and 1915 (Rischin 1977:10). According to the U.S. Industrial Commission (1901, XV: 467), "the foreign element in New York in 1890, then, made up four-fifths of its population, while the strictly native element was less than one-fifth." By 1910 the strictly foreign born comprised nearly 45 percent of New York City's population. Although Ireland and Germany had initially led in providing low-wage immigrants to New York employers, by the last decade of the nineteenth century they were eclipsed by Russia and Italy as the new leading areas of origin of the city's working poor. In 1910, Russian Jews comprised about 23 percent of the city's foreign-born population, and Italians, 18 percent (Claghorn 1901: 465–68; Rosenwaike 1972:42; U.S.Census 1910, IV:180–92; Rischin 1977:271).

The impression of an overwhelming and unending deluge stamped the depiction of turn-of-the-century migration to the United States.

> Out of the remote and little-known regions of northern, eastern, and southern Europe forever marches a vast and endless army. Nondescript and ever-changing in personnel, without leaders or organization, this great force, moving at the rate of nearly 1,500,000 each year, is invading the civilized world. (Grose 1909:16)

Fearful that unrestricted immigration would lead to the "breeding out" of the fixed, inherited, national traits that made the United States an increasingly important power in the world-system, Senator Henry Cabot Lodge, sponsor of a nativist literacy test bill in 1896, manufactured a historical precedent:

> The great influx of barbarians into Europe after the fall of the Roman Empire, so far as we can determine from all extant accounts, was small compared to the immigration to this country within the lifetime of a single generation. (Lodge [1900] 1920:51)

In 1901, Kate Claghorn, assistant registrar of the New York Tenement House Department, described how the popular press roused the fears of skilled labor in its graphic portrayal of the "new immigration":

> a recent newpaper picture . . . showed, to illustrate the evils of immigration, a vast ocean steamer, the stern touching the European shore, the bow, the American shore. Into this, on the European side poured a vast throng of people, winding down from the poorhouses of Europe; from it, on the American side, the throng reappeared, to take up the straight road to the poorhouses of America. (Claghorn [1904] 1972: 135–37)

In both popular and scholarly publications, the world was recreated to look as if eastern and southern Europe had spilled their contents into the ocean, the refuse of which washed up onto the U.S. eastern seaboard with each day's tide. Frances A. Walker, economist, President of Massachusetts Institute of Technology and outspoken racial nativist, depicted eastern and southern European immigration as natural selection in reverse:

> So broad and smooth is the channel, there is no reason why every foul and stagnant pool of population in Europe, which no breath of intellectual or industrial life has stirred for ages, should not be decanted upon our soil . . . These people have no history behind them . . . They have none of the inherited instincts and tendencies which made it comparatively easy to deal with the immigration of the olden time. They are beaten men from beaten races; representing the worst failures in the struggle for existence. (Walker [1899] 1920:369–70)

Walker feared that unregulated natural selection might lead to the survival of the least fit. Concerned with dwindling birth rates among the native-born population, he concluded that Americans had made the disastrous choice to reduce the size of their families rather than to lower their standard of living, in order to better compete with low-waged immigrant labor. In short, Walker argued that in their attempt to maintain U.S. economic and cultural superiority, native-born Americans naively fostered their own biological defeat (Higham 1955:142–44).

Walker's writings introduced pseudoscientific, biological, and "natural" dimensions to the racial nativist discussion of "the foreign danger within." Initially, biologically pessimistic views such as his were challenged by a brief wave of "optimistic racial nationalism" following U.S. expansion in the Philippines, Hawaii, and Puerto Rico. The capacity of the Anglo-Saxon race to merge with other peoples yet retain its dominance seemed undisputed. However, by 1905, when Japan emerged as a new world power to contest recent U.S. acquisitions, popular opinion reassumed an even more pessimistic and defensive posture on the possibility of absorbing the foreign born into the American "social body."

Increasingly, immigration was discussed in terms of uncontrollable natural disasters, weakened bodies, illnesses, and quasimilitary invasions, for example, tide, stream, wave, flow, flood, torrent, tidal wave, fevers, hemmorages, and the like.[8]

Like a mighty stream, it finds its source in a hundred rivulets. The huts of the mountains and the hovels of the plains are the springs which feed; the fecundity of the races of the old world the inexhaustible source. (Grose 1909:17)

Alfred C. Reed, a physician in the employ of the U.S. Public Health and Marine Hospital Service in 1912, considered the different sources of immigration and their "relative desirability from the medical standpoint." "The best class," for Reed, was drawn from northern and western Europe, and the worst, from eastern and southern Europe and the Middle East (Reed [1912] 1920: 305–6). Reed's criteria exemplified the pseudoscientific basis of early twentieth-century racial nativism.

The first rule of national life is self-preservation . . . [R]ecall a principle which is as valid from the medical standpoint as from the economic or social. Only those peoples should be admitted whom experience has shown will amalgamate quickly and become genuine citizens . . . No race is desirable which does not tend to lose its distinctive traits in the process of blending with our own social body. (Reed [1912] 1920:299, 306)

As H. H. Boyesen put it, "Just as a body cannot with safety accept nourishment any faster than it is capable of assimilating it, so a state cannot accept an excessive influx of people without serious injury" (quoted in Davis 1920:122). For Dr. Charles E. Woodruff, U.S. Army surgeon in the Philiippines,

. . . the growing distrust of the immigrant is the realization by the people that the body politic is sick . . . instead of the healthy, normal Aryan tissue harboring few commensal, healthy Semitic, Hamitic and Turanian organisms, it is swarming with them . . . Some of the parasites have grown large, fat and rich and powerful and bid fair to make the host very sick. (quoted in Drachsler [1920] 1970:45)

Depictions such as these of "the bodies" belonging to "the new immigration" both shaped and reflected the thinking behind the various efforts to selectively restrict immigration. They were incorporated into the U.S. Immigration Commission Reports of 1911 and used to legitimate the type of reception afforded new immigrants and the eventual closing of the door to them in the 1920s.

The 1911 Immigration Commission's *Dictionary of Races or Peoples* exemplified the use an emerging core state could make of racial nativism. The underlying objective of this volume was to demonstrate the extent to which certain races were hereditarily incapable of Americanizing, in the light of the popular assumption that both physical and cultural characteristics were biologically heritable. Given their influence over subsequent immigration policy and Americanization efforts, these definitions merit examination.

> CAUCASIAN, CAUCASIC, EUROPEAN, EURAFRICAN, or WHITE race. Although the white race would be supposed to be the one best understood, it is really the one about which there is the most fundamental and sometimes violent discussion (USIC 1911 V:30–1).

> ENGLISH or ANGLO-SAXON . . . Of course there is no necessity in this dictionary for discussion of a subject so well understood by all . . . It may be assumed that all Americans understand the race which has given us our language and laws and political institutions. Yet there may be some doubt as to the ethnical position of the English—as to which of the present components of the mixed English nation are to be considered as unassimilated immigrant elements and which as truly English (USIC 1911 V:54).

> HEBREW, JEWISH, or ISRAELITE . . . Scattered throughout Europe, especially in Russia, yet preserving their own individuality to a marked degree . . . Physically the Hebrew is a mixed race . . . In every country they are found to approach in type the people among whom they have long resided . . . The "Jewish nose," and to a less degree other facial characteristics, are found well-nigh everywhere throughout the race . . . Taking all factors into account, and especially their type of civilization, the Jews of today are more truly European than Asiatic or Semitic. The classification of the Bureau of Immigration separates the Hebrews from the Semites and places them in the Slavic grand division of the Aryan family, although as is explained above they are not Aryan (USIC 1911 V:73–74).

> ITALIAN. The race or people of Italy. The Bureau of Immigration divides this race into two groups, North Italian and South Italian. These two groups differ from each other materially in language, physique, and character, as well as in geographical distribution . . . [T]he South Italian [is] excitable, impulsive . . . an individualist having little adaptability to highly organized society. The North Italian, on the other hand, is . . . cool, delib-

erate, patient, practical, and as capable of great progress in the political and social organization of modern civilization . . . [A]ll crimes, and especially violent crimes, are several times more numerous among the South than the North Italians . . . Italian immigration to the United States is perhaps of more significance in the study of immigration than any other at the present time, not only because it is far larger each year than that of any other race . . . More significant still is the fact that this race has a larger population than any of the dozen other races ranking highest in the rate of immigration. In other words, out of its 35,000,000 population and the high birth rate that characterizes the race, it can continue to lead in immigration when the other races . . . are depleted . . . The heaviest transatlantic emigration from Italy is chiefly . . . South Italians. (USIC 1911 V:81–5)

Those who were considered close to the "English" or "Caucasian" races were viewed as more capable of assimilation into the American social body. In its attempt to define or distinguish racial characteristics of distinct groups, the *Dictionary* exposes the process of racialization at the state level. Contradictory and illusory categories were invented in relation and in opposition to each other (e.g., Anglo-Saxon/Hebrew, White/North Italian, North Italian/South Italian, Hebrew/Italian). Especially ironic was the ambiguity and the utter lack of specificity concerning the definition of those groups considered the benchmark or standard against which all other groups were evaluated and ranked.

What is behind these depictions of the "new immigration"? What underlying anxieties and global material processes did racialized images of transnational migration (as invasion, natural calamity, and disease) symbolize? Most important, what did these racial nativist images say about and to Russian-Jewish and Italian immigrant women? In short, how did nativism as a simultaneously racialized and gendered ideology shape their reception in the U.S.?

At a global level, the representation of human migration as "natural" obscured the historically specific social relations that had initiated, organized, and sustained mobility between the United States, Russia, and Italy. Shifts in both world economic and interstate relations and in the nationality/ethnic, gender, and class composition of immigrants in the United States provided the context for describing migration as an uncontrollable, overwhelming, inevitable force of nature. Hidden from view were the processes of an overarching world-economy gradually weaving the United States, Russia, and Italy closer together into an increasingly unequal interdependency. It is no coincidence that just as the U.S. ascended to the position of core in the world-economy immigrants from peripheralized regions became "racialized" peoples. From the 1870s until the 1920s when the U.S. immigration doors virtually shut, neither Russia nor Italy, as peripheral regions in the world-economy, were in a position to control traffic across their borders. The United States, however, as an emerging core power, stood to benefit from the flow of low-wage controllable labor and was unwilling to limit it (Sassen-Koob 1981:69). Imagery representing sending and receiving states as either victims or beneficiaries of "natural forces" reflected the changing balance of power in the world-system, and the inability and/or unwillingness of states to control it against the protests of threatened classes and social groups within their borders. Explanations for the disruptions engendered by early twentieth-century social change, couched in racial nativism, or "scientific racism," powerfully conveyed the fears, frustrations, and loss of privilege of particular social groups. Higher-waged, skilled labor and fairly autonomous artisan workers had been especially disempowered by a gradual proletarianization process occuring within an increasingly integrated global economy, with a qualitatively new racial/ethnic division of labor.

Turn-of-the-century nativism, as a racialized and gendered ideology, affected the reception of immigrant women differently than immigrant men, married women and mothers differently than single women, and Russian-Jewish and Italian women differently than other immigrant women.

From the start, women had more difficulty gaining entrance to the United States than men. Unaccompanied adult women from eastern and southern Europe were treated, at best, as children in need of supervision. In the words of Edward Corsi, director of Ellis Island at the time,

> A woman, if she came alone, was asked a number of special questions: how much money she had; if she were going outside of New York; whether her passage had been paid by herself or by some charitable institution. If she had come to join her husband in New York or Brooklyn, we could not let her loose on the streets of a strange city looking for her husband... Sometimes... the man could not be located... Sometimes these women were placed in the care of a social agency... but

if everything possible had been done, and the missing husband or fiance still could not be traced, the poor alien, despite all her tears, had to be returned to her native country. (quoted in Seller 1981:35)

Women's intended destinations were more likely to be questioned by inspectors than were men's. Immigration agents considered women, regardless of age or marital status, as economic dependents and, therefore, more likely to become public charges if unaccompanied by a man (Weatherford 1986:179).

Once allowed entry, immigrant women confronted the fears of racial nativists regarding their fertility rates compared to native-born women (Jenks and Lauck 1920:291). According to the U.S. Immigration Commission, the average new immigrant woman had a child once every 3.2 years, in contrast to the 5.3 years for a native-born white woman of native parentage. Italian and Jewish women were said to be the most prolific (USIC 1911 II:499–501).[9] In response to these numbers racial eugenists claimed that "Yankee stock" would be overwhelmed culturally and politically (Gordon 1976:137). Surveillance and documentation of immigrant women's birth rates provided more ammunition in the struggle to ward off "race suicide." The race suicide alarm nourished nativists' fears that institutions of "American civilization," particularly motherhood and the family, were in danger of subversion. Blaming immigrant women for keeping their birth rates up, however, was but the reverse side of blaming relatively privileged white native-born women for keeping theirs down. As Margaret Sanger and other "feminist eugenists" opened birth control clinics and distributed handbills in Italian and Yiddish on the lower east side, "anti-feminist eugenists" followed Theodore Roosevelt's lead in condemning the Yankee "man or woman who deliberately avoids marriage and . . . children" as "a criminal against the race" (Cowan and Cowan 1989:163; Van Vorst [1903] 1974:3).[10]

"Bodies" had become metaphors for national strength/weakness in the migration debates of the turn-of-the-century world-system. As such, the fate of nations, if not of civilization itself, was viewed as dependent upon the "scientific" discovery and classification of differences between the bodies of Jewish men and women, Italian men and women, and native-born American men and women. In the early twentieth-century context of capitalist rationalization and scientific management, precise determination of differences meant the subjection of Russian-Jewish and Italian immigrants to scientific racism.

Ironically, the ideology of scientific racism played a curious part in reducing the perception of threat to American supremacy by promoting notions of the inherent docility and congenitally weaker bodies of inferior immigrant peoples. Immigrant women's racial (physiological and cultural) inferiority, it was widely charged, was evidenced by their notoriously high rates of fertility. Denigrated for their inherent submissiveness to traditional patriarchal norms in sexual matters, immigrant mothers were belittled further by most Americanizers for their lack of parenting and homemaking skills. The incorporation of racial nativism and eugenic thinking into immigration policy, progressive social reform, and early feminism provided both racial explanations for the status of immigrant wives and mothers and "scientific" justifications for social inequalities in an expanding and productive economy. When warnings about Anglo-Saxon "race suicide" and the "fetid fertility" of immigrant women were combined with an immigration policy still relatively open until the 1920s, eastern and southern European women together were made especially vulnerable to new forms of subordination.

During this period of U.S. ascendancy in the world-economy, racial nativist discourse about fertility and motherhood structured relations between immigrant women, the U.S. state, and a diversity of Americanizing organizations. Given the then widespread view that "no race is desirable which does not tend to lose its distinctive traits in the process of blending with our own social body," managing immigrant womens' bodies and families, particularly their fertility and homemaking activities, became the preoccupation of a variety of social reformers.

IMMIGRANT WOMEN, ANGLO-AMERICAN REFORMERS, AND THE MANUFACTURE OF AMERICAN MOTHERHOOD

Although hereditarian and racial nativist thinking dominated the conclusions of the 1911 Immigration Commission and strongly influenced the eventual rejection of the new immigrants, their report also included a minority viewpoint emphasizing the mutability of race—as physiology and as culture—if vigorous efforts were made to "heat and stir the melting pot." This reform-minded approach to immigrant adaptation eventually dominated the everyday lives of those new immigrant women allowed to pass through the "golden door" to America.

> Even those characteristics which modern science has led us to consider as most stable seem to be subject to thorough changes under the new environment, which would indicate that even racial physical characteristics do not survive under the new social and climatic environment of America. (USIC 1911 I:44)

An optimistic faith in the power of the American social environment to assimilate immigrants, despite their racial origins, *if* substantially supported by the state and other social institutions, surfaced with a new urgency in the first decades of the twentieth century.[11]

The optimism of the Progressive era was founded not simply on racial nationalism, although that certainly persisted, but on two additional and related premises. First, reformers widely believed that the benefits of American industrialism would eventually trickle down to raise the standards of living for all. Second, Progressives generally assumed, like many others of the time (e.g., racial eugenists), that the application of modern scientific principles both to the factory and to the household would eventually remedy most social ills. Of course, in the meantime, reformers, such as they, were needed to grease the wheels of change.[12]

By the turn of the century, most Progressive reformers conceded that character or moral defects were not the cause of poverty, but that poverty and immorality might themselves be products of the unhealthy social environment produced by rapid industrial expansion (Beard [1915] 1972: 237ff.; Rodgers 1978: 226). As one worker at the University Settlement House on the Lower East Side explained

> Account should be taken of the poor condition under which the Italian works ... and the unscrupulous American employers who are likely to take advantage of his ignorance of our laws and save money on appliances necessary for the safety of the laborers. Thus the Italian is often the victim of sickness and accident which make him a public charge. (Aronovici 1908:31)

Although increasingly more aware of the social nature of the problems confronting immigrant wives and mothers, social reformers were nonetheless divided with respect to their goals and strategies. These were primarily shaped by their own ethnic and class identities and the nature of the ethnic communities or institutions they represented. In short, the Americanizing institutions encountered by newly arrived immigrant women were of two main types: those organized and administered primarily by white/Anglo-American middle-class reformers, and those by middle-class nominal coethnics (e.g., German/Jewish-Americans). The extent to which immigrant women were received more by one than the other had a significant effect on the nature and outcome of their adaptation. Even more important, the distinctions between the experiences of Italian and Russian-Jewish women were located primarily in their different interactions with these Americanizing organizations. Thus, it mattered profoundly to Italian Catholic women whether they became "targets" of Protestant Evangelists, "patrons" of Irish Catholic churches, "projects" for old-stock Anglo-American "friendly home visitors," or members of Italian organizations. It made a crucial difference to Russian-Jewish women whether they were subject to the surveillance of Anglo-American settlement workers, the invasiveness of nominal coethnic (German-Jewish) reformers, or members of Russian-Jewish associations.

What were the goals and strategies of the middle-class Anglo-American reformers with whom immigrant wives and mothers came into contact? What was the nature of their interactions?

Robert Woods and Albert Kennedy, two authorities in the social settlement movement, saw as their primary task "to impart American standards and ideals . . . and to assist [immigrants] in adjusting their life to ours." For them, "Americanization [was] an evolution into national fellowship through mastery of our standards of living" (1922; quoted in McBride 1975:27). They identified the aims of immigrant adaptation with that of Anglo conformity, a linear progression towards cultural homogeneity.

Sophinisba Breckinridge, professor of social economy at the University of Chicago and contributor to an eleven-volume series on methods of Americanization, characterized the goals of social settlements somewhat differently. "The settlement ideal," wrote Breckinridge, "has included the preservation of the dignity and self-esteem of the immigrant, while attempting to modify his habits when necessary and giving him some preparation for citizenship" (Breckinridge 1921:238). Breckinridge supported the addition of mother's clubs and housekeeping courses to settlement classes in English and Civics. Settlement worker Cecilia Razovski supported this practice enthusiastically. She took special pride in her role as bearer of progress to "the thousands of foreign women who have come to us without any training, whatsoever, doing what their mothers and grandmothers did before them." For Razovski, "old standards must be changed if we are sincere in our desire to attain a higher form of civilization. The strangers from across the water must be taught to discard un-American habits and conventions, to accept new ideals" (Ewen 1985: 85).

Jane Addams, a nascent cultural pluralist, tried to mitigate the conflicts between first-generation immigrant mothers and their rapidly Americanizing daughters by acknowledging and preserving the mothers' handicrafts in her Labor Museum at Hull House in Chicago (Addams [1904] 1972:80–81). Ironically, Addams heralded immigrant mother's old world, informal, sometimes non-waged, production, just as married women and their skills were increasingly devalued in the new world paid labor market.

Mary Kingsbury Simkhovitch, founder of Greenwich House, which served an increasingly Italian immigrant population in New York City, was embarrassed by the problems resulting from social reformer's general ignorance of immigrant customs. For her, the goal of settlement house work was

> not so much in the rendering of specific services . . . as in the fruitful knowledge obtained through firsthand contact with the people in the neighborhoods. To voice their wrongs, to understand their problems, to stand by their side in their life struggles, to welcome their leadership, to reveal to others who had not the opportunity of direct contact . . . is the primary task. (Simkhovitch 1938:86–87)

Simkhovitch assumed the role of advocate on behalf of new immigrants in their struggle to improve social conditions. Many settlement house workers viewed themselves, like Simkhovitch, as a contrast to the "pressure cooking" assimilation of the Anglo-conformists and attempted to counteract the tendency of reformers to divide immigrant families by generation. But, despite protestations to the contrary, even Simkhovitch was not immune to conventional middle-class assumptions and a Progressive's faith in the fruits of industrial progress. Neither was she removed from the pattern of maternalism that typically characterized relationships between female Anglo-American university-educated reformers and immigrant mothers. This was evidenced in her reflections on another resident worker at Greenwich House, a Tenement House inspector who

> taught us how to keep on the watch for violations as we went in and out of our neighbors' homes. In all these matters our position was and is to this day a delicate one. We cannot give away our neighbors, we cannot get them into trouble, and yet we cannot be blind to the evils we see. But as a wise mother may overlook a wrongdoing from time to time in order to emphasize something more important when it comes up, so it is inhuman and unwise for a settlement to take over the office of law enforcement. (Simkhovitch 1938:101)

The nature of the maternalism between female social settlement workers and recently arrived immigrant mothers was in some respects analogous to the superordinate-subordinate relationships some researchers have noted between female employers of paid domestic workers and female domestics.[13] Here, the concept is used to call attention to the dynamics of the relationship between female reformers and immigrant mothers, which protected and nurtured as it degraded and insulted. The benevolence of the female settlement worker, sometimes referred to as "the neighborhood mother," was based on a fundamental lack of respect for the female recepient as an autonomous adult (Mangano [1917] 1971:146).[14] Despite her own subordinate status as a woman, the power of the social settlement worker to reproach and to intervene in immigrant lives was enhanced by her own racial/ethnic and class identities. Moreover, as social settlement work continued to produce and reproduce the perception of a childlike immigrant mother, it simultaneously validated and strengthened the new professional status of university-educated women. Americanization efforts such as these complemented selective immigration restriction by attempting to transform or alter the "undesirable" behavior of new immigrants without curtailing the "golden stream" or seriously challenging the systems of gender, racial/ethnic, or class stratification.

Married women and mothers emerged as an early and especially important target of the movement to assimilate eastern and southern European immigrants. Impressed by studies on the rationalization of factory production, Americanizers made concerted efforts at a parallel transformation of the immigrant "homemak-ing enterprise." An economically dependent wife/mother, non-working children at least until age fourteen, and a husband/father who earned enough to support the household comprised the inflexible middle-class core of the Progressive's domestic ideal.[15] For Louise Bolard More, who conducted an evening women's club at Greenwich House, a good mother was one who judiciously managed the household income that her husband provided. The mother who takes in sewing or goes out to do what she can to increase the family income as the children grow older, even if nec-essary, was reproached by More for her "disastrous effect on the ambition of her husband. As soon as he sees that the wife can help support the family, his interest and sense of responsibility are likely to lessen, and he works irregularly or spends more on him-self" (More 1907: 87). More's fears were borne out in the New York City Consumer's League study of Italian artificial flower makers in Greenwich Village. Investigators made special mention of one woman who made flowers from six in the morning until as late as one or two o'clock at night, commenting that her unem-ployed husband stayed home and did "her housework in order that she might devote all her time to the work" (Consumer's League 1915:9).

The domestic ideal of reformers conflicted with the needs and practices of recently arrived immigrant mothers whom they tried to persuade to perform housework more productively and child care more efficiently. Moreover, it contrasted with the life experi-ences of most female social reformers themselves, whose privi-leged racial/ethnic and class positions allowed them to pursue new gender options—university educations and professional careers in "social homemaking."[16]

In the eyes of assimilationists, immigrant mothers were the guardians both of the present home and of the future generations of American citizens. A few female reformers exaggerated and romanticized the "strong" position of the immigrant mother in her family and overlooked the patriarchal restraints and limits on her alleged power of the purse. Mary Kingsbury Simkovitch viewed the new immigrant family through just such a lens:

> The position of the [immigrant] mother was a strong one, much stronger than often obtains in families of a higher economic level, since the family funds were in her hands. She paid not only

for the rent, insurance and food, but also the family's clothing and gave to the husband and earning children enough for their carfare and lunches. This built up a solid family life where each was dependent on the other. Clash and conflict were necessary corollaries of this closeness, but there was something warm and loving about such a home in which no individual could live for himself alone . . . It made of sacrifice not a beautiful thought but a common custom. (Simkhovitch 1938:136–37)

Most Americanizers, however, viewed immigrant mothers as obstacles to the assimilation and advancement of their children, families, and ethnic communities. Americanization of the immigrant mother, they claimed, was the key to the elimination of a myriad of urban problems, including the attraction to "radicalism" and juvenile delinquency. Protestant evangelist, Antonio Mangano argued that "the greatest problem is not the foreign child but the foreign mother" (Mangano [1917] 1971:144). Dr. Kate Waller Barrett, Special Agent of the U.S. Immigration Service argued that "reaching the alien mother is paramount if we are going to Americanize our foreign population . . . [since] her attitude towards the problems of daily life unconsciously are reflected in the other members of the family" (Barrett [1915] 1920:228).

For social settlement workers, motherhood was too essential to a democratic culture to abandon to the untrained hands of the unassimilated. As Sophinisba Breckinridge instructed "no doubt, many foreign-born housewives have learned to care for their homes and raise their families as systematically as their American neighbors . . . it is, however a wasteful system which leaves the instruction of the immigrant housewife to the chance instruction she can gain from fellow countrywomen who have themselves learned only imperfectly" (Breckinridge 1921:84).

Activities undertaken by settlement workers on behalf of immigrant wives and mothers stressed instruction in the "American style" of infant care, parent-child relations, family organization and finances, nutrition, and hygiene. Preoccupied with the seemingly chaotic and unregulated nature of immigrant mothers' homemaking, they sought to apply factory-based models to household and family management.

High on their list of maternal behaviors to transform was the irregularity of infant nursing habits, that is, feeding on demand (Ewen 1985:136). Incorporating the competitive ethic of industrial capitalism into baby saving and child care, some workers found that "one of the most effective ways of stimulating the interest of mothers in educating themselves in the care and feeding of young children is through baby contests or shows or 'derbies'" (Beard [1915] 1972:59). The practice of hygienic child care was of paramount importance to the nurses and home visitors sponsored by the North American Civic League for Immigrants, who seized every opportunity to "teach the mother to bathe the child gently without disturbing it." Reporting on these visits, Olivia Howard Dunbar betrayed the underlying attitude of the League in stating that "while it may be easy to interest untaught but strongly prejudiced women in cooking and sewing, it is never anything short of a heroic labor, as all missionaries to the poor have discovered, to reconcile them to water and air" (Dunbar [1913] 1917:253). She would no doubt have been shaken upon discovering the reasons for one Italian woman's disappointment with America:

> Good money, good people, but my country . . . good air, much air, nice air down [in] Italy. Blue sky, the water laugh[s] in the bay . . . in my country people cook out of doors, wash out of doors . . . America . . . many people [in] one house, work, work all the time. Good money, but no good air. (Watson 1911:777)

The imposition of middle-class Anglo-American dietary standards followed closely on the list of reformers goals. "Sympathetic questioning would reveal that the unhappy mother was utterly at a loss as to how to feed her brood in this strange country . . . where nothing was as it been at home" (Dunbar [1913] 1917:253). Simkhovitch boasted that at Greenwich House, staff "actually got our Italian neighbors to use brown flour for their macaroni!" (1938:183). The New York Association for Improving the Condition of the Poor (A.I.C.P.) opened the Mulberry Health Center in the heart of an Italian immigrant district in 1918 with the aim of changing the nutritional habits of the population. The findings of surveys conducted by the center reveal their preoccupation with the behavior of immigrant mothers. The "chief problems" in 275 malnutrition cases recorded in 1921–1922, were "instruction in preparation of food" (227 cases) and "help in planning of meals" (198 cases). The "indifference" of employed mothers was also duly noted. In only twenty-seven cases did the center find material and/or monetary relief necessary. Demeaning immigrant mothers further, the center developed a system of temporarily discontinuing home visits after three months in order to "test . . . whether the mother had been sufficiently impressed with the need of proper attention to the food and health habits of the children to enforce them." This practice enabled the worker to carry a larger number of cases (Gillett 1924:10–12). In her recommendations for securing the cooperation of Italian mothers, Lucy Gillett, Superintendent of the Nutrition Bureau of the New York A.I.C.P. claimed that "if the mother can be made to understand that the worker has only the good of her child at heart, she is usually willing to do her part." But, when the mother was uncooperative or ungrateful, Gillett suggested appealing "through reason"to the Italian father. "The worker can usually convince the man more quickly than the woman, who has grasped only an impression which she cannot repeat or explain in words" (Gillett 1924:28).

As part of their Americanization effort, social reformers also encouraged immigrant homemakers to use household budgets and account books and refrain from recourse to credit, installment buying, or pawn shops (Gibbs 1917; Breckinridge 1921:85–148; Mussey 1903:236–44; Dickinson 1984). Many settlements contained branches of the Penny Provident Fund, in order to induce women to save small amounts and later to start regular bank accounts (Union Settlement, Annual Reports 7, 1902). Howard Brubaker of the University Settlement claimed that "the provident habit acquired here will make the family more self-reliant, better prepared for adversity, less at the mercy of dishonest merchants, usurious money-lenders, or avaricious landlords" (University Settlement Studies 1906:64–65).

Instruction in sewing and needlework for immigrant women was pervasive throughout the social settlement movement. The Union Settlement, in cooperation with the Harlem Branch of the New York Charity Organization Society and the Harlem Relief Society, gave instruction in needlework and sewing to mostly Italian mothers in their south Harlem neighborhood (Union Settlement, Annual Reports 11, 1906:8; 1915:41).

Americanizers seldom recognized or acknowledged the informal training and "apprenticeships" in clothing construction that had been a part of ordinary girlhood experiences for most immigrant women. Their ignorance in these matters could, however, become a subtle source of power for immigrant women. The following passage by just such a reformer exemplifies not only her maternalist perspective but, perhaps more importantly, how her immigrant clients turned both maternalism and ignorance against her to meet their own needs.

> In the matter of clothing the [immigrant] women were equally ignorant and equally teachable. The mothers were sincere in protesting that they would be glad to make cheap, simple garments for themselves and their children if they only knew how. In these cases they were supplied with a pattern and enough material for one garment and given one or more lessons in cutting, fitting and fashioning it. These lessons, like those in cooking, proved to have an irresistable fascination for whole communities. The Educator . . . found that if she made an appointment with one ambitious Italian housewife to cut and fit a skirt, a relative would appear within five minutes . . . while at more or less regular intervals during the afternoon neighbors with soft, persuasive voices and bewitching Italian smiles would present themselves with their individual bundles and the entreaty, "Oh, please, missis, me, too!" And as she left the house, the exhausting but profitable session finally concluded, still other candidates for instruction would pounce eagerly from dark doorways to accost the "teacher" and gain her promise of help. (Dunbar [1913] 1917:254–55)

In 1905 the Scuola d'Industrie Italiane, a lace and embroidery crafts school for Italian women, was established on the upper floor of New York's Richmond Hill Settlement House. One of the purposes of the school was to "rescue" Italian mothers and their daughters from the low-waged sweatshops and factories of the city by offering them higher wages for their work and paid vacations. However, prices for the school's handmade products were extremely high and, in spite of its annual subsidy from the Italian government, the school closed down after only two years (Pozzetta 1971:262). The Richmond Hill Settlement's experiment of drawing in Italian mothers and daughters by reviving hand industries at the Scuola d'Industrie Italiane is reminiscent in some ways of Jane Addam's Labor Museum at Hull House in Chicago. Both embodied racial nativist and gendered assumptions. The Richmond Hill Settlement disregarded the more flexible gender division of labor among Russian Jews and Italians in garment production. Moreover, the emphasis on training young women in handsewing ill prepared them for the early twentieth-century clothing factory. Women who specialized in handwork were positioned only to take places as the most exploited and lowest-waged workers in tenement sweatshops finishing garments with their young children at home or in the backrooms of small shops where the nonmechanized parts of the production process remained.

A survey of the activities of eighty settlements in Manhattan, Brooklyn, and the Bronx revealed that as late as 1926 and 1927, forty-eight of them still offered classes for women in "homemaking, cooking, sewing, [and] house decoration." By that time, however, settlement authorities were more forthright about their objectives. Even if immigrant women sold their handicrafts from time to time under the auspices of the settlements, reformers clearly distinguished income production from their primary purpose: learning how to become more competent homemakers in their own households (Kennedy, Farra, et al., 1935:6, 223–27).

Between 1913 and 1919, the International Institute of the Young Women's Christian Association established thirty-one organizations across the United States to assist immigrant women (Breckinridge 1921:244). In New York City, the YWCA targeted Italian women for special attention and encouraged them to learn English, as well as to identify personal goals and needs (Treese 1990:33). Accused of breaking apart the family by focusing on individual members rather than the needs of the unit as a whole, it did not take long before the YWCA was forced to take up the theme of intergenerational conflict between Italian immigrant mothers and daughters. But only in 1934, did the New York City Uptown YWCA invite an Italian woman, Elba Farabegoli, a second-generation Italian-American with university educations both in Italy and the United States, to organize an Italian Mother's Club. Not unexpectedly, the club specialized in "mothercraft." By 1943, it seemed as if conflict and tension between the objectives of the social settlements and the family ideals of Italian mothers had reached some accommodation. In a play performed at an Italian Mother's Club meeting, entitled "Why, It's Mother!" an Americanized daughter's rudeness to her old-fashioned immigrant mother becomes the catalyst for the mother's quick gender, class and cultural makeover. The mother finally learns English, subscribes to *Good Housekeeping* magazine, begins to cook nutritious American meals, and takes up first aid and interior decorating. What made this miraculous transformation possible? Why, a recent membership in her local Italian Mother's Club! (Treese 1990:25).

IMMIGRANT MOTHERS, COETHNIC COMMUNITIES, AND EMPOWERMENT

Many Anglo-American social reformers professed a maternalism that sought to protect recently arrived immigrant wives and mothers from subordinating their interests as autonomous individuals to the priorities of their families and communities. Yet their benevolence was based on racial nativism and a fundamental lack of appreciation of the economic needs of immigrant households for multiple sources and contributors of income, which included children. Most importantly, it reflected a basic lack of respect for the mothering skills passed on to immigrant women through childhood apprenticeships to their own mothers and female kin. In these ways, reformers diminished the dreams held by many immigrant mothers to finally, once in America, be in a position to realize their "old world" ideals, including the assumption of responsibility for their own households. These Americanization efforts complemented selective immigration restriction by attempting to transform the "undesirable" behavior of the new immigration without curtailing "the golden stream" entirely, or seriously challenging the systems of gender, racial/ethnic, or class stratification.

Much research on immigrant adaptation has demonstrated that immigrants were far from passive victims of zealous reformers and has shifted the focus to the resilience of ethnic communities. More recently, this research has concentrated on the economic significance of coethnic organizations and community networks and, in particular, on the ways in which ethnic ties have been used to create small businesses and other employment and income-producing opportunities.[17] In other words, the coethnic community has itself increasingly been viewed both as a source of income, and as an "edge" for recently arrived coethnics, one that was unavailable to immigrants competing for work in the open economy. Yet few have questioned the effect of coethnic solidarity and community institutions on immigrant women or the extent to which ethnic economic networks worked to their advantage.[18]

While both Russian-Jewish and Italian Catholic immigrant mothers came into contact with the middle-class Anglo-American social settlement worker, Italian immigrant women faced the racial nativism and maternalism head-on, directly and immediately, without significant support or protection from a coethnic community organized specifically to receive immigrant women or families. The relative absence of Italian coethnic institutions in New York that were oriented to female immigrants was primarily the legacy of a transnational migration system dominated by the temporary circulation of low-waged male labor and promoted by an only recently unified and still weak Italian state (Piore 1979). Only 25 percent of all Italians arriving at the turn of the century were women, compared to nearly 50 percent of Russian-Jewish immigrants (Furio 1979; Kahan 1978).

The Italian-organized associations that emerged to assist labor migrants in the U.S. did not address the adaptation of women, much less married women or mothers. Formal Italian organizations in New York were, with few exceptions, limited to three types of activities. The largest and best funded were the various Italian government-subsidized efforts to remedy the most obvious problems and abuses of Italian male migrant workers, in order to avoid the twin evils of numerical restriction and permanent detachment from Italy, both of which would have considerably diminished migrant remittances, for example, Society for the Protection of Italian Immigrants (Pozzetta 1971:254–59).

The National Order of the Sons of Italy developed as both a protective social organization and a political action group, in order to defend a united Italian-American community against discrimination. Working "to keep alive a love for Italy" did not prevent the Sons of Italy from promoting the virtues of U.S. citizenship at the same time (Mangano [1917] 1971:129; Briggs 1978: 153). Naturalization had become increasingly necessary to protect the community from nativist prejudice and discrimination (Ware 1935:169). The Italian parliament admitted as much when, in 1912, it revised its citizenship law to facilitate the rapid recovery of Italian citizenship by repatriated emigrants (Briggs 1978:134). The easier it was to maintain ties to the Italian homeland and the longer those ties could be maintained, the more likely it was that immigrants would continue to send remittances. And, as long as any family members remained in Italy, remittances continued (Orsi 1985:19–20). It should go without saying that the Sons of Italy was not oriented specifically towards the protection of Italian immigrant women.

The most numerous ethnic organizations were the mutual benefit societies. Some were hometown associations in which membership was restricted to males from particular regions (LaRuffa 1988:100–1).[19] Others were based on church affiliation or occupation (Briggs 1978:141–47; Gabaccia 1988a:ch. 5). As a consequence of the large numbers of such societies, Americanizers came to view Italian immigrants as "most generous in assisting one another" and thus in "maintain[ing] themselves independent of outside assistance," that is, off relief (Pozzetta 1971:165–67).[20] Yet, wives and children were generally permitted only as guests at special events and as recepients of death benefits.

Italian immigrant women thus faced the harshness of racial nativism and the invasive benevolence of reformers' maternalism without the protection or assistance of a coethnic community organized on their behalf. Their response was to create their own informal networks and rely primarily on other working-class Italian immigrant women in their neighborhoods. They transformed their close kin, often both female and male, into their neighbors, and formed stem-, partner-, and joint-family households with them, partly to reduce rent.[21] They created a variety of informal social support and household income-producing strategies to meet their needs, and in these ways constructed their own "reception centers."

Russian-Jewish immigrants included a significantly higher proportion of women, in contrast to the predominantly male and low-wage temporary migration of Italians. But, more important, Russian-Jewish women, as well as men, were incorporated into an ethnic community formed by predominantly middle-class/entreprenurial German and central European Jews in New York by mid-century (Grinstein 1945; Supple 1957; Rischin 1977). The organization of New York Jewish immigrants into an "ethnic economic enclave,"[22] produced important differences between the migration experiences of Russian-Jewish women and Italian women. An enclave economy differs from some other types of close-knit ethnic neighborhoods, such as those formed by Italian immigrants, in its economic and social organization. Ethnic economic enclaves were "areas where a substantial proportion of immigrants were engaged in business activities and where a still larger proportion worked in firms owned by other immigrants" (Portes and Bach 1985:38). For some Russian Jews in New York facing racial nativism and lacking capital and connections in the wider economy, the ethnic community itself represented a potential source of economic resources (i.e., a low-waged labor force comprised of the most recent immigrant arrivals, a controlled market of coethnics, a source of credit and capital) that could be

Figure 10.
Hester Street (near Essex Street), the center of the immigrant Jewish
ethnic economic enclave in New York's Lower East Side, 1899.
Museum of the City of New York.

tapped prior to significant acculturation (Waldinger 1985, 1986; Moore 1981; Model 1985; Rischin 1977; Tenenbaum 1993). The Jewish enclave in New York City also included Jewish organizations aimed at protecting the reputation of the entire community, as well as promoting solidarity and loyalty among the diverse classes and nationalities of Jews. But, within this coethnic enclave, how did mothers and wives fare?

The largest and perhaps best-funded organization serving Russian-Jewish immigrant wives and mothers was the National Council of Jewish Women, established in 1893, with fifty sections nationwide by 1896. The president of the New York section, Sadie American, explained that the Council helped women and girls because other Jewish organizations ignored their special needs (Baum et al. 1976:166, 176). Council members sought to "throw about Jewish women those safeguards which will make of them creditable citizens in as short a time as possible and prevent their becoming the public burdens . . . which modern competitive labor conditions all too readily tend to make of them" (Beard [1915] 1972:180; National Council of Jewish Women 1897). Staff and volunteers of the NCJW's Department of Immigrant Aid offered assistance at Ellis Island to 19,377 girls, 4,020 women, and 6,427 children between 1909 and 1911. They acted as interpreters, helped to locate relatives in America, and found lodgings for women without relatives. Like their peers in other Americanizing institutions, the Council sent out home visitors to help "adjust" immigrant mothers to American conditions. They provided classes in English, sewing, health, hygiene, and nutrition (Baum et al. 1976:166–69). Like their Anglo-American counterparts in other Americanizing institutions, the German-Jewish women who organized the Council were virtually all well educated and middle class. Although maternalism and class bias were similarly much ingrained in their practices, so was the fear that racial nativism unleashed might endanger the more established German-Jewish community in America. In 1896 they decided to recruit the rare but "cultured Russian-American Jewesses" who had the "leisure, refinement, and education which would guarantee them as desirable members" (quoted in Baum et al. 1976:180).

Even before they departed Russia, the National Council for Jewish Women was involved in the lives of Russian-Jewish women. In *Der Yiddisher Emigrant* (1911), a Yiddish newspaper published in St. Petersburg, the Council provided detailed information on the rights of women in the United States concerning divorce and desertion (Karp 1976:87–88). Once in the United States, the National Desertion Bureau of the Jewish Educational Alliance assisted abandoned wives. The Bureau aimed to reunite husband and wife wherever possible. If that were not possible they attempted to obtain support for the wife and children. If all failed, the Bureau sought the aid of the District Attorney to enforce the law and help the immigrant wife and mother (Glanz 1976:62; Fridkis 1981; Friedman 1982). The Yiddish press assisted women in their search for deserters. The *Jewish Daily Forward* regularly printed photographs of the men in their "Gallery of Missing Husbands" and letters from the abandoned wives elaborating on their plight (Baum et al. 1976:116–17).

German-Jewish women sponsored activities for Russian-Jewish wives and mothers through the "sisterhood" organizations of various New York City temples. They gave material and medical relief, and formed day nurseries, kindergartens, mother's clubs, classes, and employment bureaus (Frankel 1905:69).

Middle-class German-Jewish women, however, had to compete with Jewish socialists in New York City for the loyalty of Russian-Jewish immigrant wives and mothers. The socialist prescription for Jewish motherhood was printed regularly on the women's page of the popular *Jewish Daily Forward* (Seller 1987: 416–38). While the masthead of the page pictured an older woman knitting and a mother with her infant child, housework was depicted as repetitive and restrictive. An article on special housekeeping requirements during the Passover holiday was entitled "Her Realm—Slavery." Yet, like their German-Jewish and Anglo-American middle-class counterparts, socialist columnists assumed that Jewish women, dedicated to the well being of husbands and children, would leave the labor force upon marriage. Caught up in the feminist eugenics of the time, the socialist women's page further recommended that Russian-Jewish mothers limit the number of children they had—not for the "improvement of the (white) race"—but, in order to improve the mother's quality of life, especially given that they were expected to leave paid work.

The central feature, however, that distinguished Jewish from Italian women's mode of incorporation pivoted upon the extent to which Jewish coethnic organizations and enclave entrepreneurs viewed and used Russian-Jewish women as a source of low or nonwaged labor which could be relied upon to advance the ethnic economic enclave. The United Hebrew Charities of New York organized a work room for "unskilled women" where they were taught the needle trades, much in demand in the enclave economy. There, Russian-Jewish mothers and wives were instructed to become "sufficiently accomplished to work in their own homes and thus supplement the family income." Staff at the work room, who frequently complained about the competition of factory work against waged home work, located positions for the women from among the lowest paying, most exploitative home industries in the enclave economy (Frankel 1905:69).

Nearly all institutions of Americanization and assimilation were, however, formally committed to ridding the home of child labor. Female social reformers had not elevated the work of home-making and mothering to the level of a modern vocation or enterprise only to see exploitative working conditions reenter the household and destroy it. Many were strong advocates for, if not activists within, struggles for trade union recognition and a family wage for the immigrant husband and father, in order to keep mothers and children from the necessity of wage earning (Payne 1988:128; Dye 1980).

Organizations like the Child Welfare Exhibit and the New York Child Labor Committee made concerted efforts to end the practice of child labor. The following rhyme, taken from their volume *Sorrowful Rhymes of Working Children*, exemplifies the perspective of the Child Welfare Exhibit:

> Jack Sprat Had Little Work
> His Wife Could Get Much More
> She And The Children Worked All Day
> To Keep The Wolf From The Door
>
> This Little Child Made Laces,
> This Little Child Made Flowers
> This Little Child Made Willow Plumes
> This One Held Baby For Hours
> And All Of Them Worked In A Close Warm Room
> Through The Good, Bright Summer Hours
> (Watson 1911:774, 776)

From 1905 to 1912 the New York Child Labor Committee aided 494 families with weekly payments in order to replace their

Figure 11.
Two children sewing and a man bundling.
Lewis W. Hine Collection.
United States History, Local History & Genealogy Division,
The New York Public Library.
Astor, Lenox and Tilden Foundations.

children's earnings. Yet, at the same time, the Committee refused to acknowledge problems in 75 percent of the households that were brought to their attention where the child labor law was said to be causing economic hardship. These families received only advice or, at best, temporary assistance (New York Child Labor Committee 1914). Frequently, the interest of social reformers in ending child labor launched them into the campaign to regulate tenement production, or waged industrial homework, which employed many immigrant mothers and children (Watson 1911; New York Child Labor Committee, pamps., n.d.; University Settlement Society Bulletin 1893:5–6; Van Kleeck 1910:145–49)

Yet, despite formal instruction and informal home visits by Americanizers, coethnic and otherwise, immigrant wives and mothers continued to draw upon all available hands, including their own and their children's, in order to maintain their households. But, the maternalism (often based on racial nativism), the refusal to acknowledge their skills and competencies or recognize their material needs apart from the needs of a coethnic community, contributed nonetheless to women's increased vulnerability to exploitation.

Although by 1890 more than half of New York City's population (aged ten and older) had been incorporated into the waged-labor force, women comprised only 26 percent of it and married Italian and Russian-Jewish immigrant women, even less (U.S. Census 1890, III:570–71). In 1880 only 7 percent of married Italian women had formal waged employment (excluding self-employment and work in family enterprises); by 1905 the number had dropped to fewer than 6 percent. For Jewish households, the proportions are smaller. In 1880, only 2 percent of Jewish wives took jobs outside their homes; by 1905, only 1 percent did (USIC 1911, I, 2:229; Kessner 1977:72, 75–77). One might be tempted to conclude from these numbers that newly arrived immigrant women had adapted themselves according to the domestic ideal prescribed and promoted by Americanizers and other Progressive social reformers. But a closer examination of their income needs as well as their practice of combining diverse types of income from a multiplicity of contributors contrasts sharply with this interpretation.

The clothing industry dominated the city's employment structure, as it did the paid labor force participation of eastern and southern European immigrants—men, women, and children. By

1890, 91.5 percent of male tailors were foreign born (U.S. Ind. Cmsn. [1901] 1970:319). Although the average annual wage for a New York City garment worker in 1890 was approximately $565, a family of five required at least $850 to maintain itself (U.S. Census 1890, Man. Ind.; More 1907:92). By 1910 clothing workers earned on average only $567 (this was actually quite high, compared to the national average wages in manufacturing that year of $518, or $477 for the garment trades) (U.S. Census 1910, III:514–24, 703–704, 746–51). By 1914, however, the minimum cost of living for a family of five had risen to $876 and, by 1917, was $980–$1018 (Kyrk 1933:206–7). How did Jewish and Italian immigrant women, with such high expectations of life in America, survive on such meager incomes? The wages of an adult male breadwinner alone would have guaranteed household survival for very few, and mobility for none.

With claims that the "most important of the mother's duties [childcare] . . . cannot be thoroughly done . . . unless the mother has leisure to inform herself," reformers and Americanizers set about documenting the extent to which immigrant women engaged in work at home, so that they could eliminate it. (Breckenridge 1921:39, 41–42, 149–51)

Isabel Eaton, of the College Settlements Association, set about interviewing numerous city clothing workers, from the better-paid cap maker to the poorly paid shirt maker in the depression years of 1893 and 1894. Her meticulous investigation of garment households provides us with a lens to focus on the numerous ways immigrant families made ends meet during a time when they found their customary wages in the clothing industry reduced by half (Eaton 1895:4). Clearly, most families could not and did not get by on the wages of the adult male garment worker. In order to remain viable economically and as a family, members stretched income by stretching that Americanizer's middle-class domestic ideal to fit their needs and opportunities. Family members formally employed in the clothing trades—usually adult men, widows, and unmarried daughters—became the conduit through which waged industrial homework was channeled to immigrant wives, mothers, and young children. During the busy season, tailors and operatives commonly ran their machines fifteen to sixteen hours a day in the shop and then took home large bundles of unfinished garments for their wives and children to make up at piece rates for additional waged income (Eaton 1895:19–22).

Thus, in the "pauses" of her cooking, child minding, or other unremunerated domestic labor, a full-time immigrant wife and mother was simultaneously an unreported wage-earning home finisher, sewing underwear or children's kneepants.

Until the turn of the century when legislation on tenement manufacture, mechanization, and competition with lower-paid Italian women diminished their job prospects, Russian-Jewish wives participated widely in waged homework. But after that time period, and customarily after their marriages, Russian-Jewish wives and mothers refused clothing work. A 1908 survey of home finishers in New York City by the U.S. Immigration Commission found no Russian Jews (Kessner 1977:77). According to the Bureau of Labor, "no matter how great the poverty, the Hebrew men seldom allow the women of their family to do the [clothing] work at home, even though they may have been shopworkers before marriage" (USBL 1911, 2:221; Willett 1902:89). But it was only when Russian-Jewish male heads of households began to reap the financial benefits of their more formal participation or "apprenticeship" in the ethnic enclave economy, that the improved economic conditions of their households permitted wives and mothers to withdraw their labor from one of the most exploitative segments of the workforce (Cohen 1978:115, 120–21).

As Russian-Jewish women drew away from industrial homework, Italian wives and mothers came to dominate skilled hand sewing and other nonmechanized parts of garment production. By 1908 at least 98 percent of New York City's home garment finishers were Italian women, with earnings that fluctuated between $50 and $125 annually (USIC 1911, I:2; Kessner 1977:75; Foerster 1919:347).

> The price paid for labor to a home finisher is about one half that formerly paid to a woman regularly employed in the shop. A pair of pants is lined, bottoms basted or felled, and the buttons sewed on for from 5 to 7 cents at home, while formerly, before the Italians came in, it was 10 to 14 cents in factories and 7 to 10 cents in the homes of German finishers, so that the Italian finisher works for about two-thirds of the price which other nationalities formerly received for the same work. (U.S. Ind. Cmsn. 1901:370)

According to one investigator, "wherever [home finishers] exist in large numbers we may be sure that they are Italians . . .

among the Italians may be found blocks that are practically colonies of home finishers." In contrast to Russian-Jewish women, many Italian women in New York City continued to work in "outside shops," or formal employment, after marriage, and only moved into home finishing after having children (Willett 1902:89–90, 99). Their continuous participation in the lowest-paid and most exploitative segments of clothing production owed largely to the low-paid and highly irregular employment available to the Italian immigrant men of their households.

Because home finishing paid so little, Italian immigrant wives and mothers were compelled to locate additional work opportunities in order to support their households. Russian-Jewish wives and mothers, having moved out of home finishing, still faced the need for additional household income, but found their opportunities in the ethnic economy.

A brief walk down Orchard Street, a densely populated Russian-Jewish immigrant neighborhood on the Lower East Side, suggests additional informal waged and nonwaged work undertaken by immigrant wives and mothers.

> A street full of push carts, a pushing to and fro of Jewish men and women—the former predominating among the sellers, the latter among the buyers—the bargaining not confined to the pavement . . . this is the first view of Orchard Street to the passer-by. Looking up . . . five story tenements housing families and "boarders" living with the families. The basement fronts and the first floor fronts are often shops and stores. (Bernheimer 1908:26)

Provisioning the most recent immigrant arrivals (sometimes kin or old country neighbors) as boarders and lodgers in order to both meet the rent and to save money for family remaining in Europe was another income-generating strategy frequently utilized by wives and mothers. This, too, pulled at the tight corners of the American middle-class notion of family/household privacy. The practice of taking in boarders often occurred as a stage in a family's life cycle, when children were too young to contribute significantly to household income (More 1907:58). The *Jewish Daily Forward* in 1903 noted that "during the 1890s desperate families had put 'three boarders in the front room and two *borderkes* (female boarders) in the kitchen, but today the rooms are too small (quoted in Howe 1976: 171). Although only 4.4 percent of

Russian-Jewish immigrant wives were formally employed outside the home, 56 percent of them contributed income, presumably by keeping boarders (USIC 1911, I, 2:231).

On Elizabeth Street (a Sicilian district on the Lower East Side) in 1905, almost one-fifth of all apartments contained a "partner household." The two to three families remained financially separate, with one subletting rooms and sharing the kitchen with the others. In this way, families with children too young to work were able to reduce their rent to less than $10 per month, or one-quarter of a laborer's wage (Gabaccia 1984b:76–77). An identical proportion of households contained boarders or rent-paying relatives, usually male. A typical Elizabeth Street family kept two boarders, each of whom contributed approximately 10 percent of the household income. While women's work of provisioning boarders produced additional monetary income, the work of setting up a partnership household was, in contrast, a way to reduce household monetary expenditures by increasing women's non-waged domestic labor. Households with boarders also frequently included older children who contributed their labor and wage earnings. More Sicilian clothing workers lived in partnerships than in nuclear family households (Gabaccia 1984b:80–81,92).

Immigrant wives and mothers devised still additional ways to stretch income and reduce money expenditures. These required the application of considerably more nonwaged domestic labor. During the early years of resettlement in New York, they organized frequent moves to smaller and less costly apartments and aggressively shopped for other bargains. The availability of cheap second-hand goods and ever-cheaper new manufactured goods wholesale (e.g., clothing, shoes, furniture) in neighborhood shops and pushcarts assisted a mother's efforts to maintain her family's standard of living on low wages (Rischin 1977:55–56). After the first Tenement House Law in 1867 had prohibited the keeping of horses, cows, sheep, goats, or swine in apartments, the importance of this informal component of household income declined, although it never vanished entirely. A number of women continued to raise caged rabbits, chickens, and other birds (Gabaccia 1984b:93).

Jewish wives and mothers had been peddlers and small shopkeepers in Russia, and they continued at similar work in New York's ethnic enclave economy. Active in the pushcart trade, women nonetheless had to rent their carts "by proxy," and "[del-

Figure 12.
Jewish women sell eggs from their stand on Hester Street in New York's Lower East Side, 1895. Staten Island Historical Society.

egate] to some men the task, it being a law, unwritten but acknowledged, that women should not undertake pushcart trundling" (Baum et al. 1976:100; Ewen 1985:168–69). Italian women married to grocers were always recorded as "housewives" by census takers, as were nearly all the wives and mothers who worked long days behind counters in family enterprises (Gabaccia 1988:136).[23] Small businesses located in or close to the household absorbed the labor, usually unpaid, of both women and children (Sherman 1906; Anthony 1914; McLean 1898:15–19). A wife or mother could extend her homemaking, her child-care responsibilites, as well as the length of her working day in a family enterprise. Nonwaged and nonremunerated work in family businesses was especially common for women in Russian-Jewish neighborhoods. Most of this work has gone unrecorded except as scattered in short stories, novels, and some memoirs and oral testimonies (Smith 1985:58; Schwartz 1983; Weinberg 1988). Mary Antin remembered her mother conducting business in the U.S. much as she had back in her old store in Polotzk, Russia. "[B]ehind the store was the kitchen, where in the intervals of slack trade, she did her cooking and washing. Arlington Street customers were used to waiting while the storekeeper salted the soup or rescued a loaf from the oven" (Antin [1911] 1969:196).

Despite the multiple formal and informal, waged and nonwaged strategies immigrant wives and mothers created to maintain and reproduce their households, the income squeeze was a burden many women found too heavy to shoulder. Among the group of clothing workers interviewed by Isabel Eaton in 1895, only 4 percent were able to get by on their money income; the remainder were forced to borrow from grocers, butchers, landlords, kin, friends, and neighbors (Eaton 1895:34–37; Herzfeld 1905).

To fulfill their own gender ideals and expectations of motherhood, negotiated through their interactions with kin and communities in Europe and America, immigrant women were sometimes compelled to take to the streets. During the depression of 1907–1908 when more than a hundred thousand men and women on the Lower East Side were unemployed, six hundred women joined together and marched from house to house organizing a rent strike (Ewen 1985:126–27). When food prices rose rapidly in late 1915 after gradually creeping up since the 1890s, immigrant wives and mothers reached the limits of adding and stretching income to sustain themselves and their families according to the standards to which they were accustomed, so they protested once again (Frank 1985; Hyman 1980; Ewen 1985:176–83). On February 20, 1917, more than one thousand women gathered to hear speeches in the East Side's Rutgers Square and then marched to see the mayor. That night the Mother's Anti-High Price League was formed, as a suborganization of the Socialist Party. Four days later they held a massive demonstration in Madison Square; of 5,000 protestors, 80 percent were women and 90 percent were immigrants (Frank 1985:266–70). From 1917 to 1920 immigrant districts all over New York City exploded with food boycotts, food riots, and kosher meat strikes. Immigrant wives and mothers organized and enforced most of these actions (Ewen 1985:176). Mothers in Italian East Harlem continued this pattern of protest into the early 1940s, when in disgust with the filthy conditions and the dangerous pushcarts surrounding their children's play area, they organized a campaign against pushcarts, as "the mothers of East 114th Street" (Orsi 1985:42).

CONCLUSION

Immigrant wives and mothers at the turn of the century found themselves living a paradox. On the one hand, migration to the United States promised the fulfillment of old world dreams in a new land, or at least a degree of emancipation from old world hierarchies and greater self-determination. At the same time, however, migration had the potential to intensify existing subordination, as well as to subject women to new forms of control and domination. What was the impact of migration to the United States at the turn of the century on married immigrant women? Although we have heard much from social reformers and from immigrant sons, how did wives and mothers themselves evaluate their migration experiences?

Americanizers perceived the immigrant mother as isolated and estranged from U.S. society, and as bound to traditional and alien family patterns that refused to recognize her role in assimilation or to elevate her status as homemaker to that of a vocation. Immigrant sons, in contrast, remembered their mothers as powerful guardians of the family. Although few women, whether Italian or Russian-Jewish, ever returned to Europe, or even expressed the desire to do so, their experiences of migration were nonetheless

Figure 13.
Jewish women organize kosher meat boycott due to high prices on New York's Lower East Side, April 1910. Library of Congress.

principally disempowering. Immigrant wives and mothers, however, did not speak with a single voice. The diverse patterns of their experiences are exemplified by the lives and words of the following women.

The most devastating is illustrated by the author Kim Chernin's mother, Rose, who one evening recalls the migration story of her own mother, Perle, in 1914.

> In Staten Island, during those years, there weren't many Jews. We could never understand why my father went to live there . . . My mother stayed in the house. My father never took her out with him, never. So how could she adjust to life in the United States? Everything was new to her and there was nobody to show her anything . . . she had no one to speak with . . . all this that to us seemed a paradise, to her was a living hell . . . They called her "the green one." I think she suspected that one woman there, in Brooklyn, was in love with Papa. Mama was so unhappy that she attempted suicide . . . He broke her spirit. He broke her mind . . . In two years she was destroyed. (Chernin 1983:37–38)

Perle Chernin, a competent and educated woman in Russia, known for her cooking, baking, embroidery, and letter-writing business, was thus ruined after she and the children joined her husband in America.

Mildred Hecht was a skilled tailor in Russia. In the United States she became one of the few married women to work in a garment factory, an experience that confirmed her worst fears.

> I was a tailor in Russia and a good one too. I liked my work. I liked it like a painter likes his work. When I used to finish making a coat it was good and I would get much pleasure from it . . . like I made a beautiful sculpture. I used to think that in America human beings are like machines, and I wasn't fooled. In America, when I went to work in a factory, I felt like a machine. Here is a bigger speed-up, hurry-up. I wasn't enthusiastic about going to America. (quoted in Schwartz 1983:670)

Mildred Hecht complained bitterly about her job as dressmaker. Yet, despite her disappointing job and the burden of unpaid housework after a long day, she nonetheless felt a sense of pride that her wages had made her "independent" and allowed her a measure of autonomy from her husband (Schwartz 1983:670–71,641).

Rosa Cavalleri, who emigrated from Italy to the United States in 1884, cooked and cleaned for more than forty years for the female social reformers of the Chicago Commons Settlement House. "How can I not love America," she proclaimed to a settlement worker, an "angel woman," taking down her life story (for which she was never paid, even when published). "I hope I do my work so good so I never have to leave this place! . . . Even if they didn't pay me I would not want to stop working in the Commons" (Ets 1970:221). How could Rosa Cavalleri not love America, given her previous suffering at both the hands of a cruel foster mother in Italy and an abusive husband who had summoned her to a mining camp in America to keep house for him and the other miners.

Writing at about the same time as Rosa Cavalleri, Russian-Jewish immigrant Anzia Yezierska, expressed a contrasting view of migrating women's experiences in America. In an autobiographical short story, "The Free Vacation House," Yezierska sharply criticized coethnic reformers of the "Social Betterment Society." "For why do they make it so hard for us," an immigrant mother implores. "When a mother needs a vacation, why must they tear the insides out from her first, by making her come down to the charity office? . . . And when we live through the shame of the charities and when we come already to the vacation house, for why do they boss the life out of us with so many rules and bells? . . . Do they need worn-out mothers as part of the show?" (quoted in Seller 1981:194).

The presence of an ethnic enclave economy and coethnic organizations specifically oriented to incorporating immigrant women had the potential to blunt the harshness of racial nativism and the ethnic bias of Americanization, and even to offer recent arrivals an economic edge in America. Yet, the historical outcome for many Russian-Jewish women differed substantially from this ideal. Italian immigrant wives and mothers, like Rosa Cavalleri, were indeed more directly exposed to the racial nativist and class-biased agenda of Americanizers and experienced new forms of subordination. Their economic and social options remained few as the result of a globally and historically structured system of male labor migration. For Russian-Jewish immigrant wives and mothers, coethnic Americanizing organizations could be equally maternal, condescending, and impractical with respect to the needs of recently arrived immigrant women and their families. But most important of all, Russian-Jewish women were channeled by these coethnic organizations into the underside of a well-organized ethnic economic enclave. In the process of immigrant incorporation, women's ethnic loyalty and labor constituted a significant resource towards the advancement of the American Jewish coethnic community.

"So, we have crossed half the world for this?" Maria Ganz' mother reproached her father upon discovering the rear tenement he had prepared for their arrival in New York's Lower East Side ethnic enclave (Ganz 1920:4).

CHAPTER 5

"The Right to a Personality": The Experiences of Young Single Immigrant Women in New York, 1870–1924

What do you have at home? Nothing. You only have trouble. But look at Basha. She has all the pleasures of life that one can acquire. It is a pity that she stayed at home so long. She wears pretty clothes; she is learning how to dance; she goes to parties and to the theatre. She participates in everything she wants to. This is so much more than anyone could have at home.

> —Letter from Mary Bander in Buffalo, New York,
> on December 22, 1890 to sister-in-law, Minna,
> in Rypin, Russian Poland [1]

Oh, for a place to myself. It's people all day and people all night. It's the ugly shop all day and this hideous tenement at night. It's work all day, then coming home to wash and iron and sew. It's going without breakfast or an apple, it's scrimping together a ten cent lunch. That's what my six dollars [weekly salary] brings me.

> —Immigrant girl working in basement tube room
> of New York department store[2]

More than half a million single non-English-speaking women migrated to the United States between 1910 and 1915 (Seller 1981:20–21).[3] Although most young and unmarried immigrant women came to America with their families, there were a significant minority who migrated alone, sometimes in advance of their families or sometimes to rejoin earlier family arrivals. Those who did not join parents in the U.S. lived with siblings, aunts and uncles, or as boarders. Most single women put aside part of their wage earnings in order to support aging parents in Europe or to assist other family members to migrate.

What was the experience of migration to the United States at the turn of the century for young and unmarried Jewish and Italian immigrant women? To what extent was their subordination intensified, diminished, or transformed? How did they evaluate their own experiences of migration?

This chapter is concerned with understanding the diversity of immigration experiences of young single Jewish and Italian women at the turn of the century. Among them were "women adrift" from families attempting to support themselves and possibly kin remaining in Europe, women who arrived as part of family-based households, as well as some who were born into recently arrived immigrant households before the so-called golden door to the U.S. closed to southern and eastern European immigrants in 1924.

If migration to the United States empowers women, as modernization and assimilation theorists imply, then this ought to have been especially true for young unmarried immigrant women arriving at the turn of the century. In stark contrast to their mothers, these young women, presumably, would have been unencumbered by children and other homemaking obligations. Once educated in the values and practices of the new world, they could be expected to assimilate smoothly and thus enhance their status (Kuznets 1975:100; Odencrantz 1919:300).

If nothing else, according to many of the women's contemporaries and those students of immigrant and working-class women's history who take a revised modernization approach, single women's increased wage labor force participation would change their consciousness, smooth their way towards emancipation from the constraints of old world patriarchies, and thus improve their overall life chances (e.g., Eisenstein 1983; Glenn 1990). Abraham Bisno, an organizer for the International Ladies Garment Union, claimed that unmarried immigrant women's labor force participation "allowed them the right to do whatever they pleased with their own money" and "gave them standing and authority." "They acquired the right to a personality," he maintained, "which they had not ever possessed in the old country" (Bisno 1967:212).

On the other hand, some scholars have underscored the extent to which young, working-class and immigrant women's gendered experiences at school and in their patriarchal families unambiguously reinforced their subordination in the capitalist workplace and encouraged them to marry in order to escape their jobs rather than challenge their exploitation (e.g., Tentler 1979). Speaking of her job in a paper-box factory one young woman worker exclaimed, "You never rest until you die, but I will get out by marrying somebody, but my mother won't marry me off yet. I had a fine chance last week, a nice fellow with a good job, who wanted me. But you see I got to work until my brother begins to make some money. I am making $10 and my father $15. It is no cinch I tell you. There are eight of us" (N.Y. St. FIC IV, 1915:1577–78). Migration, in this view, simply reinforced young women's premodern family-centered sense of identity.

In contrast to these two polarized conceptions of the outcome of single women's migration, this chapter suggests that turn-of-the-century migration to New York City did indeed increase the possibility that an unmarried young woman might become a more self-determining person (especially in comparison to her immigrant mother), realize some of her aspirations, and sometimes even imagine new ones. But the conditions upon which a single immigrant woman's empowerment rested were much more multifaceted and much less linear than the dichotomous alternatives of either entering or avoiding wage employment. As the two young women's remarks at the start of this chapter illustrate, the circumstances and outcome of single immigrant women's incorporation into the U.S. social structure were far from identical for all women. Significant and patterned differences regarding the emancipatory posssibilities of immigration existed among unmarried women, based on a complex interrelationship between their region of origin and its position in the world-system (hence, their premigration racial/ethnic/national identities), the nature of their reception by both dominant U.S. institutions and nominal coethnic communities, and finally, their status in their families and households vis-a-vis other members. Moreover, in the interaction among these contextual components, young unmarried women, like their mothers, were not passive observers of their fate but rather active participants and "strategists,"[4] imagining alternatives, weighing possibilities, and devising various means to realize goals. Finally, each woman's experience of immigration evolved out of her own way of negotiating between and reconciling structurally constrained options and possibilities.

The analysis of young unmarried immigrant women's experiences in this chapter is framed through a specific lens, which explores how they attempted to meet personal and/or kinship expectations in the midst of two campaigns for social reform at the turn of the century. The campaign against international white slave trafficking and the movement for women's vocational education were paradigmatic of the maternalist ambivalence of many female Progressive reformers, including coethnics of previous migration waves, towards "the immigrant girl problem."[5] Reformers and policy makers, in other words, vacillated between expressions of protective and nurturing benevolence that improved the immediate conditions of some women, on the one hand, with, on the other hand, degrading and insulting condescension that reinforced or transformed women's subordination without diminishing it. But most importantly, in these two campaigns, single women confronted nearly all the interlocking assumptions about gender, about nativity/race/ethnicity, about social class, and about the meaning of work that were to structure the most relevant contexts of their incorporation in America.

"THE IMMIGRANT GIRL PROBLEM": RACIAL NATIVISM, THE ANTI-WHITE SLAVERY CAMPAIGN, AND THE MANAGEMENT OF FEMALE WORKING-CLASS SEXUALITY[6]

Racial nativism affected unmarried immigrant women differently than single men, and differently than their mothers and married sisters. In its application, it differentiated furthermore between Russian-Jewish and Italian immigrant women, attaching distinct stereotypes to each but targeting Jewish women in particular. Whereas immigrant mothers and wives had been characterized as incompetent housekeepers and inadequate mothers, immigrant daughters and unmarried working-class immigrant women were portrayed as "loose" and sexually immoral. Whereas mothers and wives had been subjected to intrusive instruction in American homemaking and mothercraft that demeaned their competence and diminished their authority in these domains, their unmarried daughters and sisters found themselves in an environment which not only redefined and regulated what was appropriate feminine behavior, but demanded the increased self-management of sexuality as well. Racial nativist stereotypes, sexist ideologies, and class bias all interacted in the construction of a working-class 'immigrant girl problem,' the solution to which Americanizers and social reformers attached great urgency at the turn of the century.

The Progressive Era (1897–1918) was witness to one of the most zealous campaigns in U.S. history against prostitution. As counterpart in tone and theme to the racial nativist preoccupation with the fertility of immigrant mothers, antiprostitution reformers enlisted the aid of both the newly influential scientific and medical communities and the state to alert the public to the threat posed by uncontrolled venereal disease. New York in 1900 was one of the earliest cities to "scientifically" investigate prostitution. Between 1910 and 1917, forty-three other U.S. cities conducted large-scale surveys of the "great social evil" (Rosen 1982:14). In 1907 the United States Congress, in response to growing national panic over "white slavery"[7] appointed a commission to investigate "the importation and harboring of women for immoral purposes." The Commission's findings, which drew upon, confirmed, and further fueled reformer's anxieties, were published in 1911 as part of the massive forty-two-volume Dillingham Immigration Commission Reports. "In the opinion of practically everyone who has had an opportunity for careful judgment," the Commission warned, "the numbers [of foreign-born prostitutes] imported run well into the thousands each year" (U.S. Imm. Comm. 1911, v.37:60). As a consequence, government officials tightened immigration regulations and procedures; and social reformers, in conjunction with the state, made efforts to increase their surveillance and their control over the lives of all women suspected of being or becoming prostitutes. Against the background of the increasing migration of the rural native born to cities, the increasing immigration from the eastern and southern European peripheries, and the changing behavior of working-class and middle-class young women, the moral behavior of most women in public drew suspicion.

Middle-class reformers were divided in their approach to controlling prostitution, just as they were on nearly all strategies of Americanization and assimilation. The measures they promoted reflected their own diverse social origins as well as their contrasting explanations for the causes of prostitution. Coinciding with widespread fears about "race suicide" and the racial quality of the population, and in the global context of intensifying international rivalries, many antiprostitution reformers adopted a so-called scientific or hereditarian perspective of racial eugenics. They differentially categorized, stigmatized, and tried to regulate the behavior of racialized women of particular ethnicities and nationalities. It is this view that predominates in the Immigration Commission's findings, supporting the special scrutiny and sometimes even the deportation of particular social groups and classes of women.

But many other middle-class female reformers and social feminists, influenced by the new social science, viewed prostitutes instead as victims of social injustice and of the intrusion of cruel, impersonal market forces into the private lives of families. For them, prostitution represented the evil underside of industrial capitalism and posed a deadly threat to the sanctity of the private sphere and the purity of their own families (U.S. Imm. Comm. 1911, vol. 37:85). In their eyes, if the traffic in poor and immigrant young women was not suppressed, no woman regardless of class standing or racial/ethnic/national origin could hope for elevation of her status in society.

Antiprostitution reformers sought preventive measures based on their own particular explanation of prostitution, but as in the Americanization movement in general, racial nativism also insinuated itself into even those perspectives that most seemed to stress social environmental causes. This is seen most clearly in the targeting and scapegoating of particular racial/ethnic groups for special scrutiny as either prostitutes or procurers. In contrast to much of the data they collected, some antiprostitution reformers continually portrayed those involved in the traffic, as primarily new immigrants, and most often eastern European Jews.[8] In the words of the U.S. Immigration Commission,

> According to those best informed, a very large proportion of the pimps living in the United States are foreigners . . . The Jews often import or harbor Russian, Austrian, Hungarian, Polish, or German women, doubtless usually of their own race . . . There are large numbers of Jews scattered throughout the United States, although mainly located in New York and Chicago, who seduce and keep girls. Some of them are engaged in importation, but apparently they prey rather upon young girls whom they find on the street, in the dance halls, and similar places, and whom . . . they deceive and ruin. Many of them are petty thieves, pickpockets, and gamblers. They also have various resorts where they meet and receive their mail, transact business with one another, and visit. Perhaps the best-known organization of this kind throughout the country was one legally incorporated in New York in 1904 under the name of the New York Independent Benevolent Association. (1911, vol. 37:76–77)

In 1908, the Police Commissioner of New York City, Theodor Bingham, falsely claimed that half of the criminals in the city were Jewish. A year later, G. K. Turner reported in *McClure's* that New York City was the world center of "white slavery," and that it was primarily a Jewish problem (Bristow 1982:161–62). By 1911, the Immigration Commission, in keeping with the xenophobic and antisemitic tenor of the time, concluded not only that immigrant Jews were the ringleaders of an international "prostitution syndicate," but in so doing cast suspicion on all immigrant Jewish working-class fraternal associations. The Commission further reported that "procurers and pimps of other nationalities [were] fewer in number, and . . . [lacked] regularly organized clubs among them." Yet, in keeping with its objective of amassing information on which to base restrictive legislation in general, the Commission also targeted "a number of Italian pimps scattered throughout the country who are apparently vicious and criminal . . . some of [whom] . . . seem to be more feared by their women than are pimps of other nationalities" (U.S. Imm. Comm. 1911, vol. 37: 78, 86).

Racial nativism interacted with class prejudices and polarized portrayals of the prostitutes. U.S.-born potentially middle-class young women of northern and western European origin were often depicted as innocent victims of their social environment. Social reformers characterized the young working girl between the ages of seventeen and twenty as "the victim of hardship and temptation" and took pains to anticipate and remedy the conditions that led to her downfall. "A low standard of family life, with overcrowding, poor and insufficient food, and lack of privacy" were said to "undermine [her] bodily strength and character." Insufficient recreation and "the necessity to rely upon men for costly and desired pleasures" easily became the source of such a girl's "moral breakdown" (Woods and Kennedy 1922:91).

Poor, working-class, and "new immigrant" young women, on the other hand, were frequently held responsible not only for their own fates but also for (indirectly) endangering (i.e., infecting) the purity (i.e., bodies) of middle-class families, especially middle-class women. Certainly the Immigration Commission found women who had been deceived and forced into the trade. Yet it made a special point of differentiating between American and foreign-born prostitutes, with important policy implications.

> Since in Europe the feeling regarding sexual immorality is much less pronounced than in the United States, the women presumably in many instances have not the consciousness of degradation from their fallen condition that in some instances causes the American girl her keenest suffering. (U.S. Imm. Comm. 1911, vol. 37:81)

This view was shared, to an extent, by some nominal coethnics. In her memoirs of the Henry Street settlement in the heavily Russian-Jewish Lower East Side of New York, Lillian Wald, an upper-middle-class German-Jewish social reformer recounted the story of an immigrant girl "leading an immoral life" who had been sent to her for help. Despite "the picture of the wretched home that she had presented—its congestion, the slovenly housekeeping, the demanding infant, the ill-prepared food snatched from the stove by the members of the family as they returned from work," Wald nonetheless blamed the girl's character, her inclination toward vanity, love of luxury, and lack of self-control in the face of temptation for her "moral deterioration" (Wald 1915:171). It seems that the girl had started wage work at age eleven and soon thereafter located a job at a department store. Once there, her single overwhelming desire was to be able to buy her own silk underwear, the same kind she had so frequently observed "luxurious women" purchasing with ease (Wald 1915:172). In Wald's view, this desire was the source of her downfall.

Information about the white slave trade, gathered by social investigators and reformers through various surveys and investigations, contradicted many of their conclusions. Concerning alleged Jewish involvement in international trafficking or, more specifically, about the New York Independent Benevolent Association, Special Inspector at Ellis Island, Helen Bullis, concluded in 1912 that "The Association did not do any importing at the time I knew it, and it is doubtful if individual members did very much. It was much easier to get girls here, with practically no risk" (quoted in Bristow 1982:157). Of men convicted under the Mann Act of 1910, which aimed to prevent the domestic traffic in women across state lines, 72.5 percent were U.S. born, 11.5 percent were Italian, and 3.5 percent were Jewish (Rosen 1982:119). Among the prostitutes surveyed in New York City in 1912, the overwhelming majority (68 percent) had been born in the United States. Of course, their numbers may have included the native-born daughters of immigrant parents. Among the foreign-born prostitute population, Jewish and Italian women were underrepresented (Rosen 1982:44, 141, 203–204). Moreover, police records for the years from 1913 to 1930 reveal that only approximately 17 percent of all prostitutes arrested in Manhattan were Jewish, less than the Jewish proportion of the population (Baum 1976:68).

But to understand the reception of young unmarried Russian-Jewish immigrant women by the state, social reform organizations, and related institutions, it is not sufficient to acknowledge the impact on them of racial nativism alone. Recommendations to suppress or prevent prostitution by both reformers and the Immigration Commission demonstrate also the underlying and mounting social anxieties over changes in family arrangements, especially concerning the morality of unmarried middle-class and working-class women's public behavior. While the gender identities, in particular, of Russian-Jewish women were becoming racialized in the context of international migration, their class positions were simultaneously reconstituted through the prisms of gender and race. In other words, not only had race/ethnic/national, gender, and class prejudices traveled together across the Atlantic, inextricably intertwined, but in the course of their passage to the so-called golden land they had become rewoven into new patterns of domination. It was these new and revised attempts at control and regulation that young women saw standing next to the "golden door."

Especially disturbing to the Immigration Commission was that its standard controls against the "importation and harboring of women for immoral purposes" were being evaded by, in its view, particularly devious "professional prostitutes." Each and every lone woman, traveling third class, entering the U.S. for the first time, and headed toward New York had been ordered to be held at Ellis Island until such time as they were retrieved by a relative or friend. If such person(s) failed to appear, Russian-Jewish women were then to be turned over to special immigrant homes, such as those organized by the upper-middle-class dominated National Council of Jewish Women. However, in the course of its investigations, the Commission alleged to have discovered a widespread practice whereby women, suspected of prostitution and thus subject to deportation orders, were marrying men of dubious character who retrieved them from Ellis Island in order to remain in the country to practice their trade. According to the Commission, these supposed husbands and fiancés, whether foreigners or not, were in fact pimps and procurers! Thus, the Commission conceded that it was "extremely difficult to prove the illegal entrance of either women or procurers. The inspector has to judge mainly by their appearance and the stories they tell." Interestingly, to explain this admission further the Immigration Commission recounted an embarassing incident on the Canadian border two years previous, when an "inspector stopped by mistake the wife of a prominent citizen of one of our leading commercial cities, a woman against whose character suspicion had never been raised. The inspector was judging mainly by her appearance and manner in replying to his questions." Immigration authorities admitted that "the possibility of such mistakes permits almost any reasonably well-behaved woman, with some ingenuity in framing skillful answers to the usual inquiries, to enter the United States, whatever her character. The higher the social standing the woman seems to have, the more cautious the inspector is about causing her unnecessary delay and trouble" (U.S. Imm. Comm. 1911, vol. 37:70–71).

Against the backdrop of transformations in middle-class family life and middle-class women's behavior such as rising divorce rates, declining birth rates, and women's public involvment in the campaign for suffrage, in the women's club movement, and in social reform work, it was no simple task to differentiate among women. For the Commission, then, many women had become suspects. Changes in turn-of-the-century family organization and middle-class women's activities had blurred the idealized distinction between the "good woman" within the private sphere of the family and the "bad woman" in the commercialized public sphere. Whereas in 1860 only 9.7 percent of women were employed outside the household, by 1910, the proportion had risen to nearly 25 percent (Rosen 1982:43). Moreover, the labor force participation rate for single women, already 40.5 percent in 1890, rose to nearly 46 percent by 1900 (Matthaei 1982:141–42). Thus, working for wages was quite rapidly becoming part of the typical experience of a near majority of unmarried women. The existence of a group of unaccompanied young women crossing international borders only contributed further to the growing anxiety over blurred boundaries and transformations of the social order.

In its suggestions for new legislation the Immigration Commission advised increasing the external restraints and surveillance of

young alien women, that is, holding poor, unmarried and unaccompanied young immigrant women where they entered the country until the persons or places to which they were to be discharged
could be thoroughly investigated and approved (U.S. Imm. Comm.
1911, vol. 37:90–91). Although some young immigrant women
more than others were stigmatized and made especially vulnerable,
given their racialized/ethnic/national identity and social class, all
were constrained by legislation and treatment based on the association of young mobile or migrating women with white slavery
and prostitution.

Middle-class female social reformers and feminists, including
some German-Jewish social reformers, differed from the Immigration Commission in their general approach to the immigrant girl
problem. But, they also differed among themselves and even fluctuated in their approaches over time. Unlike the Commission and
popular press, however, they generally opposed harsh new restrictions against prostitutes; instead, they recognized men's responsibility for the "downfall" of women, urged moral purity for both
sexes, and demanded greater sympathy for prostitutes, as well as
protection for all young women.

Some coethnic reformers, like Sadie American, a founder of
the National Council for Jewish Women (NCJW) and president of
its New York City section, hoped to remove one excuse for the
antisemitism barely hidden underneath the call for the restriction
or deportation of Jewish immigrants. Upon her return from the
1910 International White Slave Traffic Conference in Madrid, she
remarked, "Underneath it all, like powder ready for the match,
was the fear that the whole conference would be turned into . . .
denunciation of the Jew because of the Jewish traffickers of whom
there were too many, no matter how few they might be" (quoted
in Baum et al. 1976:172; Beard [1915] 1972:118–19, 180–81).
Although, at first cautioning German-Jewish community leaders
to use quiet influence to curb the problem, if there indeed were
one, by 1908 the NJCW was more informed with the findings of
its own study; of the 2,900 immigrant Jewish girls it surveyed,
only two had been deported as prostitutes (Kuzmack 1990:68–
69). Nonetheless, declaring that no other Jewish organization in
the U.S. was concerned or involved with the tragic effects of "the
white slave trade" on the girls themselves, American led the Council in developing external controls and regulations that would prevent young women from being tricked and kidnapped by white

slavers in the first place. National treasurer of the NCJW (1908–1911), Hattie Kahn, agreeing with American's assessment, declared that "the Jewish immigrant does not belong in the class in which we find her but has been forced there by untoward circumstances" against which she was powerless (quoted in Rogow 1993:137).

In alliance with government authorities and their approaches, but driven by different goals, the NCJW's Department of Immigrant Aid created a permanent station on Ellis Island staffed by middle-class professionals and volunteers to interview every female Jewish arrival between the ages of twelve and thirty (Rogow 1993:138). Between 1904 and 1907 the NCJW helped approximately 20,000 Jewish women and girls make it through customs and settle in the United States (Rogow 1993:152). In 1908 alone, the New York Section of the Council met 10,000 immigrant girls at Ellis Island; they provided some of them with transportation to Council homes or other appropriate housing. "Friendly visitors" then went to these homes to advise the young women on how to secure more permanent lodgings, employment, medical care, English-language and vocational training. The NCJW also worked closely with the police, courts, and other municipal organizations to ensure that single Jewish immigrant women would be protected. Nationally, in over 300 cities, between 1911 and 1914, the NCJW's Department of Immigrant Aid assisted 41,000 immigrant women and girls between the ages of fourteen and fifty-nine (Rogow 1993:72–73). When Sadie American visited Rome in 1913, the Italian secretary of immigration, it is said, asked her advice about what should be done to protect Italian women immigrants (Kuzmack 1990:74).

At the same time, some middle-class social reformers, including some German Jews, recognized the limits of external protection against young women's high aspirations of life in the new world amidst the reality of grinding poverty in their lives. They believed that one solution to prostitution was to assist young immigrant women to find employment or job training, respectable homes, healthy recreation, and education in American morality as preparation for eventual motherhood. They thus counseled young women in their duty to parents and loyalty to employers; they encouraged moral and sexual purity and promoted thrift and frugality with regard to consumption. In short, they aimed to induce greater self-control and self-management in the face of temptation. Although they acknowledged the sexual double standard with regard to prostitution, some members of the NCJW joined with non-Jewish reformers in associating that practice exclusively with the lower classes. One of the founders of the NCJW, Hannah Solomon, insisted in 1911 that "It is rather the love of pleasure and ease, love of society and luxury and, most of all, the absense of proper maternal care." Sadie American added only that "it [was] a well known fact that the first generation of the immigrant population produces more evil than the next generation . . . because all the old sanctions are gone and the new sanctions are not yet here" (quoted in Kuzmack 1990:71).

To encourage women to protect themselves, if they insisted on migrating alone, *Der Yiddisher Emigrant*, a Yiddish newspaper published in St. Petersburg, alerted young women, even before they left Russia, to the dangers awaiting them and provided information concerning the services that had been established on their behalf.

> From European harbor cities we have been receiving reports that lately a large number of young lady emigrants have been traveling alone. They thus are in danger of being accosted by persons who would take advantage of their loneliness and innocence. It is, therefore, important to warn such young ladies against such persons who would press them into white slavery. If such girls turn to representatives of the immigration societies, the agents should inform their colleagues in the port cities of their arrival so that they can be protected. (*Der Yiddisher Emigrant* V, 18, 1911, in Karp 1976: 88–89)

The National Council of Jewish Women frightened young immigrant women more directly into adopting internalized constraints, while still promoting dependence on their benefactors. The Council distributed the following warning on cards printed in English, German, and Yiddish.

> Beware of any person who gives addresses, offers you easy well paid work, or even marriage. There are evil men and women who have in this way led girls to destruction. Always inquire for the persons whose names are given on the other side of this card, who will find out the truth for you, who will advise you and give you all necessary information or aid. (quoted in Karp 1976: 89)

The Immigration Commission warned that

those who recruit women for immoral purposes watch all places where young women are likely to be found under circumstances which will give them a ready means of acquaintance and intimacy, such as employment agencies, immigrant homes, moving-picture shows, dance halls, sometimes waiting rooms in large department stores, railroad stations, manicuring and hairdressing establishments. (U.S. Imm. Comm. 1911, vol. 37:68)

In advice columns, in the pronouncements of immigrant aid workers, settlement workers, and social reformers, in the findings of government commissions were warnings to young single women to protect themselves from the dangers of the public sphere, the labor market, commercialized leisure—in short from the new world.

If the line between "good women" and "bad women" had become increasingly blurred at the turn of the century, a similar message about men was implied in the above warnings. Popular and prescriptive literature, in other words, warned of the increasing difficulty for young women in distinguishing "white slavers" and procurers from "good catches," or potential husbands, who promised aspiring women a chance for upward mobility in the new world.

The story of an unlucky young Jewish woman, poor eighteen-year-old Mollie Yosabowitz, who had left Romania in 1913 to join her mother in Newark, New Jersey, demonstrated what could happen if a young woman were not cautious and discriminating, but instead followed her own ambitions. Unable to find a suitable husband in the old world, presumably due to the poverty of her family, Mollie sought the services of a traditional Jewish marriage broker in the U.S., who then introduced her to Benny Winkler. Benny promised marriage, but instead seduced naive Mollie. Breaking off with Benny, Mollie followed the next best strategy to improve her life chances; she went to the Austrian-Hungarian Employment Agency. Unfortunately, the so-called employment agency sent unsuspecting Mollie to Max and Sarah Adler of Delancey Street on New York City's Lower East Side, who ran a brothel out of their apartment. Finally, Mollie gave in. Her story became part of Immigration and Naturalization Service records when she was eventually deported as an alien prostitute, one year after her arrival (Bristow 1982:155).

The lesson of Mollie's story was not one limited to prostitution, narrowly defined, but to young working-class immigrant womens' general needs and desires to improve their circumstances and, simply, to see life. Middle-class reformers often extended the label of prostitute to encompass a wide diversity of youthful female sexual behaviors—from premarital sex, to dancing and kissing young men in dance halls, to going out with young men unchaperoned. It also included going out on the town with other young working women, all dressed up in flashy imitations of more affluent women's fashions, to spend some hard-earned wages, or more likely to attract young men into "treating"[9] them to an ice cream soda or candy to supplement their meager dinners or to an evening's entertainment they could never have afforded on their own. "Gee! but I feel sorry for the girls who haven't got a steady," Miss H.A. explained to a factory investigator. "Why, if I had to buy all of my meals I'd never get along" (N.Y. St. Fac. Inv. Com. IV 1915:1677–78, 1685–86; Consumer's League 1919:8–9). As middle-class Americanizers sought to incorporate young immigrant women into their polarized and rigid framework of acceptable female sexuality and proper womanhood, they cautioned young women to avoid dance halls, cheap movie theaters, department stores, and all public amusements that seemed to clash with obligations to their parents and their own future vocation as mothers. Since procurers and pimps were said to deviously appeal to the social, economic, and psychological needs of young women, reformers warned them to suppress those needs and control those ambitions. If, in other words, a job or marriage offer, the two main paths of mobility open to women, sounded too good to be true, they probably were. By broadening and applying the label of prostitute to young unmarried women in public, especially working-class immigrant women, state authorities and Progressive reformers attempted to not only regain control over women's seemingly more self-determined public behavior but to induce their self-regulation in compliance with middle-class "American" gender expectations.

Preoccupation with unmarried women's behavior, especially sexual behavior, by state authorities and social reformers, however, did not necessarily or uniformly translate into more control over women or greater compliance by women. Certainly, various legislative and reform efforts did target unmarried women, and some classes and ethnicities more than others. But, the other side of this exaggerated attention should be read as evidence of the increased possibilities and domains for self-determination, and of the new social freedom that some women sought from their families and households in industrially expanding New York City. For

Figure 14.

Young female apprentice visiting with male friend during a lunch break in New York's garment district. Lewis W. Hine Collection. United States History, Local History & Genealogy Division, The New York Public Library. Astor, Lenox and Tilden Foundations.

a brief period in their lives some unmarried women found the space as new immigrants in New York to experiment with different class and gender images, to try on and play with new ways of being female, quite unlike the paths marked for them by their old world mothers. They were able "to become persons," wage earners, and decision makers outside the boundaries marked by customary gender, class, and ethnic/racial expectations.[10] What bothered reformers most of all was the increased flexibility young women seemed to have, so much so that it was taking an inordinate amount of effort to attach a stigma to women's behavior.

INDUSTRIAL EDUCATION AND WORK DISCIPLINE AMONG YOUNG IMMIGRANT WOMEN

If poor naive Mollie Yosabowitz was the unwitting victim of trying to make her old world dreams come true in the new world, other young immigrant prostitutes in New York were more clear sighted and candid when interviewed about their ambitions and the obstacles to realizing them. Mollie Kessler, a former cloak operative, maintained that she simply could not exist on $4 or $5 a week. One woman who worked at Siegel and Cooper's for $6 a week and who "went astray" while still at that job, said she would lead "an honest life only for $15 per week" (Bristow 1982:158; Kessler-Harris 1982:104–5).

Comments such as these confirmed the views of many feminists and Progressive social reformers that a woman with sufficient means to support herself would be less likely to succumb to the promises of procurers and pimps.[11] Representative of this perspective, middle-class German-Jewish reformer, Julia Richman (1855–1912), not only led raids on Lower East Side brothels and demanded the assignment of special agents to Ellis Island to keep young immigrant girls out of the hands of white slavers, but, most important, she organized a Working Girls Club to raise the sights of immigrant shop girls. Together with the Young Ladies Charitable Union and the United Hebrew Charities of New York, Richman was active in developing an industrial school for poor immigrant girls by the mid-1880s (Berrol 1980:39).[12] Taking a rather unorthodox view at the time of the traditional path to upward mobility for a woman, Richman argued, "It is really much better for a girl to build a productive single life rather than settle for an unsuitable husband just for the sake of being married" (quoted in Berrol 1980:49; Peiss 1986:168–69; Kuzmack 1990:91–92).

Julia Richman's own ambivalence about marriage as women's only true vocation prompted her, as it did many other feminists and middle-class Americanizers, to vigorously support increased opportunities for young women's self-development and vocational/industrial training. By the end of the nineteenth century, education came to be viewed as, if not the panacea, at least the catalyst for improving women's lives, providing opportunities not only for young immigrant women, but for middle-class reformers as well. In the wake of their successful antiwhite-slavery campaign, middle-class Jewish women in the National Council of Jewish Women broadened their social service role. They formed clubs and classes for immigrant women, cared for sick children and their parents in homes and hospitals, sponsored juvenile court officers, established homes for delinquent girls, opened evening and vacation schools, work rooms, and vocational classes. By 1910, 41 settlements in New York sponsored 160 clubs for girls and young women (Peiss 1986:180). By 1920 nationwide, there were 3,553 public and private all-day training schools and 6,731 part-time and evening schools for women (Kessler-Harris 1982:178).

On the one hand, the notion of teaching young women a trade appealed to middle-class female social reformer's vision of economic emancipation for all women, as well as a way out of the underpaid monotonous jobs typically relegated to immigrant women. A 1909 investigation in New York City had revealed that the average annual wage for young women without training was only one-third of the wage for trained stenographers and less than half for those trained as nurses (Kessler-Harris 1982:172). The New York State Factory Investigating Commission also remarked on the " tendency on the part of the employer to recognize training for girls by an increased wage" (N.Y. St. Fac. In. C. 1915 IV:1432).[13] In her study of women in the millinery trade, social reformer Mary Van Kleeck demonstrated that those girls who stayed in school longer and entered wage earning after age sixteen could earn higher weekly wages than those who entered the trade at an earlier age (Van Kleeck 1917:162–63). Thus, vocational education came to be viewed by many reformers as a kind of cure-all for unmarried women, and young immigrant women in particular.

In practice, on the other hand, vocational education for young unmarried women continued to exemplify middle-class ambiva-

Figure 15.
Young women finishing garments by hand in New York City workshop at the turn of the century. George Eastman House.

lence over women's changing behavior in society, especially working-class immigrant women. Because industrial courses were viewed from many different quarters as undermining the training every woman needed to properly fulfill her role as wife and mother, schools tended to emphasize the home-related value of their courses as much as, if not more than, their job-training potential. A comment in *The American Jewess* (1895), a periodical directed to middle-class Jewish women, asserted that "Education ought to prepare [women] . . . to be the best qualified guardian of her offspring . . . [she] should receive instructions in all branches which will promote the physical condition of future generations" (quoted in Kuzmack 1990:90; Rogow 1993:136). This view tended to be incorporated especially in the courses offered by social settlements, which focused on "training in handwork." For young women, this meant, in particular, learning "command of the needle," considered to be "so fundamental both in industry and homemaking." A different type of handwork instruction was made available by Mabel H. Kittredge, resident social worker at the Henry Street Settlement. Kittredge would rent a "typical" tenement house apartment for use as a model in order to train young working-class immigrant women in the full round of household duties "under [their] actual conditions of life" (Woods and Kennedy 1922:142–43). Leaders in the settlement movement acknowledged that they offered little in the manner of specific skill training relevent to employment in factories and stores, but claimed that training in even simple household handwork instilled "accuracy, neatness, order, perseverance, initiative, and through the attainment of these habits, strengthen[ed] the will; while appreciation of property created by one's own labor [brought] about a new attitude toward thoughtless destruction" (Woods and Kennedy 1922:140, 145). Presumably, settlement workers believed these "habits" or skills could be transferred from women's non-waged work in households to their waged employment.

In her 1910 to 1911 study of wage-earning women in trade schools, Mary Van Kleeck discovered that "a greater variety of courses [were] offered to men than to women." Young men were given the opportunity to study blacksmithing, cabinet making, carpentry, electrical engineering, electrical installation, gas engine construction, pattern making, plumbing, printing, and steam engineering. Young women, on the other hand, were limited to courses in low-waged occupations such as millinery, dressmaking, and costume designing (Van Kleeck 1914:14). At the Manhattan Trade

School (initiated by private enterprise in 1902 but incorporated into the New York public school system in 1910), course offerings for women included training in the garment trades, but with the stipulation that no young woman would be permitted to take the classes if she were not already employed or able to demonstrate that she was indeed seeking training for wage employment, rather than merely a source of "personal accomplishment" (Van Kleeck 1914:118–19). This represented yet another sign of the ambiguous and contradictory messages embodied in the movement for vocational education for single women.

The campaign for immigrant women's vocational education embraced all of the tensions and contradictions surrounding Progressive reformers' involvement in the construction of differences around race/ethnicity/nativity, social class, and gender. These contradictions are especially apparent in the variance among reformers' goals and expectations: first, to provide access to jobs and an economic independence previously unavailable to women, in part as an antidote to immoral temptations and prostitution; and second, to keep women morally "fit for motherhood" and to train them, in the words of the Federal Board for Vocational Education in 1919, to become "intelligent, discriminating, purchasing agents for themselves and their homes." The National Educational Association was forthright about its objectives: "the courses of instruction should train [women] for work in distinctly feminine occupations" (quoted in Kessler-Harris 1982:176). Lenora O'Reilly, who supervised sewing machine operators at the Manhattan Trade School for Girls, claimed that sewing would provide women access to self-expression, rather than just a skill (Kessler-Harris 1982:173, 359). The manual training committee of the National Educational Association argued that industrial education for young women would not only result in "happier and richer lives" for "future homemakers," but would raise their parents' standards of living as well (Kessler-Harris 1982:174). The training committee presumed that all young unmarried wage-earning women would have been living in their parents' households and would be continuing to contribute to them both their wage earnings and their nonwaged domestic labor. Of course, the National Educational Association was close in its assumptions. In the first decades of the century, most single wage-earning women in New York earned barely half the average wage of men and few could afford to live on their own. Among the largest industrial cities in the nation, New York City had one of the highest rates of wage-earning women residing with their parents or other relatives, between 80 and 90 percent (Peiss 1986:52).

Middle-class advocates for vocational education attempted to implement a third objective, often implicit but no less contradictory, when it came to some unmarried working-class immigrant women—that of developing docile, loyal, disciplined, low-waged workers. The point of vocational education was to inculcate in young immigrant women the values and skills perceived by middle-class reformers as appropriate to their racial/ethnic, class, and gender positions. Immigrant women from peripheral and semiperipheral regions of the world-economy were not, with few exceptions, expected or trained by middle-class feminists and Americanizers to become pioneers in well-paid occupations traditionally closed to women, or homemakers and mothers of middle-class families. Instead, depending on ethnicity, young single immigrant women were channeled into domestic service training or specific branches of the needle trades; they were, as well, lectured in "sex hygiene," and in how to avoid unnecessary household expenditures. One advocate of homemaker training for working-class immigrant Jewish women argued in 1906 that "while we have men who are able to work and make ten and twelve dollars a week, we have no women that can arrange their homes comfortably with that little amount of money, and therein lies the difficulty in the Jewish girl question" (quoted in Sinkoff 1988:594).

The enthusiasm of many Progressive reformers for the inclusion of industrial and vocational courses in public schools, social settlements, and immigrant community-based organizations was matched only by the support of numerous employers. At the end of the nineteenth century, many employers viewed the provision of training in skills specific to particular jobs as an important way of breaking craft monopolies held by workers. From the skilled worker's perspective, however, vocational education posed a threat to their relatively privileged position in the labor market, one which included controlling entry to trades through the apprenticeship system. Moreover, male craftworkers seemed especially threatened by the ominous specter of "outsiders" bypassing their authority and training young foreign-born women, in particular. One young woman, with twelve years experience in the millinery trade, addressed this contradictory goal of vocational education advocates with great clarity and foresight. In her words,

Figure 16.
Artificial flower makers pressing petals, a particularly routinized form of labor,
in an early twentieth-century factory. Lewis W. Hine Collection.
United States History, Local History & Genealogy Division, The New York Public Library.
Astor, Lenox and Tilden Foundations.

"There are too many milliners looking for work. If trade schools train too many, their training will not bring them higher wages because the increased numbers will keep the wages down" (quoted in Van Kleeck 1917:159).

While the milliner's statement was accurate enough for the few trades that had maintained a craft tradition, social reformers, like Mary Van Kleeck and Louise Odencrantz, were also reminded by other industrial employers they investigated that the rapid increase in the subdivision of tasks had already rendered training in many occupations unnecessary. "The monotony and unskilled nature of most of the processes [meant] that there was obviously nothing to learn and no chance for advancement." Speed and accuracy were the only qualifications really required for the slight advancement posssible in most trades. Of course, some employers readily acknowledged "the value of trade school training in developing in the girls a sense of responsibility and industrious habits" (Odencrantz 1919:265, 267, 270–71). One particularly candid employer explained to a horrified Mary Van Kleeck: "If the schools could get the girls started as you get a machine well-oiled up and set going it would be a fine thing for us" (Van Kleeck 1913:207–8). For Odencrantz, however, this increased "specialization" (i.e., deskilling) was not a deterrent, but rather "an added argument for better training and preparation for work, unless," as she and others feared, "the worker is to degenerate into a machine knowing only one minute process or motion of an occupation, without understanding its relation to the rest of the work and without ability to shift into any other process" (Odencrantz 1919:271). Against the background of single immigrant women's unremitting need for money income, the irregular and seasonal nature of the jobs available to them, not to mention the increasing specialization or deskilling of work, some reformers searched for new ways to develop women's abilities to shift more easily from one industrial task to another, ostensibly in order to protect them from "moral breakdown."

IMMIGRANT GIRLS AND COETHNIC NETWORKS: DIFFERENT PATHS AND MIXED BLESSINGS

Russian-Jewish immigrant women's experiences at the Clara de Hirsch Home for Working Girls, a turn-of-the-century boarding-home and vocational school, exemplified many of the contradictions and tensions between female middle-class social reformers and young unmarried working-class immigrant women. Their experiences, moreover, prefigured the characteristics that eventually differentiated Russian-Jewish women's work and community experiences from those of young unmarried Italian immigrant women.

The Clara de Hirsch Home for Working Girls was founded in 1897 for young Russian-Jewish immigrant women by affluent German Jews in New York. Migrating to the United States from Germany between the 1830s and the 1850s, this group of eventually wealthy financiers, bankers, and department store owners developed a tightly knit solidarity based on business, social, marriage, and cultural ties (Supple 1957:146, 158, 163; Rischin 1977:51–53). Founders of the Home, Oscar and Sarah Straus (son and daughter-in-law of department store magnate Lazarus Straus of Macy's and Abraham and Straus) and the Baroness Clara de Hirsch, were representative of the most affluent of this elite group. Not until the migration of eastern European Jews in the 1870s was their ethnic and class cohesiveness challenged, when they found themselves face to face with a mass of impoverished proletarians claiming a nominal coethnicity. Fearful in the context of increasing racial nativism that the arrival of Russian-Jewish immigrants would stigmatize and harm the position of the entire group, the German-Jewish community set out to incorporate them. Accustomed to pooling resources and extending credit to poorer German-Jewish businessmen, this moderately affluent community developed a myriad of coethnic organizations to help "adjust" the new immigrants to the United States (Supple 1957: 169; Tenenbaum 1993; Rischin 1977:ch. 6; Glanz 1976:ch. 4). The Clara de Hirsch Home for Working Girls was only one of many such institutions. Its express objective was "to benefit working girls and other unmarried women who are dependent upon their own exertions for a livelihood . . . [by] train[ing] them for self-support" (quoted in Sinkoff 1988:573).

Chief among the coethnic economic networks into which single Jewish immigrant women were received and incorporated differently than Italian immigrant women were the New York's garment trades, often termed "the great Jewish metier" (Pope 1905:49; Rubinow 1905:10; Rischin 1977:61–68; Waldinger 1986). German Jews predominated among the owners of large wholesale clothing establishments in most centers of the apparel trades in the

United States (Passero 1978:35–37). Historian Rudolf Glanz, among others, has suggested that "organized [German] Jewry" made it a policy to steer young Russian-Jewish immigrant women first into training courses and then into the semiskilled and unskilled sectors of the garment trades. "By the end of the [nineteenth] century it could be stated that at most places where Jewish immigrants had concentrated, the girls were helped through industrial education" (Glanz 1976:27–30; Kessner and Caroli 1978:26). By 1900, nearly 53 percent of Russian-Jewish men, 77 percent of women, and 59 percent of children, according to one estimate, had been incorporated into the lower end of New York's needle trades, within the Jewish ethnic economic enclave (Rubinow 1905:112). But, most importantly, by 1914, the German-Jewish employer had been replaced, except in the oldest and largest clothing firms, by their upwardly mobile former employees, eastern European Jewish men (Rischin 1977:67).

How did single Russian-Jewish women fare in the ascent of Russian-Jewish men from the rank of apprentice in exploited low-waged labor, to that of contractor and owner? How did they respond to the efforts of nominally coethnic middle-class Americanizers to channel their labor force participation into particular directions? What were their expectations and actual experiences of vocational education for wage-earning jobs in New York City? Most important, how did they compare with the experiences of unmarried Italian immigrant women?

The Clara de Hirsch Home, unlike some of the other more narrowly defined trade schools, attempted to meet a variety of young women's needs, as its board of directors defined them. They offered services to three types of young women: unskilled Jewish immigrant women over age fourteen, who had left school and whose family (if known) could not support them while they were learning a trade; "women adrift," (i.e., employed women with aspirations to be self-supporting, between age sixteen and thirty, who were without families and homes); and unskilled immigrant girls who were still living with their parents.[14] At its height in 1912–1913, over 140 young women lived at the Home where, following the emergent trends of scientific management and scientific homemaking, they were subject to a very tightly routinized schedule, made to resemble that of a factory (Sinkoff 1988:576–77, 579). Punctuality at breakfast as well as inflexible curfews at night reflected not only attempts to inculcate the rigors of work disci-

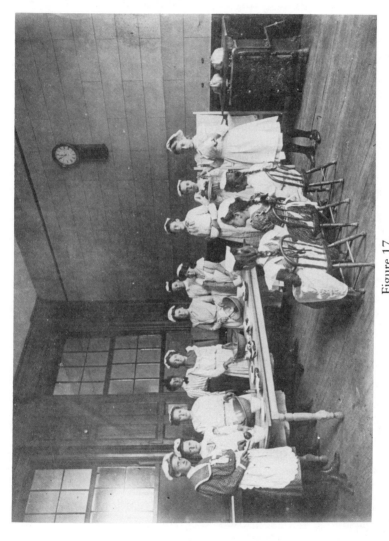

Figure 17.
Cooking class for immigrant girls at the Brooklyn Vocational School, 1902.
The Jacob A. Riis Collection. Museum of the City of New York.

pline, but when applied to young women, also meant a preoccupation with their sexual morality. Sex hygiene lectures were added to the vocational curriculum, as were closely supervised and regulated leisure activities. In addition, boarders at the Home were required to contribute to the Penny Provident Fund every week, in order to practice habits of thrift and economy (Sinkoff 1988:590).

Given the close relationship of the Home to garment manufacturers and retailers, courses in sewing dominated the school's curriculum. Following the lead of the social settlements, the young women started with a year-long program in handsewing, in which they learned twenty-four basic stitches, as well as how to construct aprons, uniforms, curtains, and so forth. Machine-sewing courses followed, and they in turn led to a more specialized education in millinery and dressmaking. Those young women who took these final courses were able to produce complete dresses for paying customers (Sinkoff 1988:580).

Although the Home's stated objective was "to fit young girls in as short a time as practicable for trade work, as a means of livelihood," immigrant women were required "to assist in the household, [as they were] being trained for their future homes," in addition to attending their vocational classes (Sinkoff 1988:579–80). The lesson in this for young immigrant women, informed by the founders' own class-based assumptions, was that wage earning should be but a temporary period in a woman's life, preceding marriage, and if necessary, following the death of a breadwinning husband, since "a woman's foremost mission . . . [was] to be the best qualified guardian of her offspring" (Sinkoff 1988:582).

But, there was an underlying or additional purpose to the Home's inclusion of courses in a middle-class style of cooking, laundry, grocery shopping, and serving. Middle-class German-Jewish female reformers were faced, during this period, with a severe shortage of servants. Their eagerness to steer young immigrant women into domestic service training programs reflected, in part, their idea of how to remedy their own household management problems.[15] Three months of the year-long program in domestic service were supposed to be spent in an apprenticeship, or in other words, working for a family.[16] In 1898, *The American Jewess* advised that it would "be philanthropy enough to alleviate the burdens of the rich by improving domestic service alone, quite apart from considerations of benefit to the pupil" (quoted in Sinkoff 1988:583).

How did the young immigrant students at the Clara de Hirsch Home for Girls respond to the contradictory messages embedded in their lessons and the none-too-subtle attempts to channel them into particular occupational directions? First, indications are that young unmarried Russian-Jewish women, like their Italian counterparts, shunned home-based employment. Only 15 percent of wage-earning daughters of Russian-Jewish immigrants and 13 percent of Italian daughters took up domestic and personal service occupations in New York City in 1900 (Van Kleeck 1913:31). Most seemed intent on not following in their mother's footsteps, but rather in striking out for higher-waged employment in less-controlled work environments, if given the opportunity. In 1900 only seven out of forty-one students at the Home elected the domestic service training program. The great majority of those who were placed as domestics left their jobs within the first year (Sinkoff 1988:585). The program was discontinued in 1902. It is a further irony that in their explicit intent to protect young immigrant women from the immoral environment of the mixed-sex factory, the benefactresses of the Clara de Hirsch Home for Girls attempted to direct them instead into the isolation of private service, where sexual harrassment was so much more commonplace.

Second, although many accounts place single Russian-Jewish women overwhelmingly in garment manufacturing, due to either cultural preference (Kessler-Harris 1982:127, 138), ethnic economic solidarity, or the immediate necessity of earning a small income without knowledge of English or specific skill training, indications are that as early as the turn of the century, they were already starting to leave this ethnic economic enclave for other types of employment. In the vocational training program at the Henry Street Settlement, out of fifty-nine graduates between 1889–1896, there were only two dressmakers, three milliners, and one beadworker. The majority became office workers, primarily typists, bookkeepers, and stenographers (Glanz 1976:32). Of those remaining in the garment trades in 1880, 95 percent "benefitting from a network of connections and experiences ... took skilled and semiskilled jobs," compared with 61 percent of their brothers and 55 percent of their fathers. By 1905, one out of four single Russian-Jewish women worked as a school teacher, clerk, salesperson, or shopkeeper in New York (Kessner and Caroli 1978:27).

Figure 18.
Young women and men mingle as coworkers in this garment workshop,
New York City, 1912. George Eastman House.

Although some single Russian-Jewish women made attempts to escape their position as dutiful daughters and loyal low-waged garment workers in the ethnic economic enclave, others embraced their long-sought status as an "earner," a "person," an "adult" in the labor market, and with it the proud right to an individual wage. In their view, the appropriate accommodation to the demands placed upon them by kin, coethnics, and social reformers, was neither to escape into marriage nor to train for a different occupation—at least not for some time. These women, pressured by their families' need for income and/or their own self-support, increasingly developed reputations as unruly and demanding workers.[17] In November 1909, thirty thousand garment workers began a thirteen-week-long strike to organize the International Ladies Garment Union. Known as the "girls' strike," because young women led it, approximately 21,000 Jewish women, 2,000 Italian women, 1,000 American women, and 6,000 (mostly Jewish) men participated (Seller 1986:255, 267). By 1913, Mary Van Kleeck found among the employers she interviewed that young Russian-Jewish immigrant women were considered "agitators." "The Jewish girl . . . has a distinct sense of social responsibility and often displays an eager zest for discussion of labor problems . . . [she] plunge[s] at once into a discussion of her trade, its advantages and disadvantages, wages, hours of work, and instances of shabby treatment in the shops, or of unsanitary conditions in the workrooms." The "Italian girl," on the other hand, was said to be more interested in craftsmanship or her own wages, rather than the general conditions in the trade. "[T]raditionally inclined to subordinate her individual desires" to her family, on whose behalf she was said to be employed, "the Italian girl is more willing than the Jewish girl to accept conditions as she finds them. The owner of a large [artificial] flower factory says he prefers to employ Italians because they 'are more tractable'" (Van Kleeck 1913:34–35).

Gradually, young Italian immigrant women replaced young Russian-Jewish immigrant women in various branches of the garment trades. Italian immigrant women faced a different set of racial/ethnic stereotypes in the workplace, and a coethnic community and household system organized according to a global migration system based primarily on the temporary circulation of low-waged adult men. Instead of bearing a reputation for leading strikes, young Italian women were regarded by employers and

Figure 19.

Striking shirtwaist workers and their supporters fill the streets of New York's Lower East Side in 1909. International Ladies' Garment Workers' Union Records, Labor Management Documentation Center, Cornell University.

non-Italian workers as especially docile and cheap labor, with a tendency to drive out other ethnicities from the trades they entered, due to underbidding (Van Kleeck 1913:30, 67–70). By 1900, 78 percent of wage-earning Italian women in New York City were at work in factories, more than any other ethnic group. And, within manufacturing industry, they were concentrated into only a limited number of trades, 52 percent were either tailoresses, seamstresses, or dressmakers. Italian immigrant women were particularly concentrated in the occupations of artificial flower making, dressmaking, hand sewing, and embroidery (Van Kleeck 1913:32–33).

In contrast to Russian-Jewish women, young Italian immigrant women were not steered to limited areas of the labor market by an affluent group of coethnic entrepreneurs or middle-class coethnic social reformers. Most were under age twenty-one (two-thirds) and obtained their jobs through friends and relatives of the same social class (Van Kleeck 1913:204; Odencrantz 1919:15, 272, 315). "Chance," rather than "any personal preferences or ideas as to [her] special fitness for certain kinds of work" was what investigators found drawing young Italian women to particular sectors of the labor market (Odencrantz 1919:272). Sometimes chance was supplemented, or perhaps driven, by unacknowledged and unrecognized skills and work experience. Many Italian women in the artificial flower trade had practice as industrial homeworkers when they were young children, before going to work in the shop (Van Kleeck 1913:196). Celestine, who had made artificial flowers at home since she was ten, declared to one investigator at the beginning of her study that she would never go into the degraded flower trade. But, on a later visit, the investigator found that Celestine had done just that. "I couldn't do anything else," she explained, shrugging her shoulders, "so I had to make flowers" (Van Kleeck 1913:201). Among a group of 894 newly arrived, young, unmarried Italian women in New York, between 1912 and 1913, more than fifty percent had been wage earners in Italy, often combining dressmaking in the winter with farm work in the summer. Most important, only forty-four young Italian women out of a group of 874 had, according to Odencrantz, "the advantage of help from a school, settlement, or agency" (Odencrantz 1919:305, 273).

During the time when so many Russian-Jewish women left the New York garment trades for employment in offices and depart-

Figure 20.

Young Italian immigrant women branching artificial roses, a remaining form of skilled labor, in this early twentieth-century New York workshop. Lewis W. Hine Collection. United States History, Local History & Genealogy Division, The New York Public Library. Astor, Lenox and Tilden Foundations.

ment stores, most unmarried Italian women remained, only gradually entering these areas in the mid-1920s and then in large numbers by the 1950s (Cohen 1978:284, 288). When pressed by investigators as to why they did not likewise prefer office work over factory work in New York, some young Italian immigrant women responded that "their mothers wouldn't stand for it" (Odencrantz 1919:35). Some operatives in the garment trades still made more money than office workers. Among female Italian artificial flower makers, industrial reformers heard persistently of Italian men's low wages and a family's dependence on the waged income contributions of its daughters.[18] In only two of 128 households of young flower makers studied, were they the only wage earners. Most of these households required as many as three and four wage earners in order to make ends meet (Van Kleeck 1913:76–78). Nearly half of 894 recently arrived young Italian women between 1912 and 1913 were contributing their earnings to the support of households either in Italy or in New York City, and sometimes to both. Reformers and union organizers recognized with dismay that this practice "made a girl readier to accept the first work and wages which were offered" and extremely reluctant to complain (Odencrantz 1919:305).

Despite these constraints, more than one-third of a group of 1,095 single Italian women supplemented their educations with classes in evening schools, social settlements, business schools, or private dressmaking schools. They viewed these institutions as far more relevent to their needs than the public high schools. In 1914, more than 27 percent of the students admitted to the Manhattan Trade School for Girls were Italian, an especially large number since Italians comprised only 11 percent of the population in 1910. Most studied dressmaking, sewing, and millinery—the typical curriculum offered to single young women in New York—but one which they expected to be a sequel to the classes in which so many had studied before leaving Italy (Odencrantz 1919:260–262). Most, however, were sorely disappointed. The subdivision of tasks had accelerated so rapidly and was so great in New York that there was no opportunity for a young woman to learn the whole of any process, and thus advance herself in the trade. At work they quickly discovered that producing the "American way" meant "cheap work" and that "everything must be done in a hurry" (Van Kleek 1913:194–95; Odencrantz 1919:39–41). Most new workers discovered the impracticality of vocational training when they started a new job. "The forelady showed me once," usually summarized how a girl learned the work. Often she simply learned from the girl next to her (Odencrantz 1919:267). In the context of much unwaged domestic labor, and possibly industrial homework, waiting for them in the evenings after at least a ten-hour day in the shops, many young women were forced to drop out of vocational training courses before completing them (Odencrantz 1919:261).

Despite the shortcomings and contradictions of the vocational education movement, it nonetheless shaped the labor force experience of young Jewish and Italian immigrant women in important ways. It exemplified the ambivalence of female Progressive reformers towards single immigrant women. And it was emblematic of the way that social reformers simultaneously constrained and promoted the empowerment of immigrant women. Vocational education projects included the unlikely combination and contradictory goals of diverse groups of employers, middle-class social reformers, coethnics, feminists, and Americanizers, not to mention the aspirations of young immigrant women themselves. This variety of goals, many of them mutually exclusive but often claimed by the same organization or institution, created a limited space within a context of constraints, for some young immigrant women to push at the boundaries of appropriate female vocations, assert their own needs, and claim their own ambitions. The intentions of employers and social reformers for young immigrant women, in other words, were not easily realized. Young Russian-Jewish and Italian women had their own plans and ambitions when they migrated—a combined product of their old world experiences as active contributors to the support of their households and the new promise of gaining "the right to a personality" in New York City with an individual wage packet to spend.

Young immigrant women were caught in the middle, trying in a variety of different ways to negotiate space for their own goals and needs, attempting to reconcile them not only with the efforts of Americanizers and reformers but, more importantly, with the increased needs of their households for waged income. As married immigrant women and mothers found themselves increasingly marginalized in the new world through the actions of state authorities and social reformers, as they were channeled into small family shops and home-based work, both waged and nonwaged, and as immigrant fathers and husbands were relegated to low-paying positions, the waged contributions of unmarried daughters to household income assumed greater relative importance (Chapin 1909; USIC 1911, XXVI:226, 232).

Russian-Jewish women ranked fourth and Italian women, seventh, among the most numerous groups of female wage earners in New York City in 1900. Most of them were young; of all women employed in manufacturing industries in New York City in 1900, 53 percent were between the ages of sixteen and twenty-five (Van Kleeck 1913:32, 25). In 1888, nearly three-quarters of all single women factory workers turned over their entire wage packet to the heads of their families, unlike their brothers and fathers who reserved a portion for their own spending money (Peiss 1986:68). Some sacrificed more. Lucy, a twenty-three-year-old Italian woman who worked in a paper-box factory, complained to factory investigator, Marie Orenstein, that she was the sole support for her mother and young brother. "She said to me pathetically: 'The other week my mother turned away a good offer of marriage because she said I must work until my brother is old enough to work'" (N.Y. St. Fac. Inv. Com. V, 1915:2650). Young Russian-Jewish women were similarly obligated to put off marriage in order to provide for their parents and siblings. Anna R. delayed her marriage for several years, until she had brought her parents and three brothers and sisters to the United States. "In three years the whole family was here. But I was the one to bring the rest of them over, because I made more money than the rest of them." What was a matter of pride and accomplishment for Anna R. was a source of bitterness for Anna Kahan, who believed that her years of hard work and saving to pay for the passage of her parents and brother had destroyed her health. "I was a healthy child, and they killed me. This life killed me. All I took on myself. Of course, I saved the family. But they killed me" (quoted in Weinberg 1988:157).

Despite a cultural ideal of household income pooling shared by both Russian Jews and Italians, based on notions of mutual obligation, mutual need, filial obedience to parents, and family unity, some young women wage earners gradually started to withhold part of their income from the "common fund" (Smith 1985; Weinberg 1988:ch. 8). According to industrial investigator Mabel Willett in 1902, Russian-Jewish women in the clothing trades "continue to live at home, but they have . . . a greater degree of freedom in the spending of their income than is common among either German or Italian girls . . . Sometimes the girl hands over her money regularly to her parents, but it is not unusual to find her retaining practically all her earnings" (Willett 1902:88–89). This increased freedom of some Russian-Jewish women to dispose of their earnings as they chose was, in part, a recognition by parents of the need to spend on clothing, in the place of a dowry. At the same time, the right to spend on oneself was not something easily acknowledged or won. In her observations of youthful rebelliousness and generational conflict, Willett remarked that "the younger generation of lower east side Jews [was] quite capable of ignoring parental advice and influence if a strong incentive is present" (Willett 1902:88).

Young Italian immigrant women, on the other hand, were forced to accept for a much longer period the practice of turning over the unopened wage packet to the head of the household, rather than holding back a portion to spend on themselves. On average, an Italian daughter's wages constituted 44 percent of the entire household's money income. She was considered the "mainstay" and the most regular of all money contributors to the household's support (Odencrantz 1919:177, 187). But even, or especially, a mainstay could claim some privileges, based on her regular contributions. Some were able to "strike an implicit bargain" for increased freedom to come and go, given the size of their contributions. Antoinette Paluzzi, who migrated at age thirteen from Sicily to New York, was not allowed by her father to date. Her mother, on the other hand, allowed her to go to the park with a girlfriend—where she met her boyfriend. Similarly, wage earner Angelina Defina and her fiancé were "always" properly chaperoned, but on occasion, each took time off from work in the afternoon to visit together (Peiss 1986:70). Between 1911 and 1913, out of a group of 1,095 young Italian wage-earning women, 86 percent turned their entire paycheck over to their parents, while their brothers held back half or sometimes all for spending money (Odencrantz 1919:21, 175–76). But 14 percent of the young women kept some of their earnings ostensibly to pay for carfare, lunches, and work clothes. In reality, however, these young immigrant women usually found a way to do without some of these items or to substitute their own labor for the money (Clark and Wyatt 1911), in order to have more to spend on their limited realm of autonomous recreation and empowerment.

CONCLUSION

In the narrow space between increased household pressure to deliver a waged income and the determination by the state and social reformers to protect their moral purity, and sometimes to develop their skills, some young immigrant women were able to experience a new leverage to pursue more self-defined goals. The degree of leverage, or bargaining power, young immigrant women possessed, with respect to determining their future occupations, had a great deal to do with both the nature of their reception by a coethnic community and the economic circumstances and composition of their households. Due to the timing and circumstances of their migration, unmarried Italian and Russian-Jewish immigrant women entered coethnic communities and became members of household systems that were organized socially and economically quite differently from one another, with differentiating consequences for their labor force experiences in America. Nonetheless, "the independent Jewish or Italian girl working in the coat, pants or vest shops, paying her board, and maintaining herself from the balance of her earnings, is largely a dream of the investigator" (Willett 1902:92).

"Becoming a person" in New York City for single immigrant women, both Italian and Russian-Jewish, meant first of all, becoming an important wage earner in her household. This was a source of self-esteem, pride, and accomplishment for many women, although never a free choice. Depending on the composition of her household and the degree to which she was permitted to learn a skilled trade and thus earn an income high enough to save or to spend as she chose, a young immigrant woman would have considered herself relatively empowered in the so-called new world.

Conclusion

The migrant has recently been designated the "central or defining figure of the twentieth century."[1] But for much of this period, the study of international migration has centered on the uprooting and transplanting processes of adult men as representative and ignored the part of women in migration.

This study set out to explain migrating women's part in the global population movements from peripheral and semiperipheral to core regions of the world-system during the late nineteenth and early twentieth centuries. In it, I have analyzed and reassessed the impact of the migration experience on Russian-Jewish and Italian women's lives. The principal organizing question throughout has been whether and to what extent migration diminished, intensified, and/or transformed the nature of women's social status and social position. Put simply, my objective was to determine whether migration was an empowering or disempowering experience for women, and what made it so.

In this chapter, I return to the initial theoretical debates and controversies that informed both the organizing question and the research strategies. This chapter also describes the more specific findings of this study concerning the contrast in migration experiences among and between Russian-Jewish and Italian women. I, then, conclude with some reflections about what a study comparing Russian-Jewish and Italian immigrant women's experiences in turn-of-the-twentieth-century New York may imply for research on other migrations, historical or contemporary.

INTERNATIONAL MIGRATION AND THEORETICAL CONTROVERSIES: GENDER AND NATIONALITY/ETHNICITY/RACE TRAVEL THE WORLD-SYSTEM TOGETHER

What had at first appeared to be a deceptively straightforward research question—on the relationship between international migration and women's social position—gradually evolved into a more complex and nuanced task, one which ultimately led to the development of an alternative interpretive framework. My inquiry into European women's experiences of migration to the United States at the turn of the century involved nothing less than traversing through all three phases of scholarship on the historical sociology of women (Boxer and Quataert 1987:112–13). It involved, at first, the task of dismantling or revealing the flawed assumptions, interpretations, and practices that had led to distorted understandings of women's part in international migrations. Second, followed the work of (re)discovering old and new sources documenting women's presence and diverse modes of participation in the global economic, political, and social changes of the period, of which migration was but one aspect. Finally, efforts to integrate new knowledge about women and international migration into preexisting theoretical frameworks evolved into the emergence of a new interpretive framework. Placing the interconnected processes of gender, national/ethnic/racial, and class formation at the center of analysis disrupted and rearranged traditional explanations and predictions of the sociology of migration. This outcome is suggestive of the implications that such an integrative, wholistic, and comparative historical perspective may hold for reshaping understandings of both women's *and* men's experiences of migration.

Two broad theoretical frameworks have tended to guide the analysis of international migration and immigrant adaptation, those emphasizing either a push-pull/modernization or a historical-structural/world-systems orientation. The most widely held perspective on the dynamics of migration has been the push-pull model, which has generally been combined with assimilationist and human-capital approaches to immigrant outcomes. An underlying assumption of this framework holds that migration is primarily a matter of individual choice and a movement of unencumbered individuals. The individual, as the unit of analysis and source of the decision to migrate, is isolated from any restraining or enabling social relationships, just as conditions in the sending country are analytically separated from those in the receiving society. Thus, the mass movement from eastern and southern Europe to the United States in the late nineteenth century is explained by means of a compilation of economic, political, and social disadvantages that prompted individuals to leave their homelands, and of a separate and wholly unconnected calculation of advantages that pulled these individuals toward the United States. Those individuals most likely to migrate were, fortuitously, those most likely to succeed in America—individuals who had been exposed to "modern Western values" and who could project themselves into the role of "Western man." When this framework considered women, although its assumptions generally rendered women's part in migration invisible, it claimed that those individuals who did migrate were exceptionally modern women in terms of their self-interest and economic rationality. "Not content to stay at home and do nothing" these women "broke out of the ghetto of passive domesticity" to pursue educations and careers in America. Push-pull and assimilationist models predicted that women such as these could expect to experience greater empowerment and personal autonomy following immigration. Those individuals or groups (aggregates of individuals) with migration experiences that seemed to contradict this linear progression were blamed for not having *yet* been sufficiently exposed to Western values, a problem that unless remedied by outside assistance could retard their Americanization and the chances of their families and ethnic communities for upward mobility.

The strongest challenge to the push-pull/modernization and assimilation tradition has been from historical-structural frameworks in which the unit of analysis was shifted from the individual to the social structures and processes of a global economic system. Proponents recast international migration from a one-way transfer of persons between autonomous and unrelated nation states to the ongoing circulation of resources, both capital and labor, within the boundaries of a single global division of labor, that is between a dominant core and a dependent periphery. A new emphasis was placed on the exploitative nature of the relationship between sending and receiving countries. Similarly, immigration, whether male or female, was characterized above all as as a source of cheap wage labor in core countries such as the United States. As a consequence, opportunities and institutions in the receiving society were structured to maintain and reproduce economic inequality. The expectation following from this position was for the continued subordination, if not greater exploitation, of immigrant women who were pulled out of their peripheral European homelands by the demand for low-cost labor in the industrializing United States.

But, when the global and interactive processes of gender, national/racial/ethnic, and class formation were placed at the center of the dynamics of women's migration, their experiences contrasted sharply with the generic descriptions and predictions embedded in either of the dominant theoretical frameworks. Situating women's multiple, intersecting, and shifting identities at the center of analysis exposed the polarized and dichotomous thinking embedded in the principal competing paradigms. When individual immigrant women described their own experiences, or the focus of research was recentered on them as this study has done, the stories that have emerged are more nuanced and ambiguous, in terms of expected aggregate outcomes or measures of empowerment and personal autonomy. No single path or purpose led women out of eastern and southern Europe in the last quarter of the nineteenth century. Nor did their experiences necessarily converge and homogenize into a singular pattern of adaptation in the United States. Women experienced migration as neither uniformly emancipating nor uniformly disempowering. Most often immigration had fundamentally contradictory, if not paradoxical, implications for women's lives. Nonetheless, despite the contradictory outcomes and the multiplicity of experiences, it was impossible to overlook one significant commonality shared by the women studied. Immigrant women, in contrast to their representation in much of the literature as passive appendages of *the real migrant* (male breadwinner) or otherwise exceptional women, were active participants in the migration process and engaged subjects of their lives. They made great efforts, which did not always meet with success, to negotiate and to reconcile, to accommodate and to resist the generally conflicting expectations and social forces that confronted them as they crossed borders and refashioned gender, national/racial/ethnic, and class identities.

New patterns of migration, such as those sketched out previously, were observed by employing an alternative framework that not only placed the processes of gender and racial/ethnic formation at the center of migration analysis, but also refused to juxtapose or privilege the world-system, as a unit of analysis, over and against the individual immigrant. In utilizing a both/and approach, rather than an either/or perspective rooted in dualistic thinking (Collins 1991:42–43), Russian-Jewish and Italian immigrant women were analyzed as individual participants in a changing world-system, interpreting and improvising their lives against shifting economic, political, and social contexts. A greater diversity of migration patterns were revealed by focusing on and reinterpreting neglected aspects of the immigrant's backgrounds as

subjects with gender and national/racial/ethnic identities in formation, as specifically Russian-Jewish and Italian women of the late
nineteenth century, and as Jewish and Italian American women of
the early twentieth century (e.g., from "not-quite-white" to "not-
yet-white" women). The particular political, economic, and social
changes in the world-system that prompted their selective departures from Russia and Italy and their arrival in the U.S. decisively
shaped their modes of incorporation into the United States. At the
same time, the varying nature of their receptions in the United
States by political and economic institutions, by the dominant
population, by kin and preexisting coethnic communities, all
played a significant role in differentiating immigrant women's
experiences from one another.

More precisely, the alternative framework developed to illuminate the diversity of women's migration experiences and to interpret the extent of their subordination and/or empowerment
located immigrant women in the context of three intersecting sets
of hierarchical relationships. It was within the context of these
stratified yet dynamic relations that their personal and social
backgrounds were examined. Through these multiple relationships Russian-Jewish and Italian women were joined to an overarching world-system.

First, Russian-Jewish and Italian women were situated within
the context of the principal economic transformations in nin-
teenth-century Russia and Italy, as their changing connection to
the world-economy rearranged the material resources and opportunities available across social groups, classes, and households.
New challenges to making a living and changing class relations
gave rise to migrant flows with distinct social compositions. These
factors predisposed women to certain patterned outcomes later as
immigrants in the United States. In order to examine economic
change in terms that had real meaning for turn-of-the-century
women and girls, I reconceptualized economic position to encompass the transformations in both paid and unpaid work, in formal
and informal sectors, which bound women to families, households, regions, and ethnic communities. Similarly, changes in
other important indicators of economic position such as education, literacy, and skill were broadened to include the socially
undervalued and invisible training Russian-Jewish and Italian
girls received since early childhood, often from female kin, in skills
appropriate to their culturally specific communities.

The second set of stratifying processes I examined, which encompassed and structured immigrant women's backgrounds, consisted of various political relationships. The politics of emigration in Russia and Italy at the end of the nineteenth century reflected not only changing domestic or internal relations but, to a great extent, the changing framework of interstate relations in the world-system. Russian and Italian emigration policies directly determined which social groups (primarily by class, ethnicity, and nationality) were forbidden, allowed, or even pressured to leave. Similarly, U.S. immigration politics directly shaped the social composition of newcomers by means of the criteria through which individuals were grouped, categorized, and then selectively allowed or denied entry. Indirectly, political decisions taken by Russia and Italy, but deeply conditioned by each state's position within an overarching world-economy, such as those concerning agricultural and industrial development, promoted migration for particular social groups as opposed to others, by constraining or otherwise altering their local income-producing opportunities.

The third and most important, but most problemmatic, set of stratifying relationships organizing women's migration to the United States was comprised of the multitude of social and cultural ties that bound women to families, households, and ethnic groups. On the one hand, kinship, friendship, and community networks made it either possible or virtually impossible for many women to migrate by providing or denying important material resources, information, encouragement, and emotional support. These networks, to a very great extent, facilitated and organized migration flows that economic and political forces had only made possible. Networks shaped the social composition, duration, and direction of migration. On the other hand, the global economic and political forces that had made migration a possibility in the abstract were themselves organized by gender and national/racial/ethnic assumptions and practices. The same was true for the social and cultural networks in which migrating women were more intimately involved. The gender division of labor and the cultural beliefs and practices regarding appropriate Russian-Jewish, Italian, and American feminine and masculine behavior determined more directly the nature of immigrant women's involvement in these potential "networks of opportunity," or relationships, and their subsequent social position in immigrant communities.

IMMIGRATION AND WOMEN'S STATUS:
HOUSEHOLD AND COMMUNITY RELATIONS SHAPE
THE NATURE OF EMPOWERMENT

Women's immigration experiences were shaped not only by the American contexts in which they renegotiated their identities but in important ways by both an overarching world-system and by the European contexts and social relations in which their lives had been deeply embedded. The position of Russia, Italy, and the United States in the global division of labor and interstate rivalries of the mid- to late nineteenth century set the broad historical parameters within which women's migration took place. Changes in these global hierarchical relationships had reverberating effects on the internal dynamics of sending states, communities, and households, the social units that ultimately released some women from their preexisting obligations and responsibilities and influenced their selection of destination. In other words, it was the interplay between global economic and political pressures, local social networks, and interpersonal relations that translated a propensity for many to emigrate from the peripheries of Europe into actual immigration to the United States for only some.

Although Russian-Jewish immigrant women, like Italian women, were active self-conscious participants in the making of their individual life chances, both were at the same time connected to large-scale and long-term stratifying processes that increasingly made overseas migration a meaningful possibility for them. Russian-Jewish women experienced quite tangibly the ramifications of these broader economic, political, and social forces over the nineteenth century through three intersecting domains: in the increasingly restrictive Russian state policies concerning ethnic and national minorities on its western borderlands, a consequence of its changing position in the global interstate system; in the acceleration of class differentiation and conflict among Russian Jews, and between Jews and peasants, a result of Russia's peripheralization in the world-economy; and in the increasing obligations and responsibilities of Jewish women for both paid and nonpaid work, a complex outcome of the relations between genders, households, and labor-force structures. The intersection of all these trends significantly influenced the timing, composition, and most of all the motivations comprising Jewish women's migration to the United States.

As the Russian government periodically tightened restrictions on Jewish entitlements to practice particular livelihoods in given localities, both the characteristics of the providers of income and the types of income to Jewish households shifted. As the commercial labor market throughout the Pale of Settlement, and particularly in the northwest, became evermore saturated, Jewish household members, in order to make ends meet, were compelled to take up alternative and auxiliary occupations. Increasingly, Russian-Jewish women joined the paid labor force as artisans, industrial homeworkers, and petty entreprenuers, sometimes displacing adult males in the process. As single women, wives, mothers, and widows, Russian-Jewish women negotiated and maneuvered changes in the definition of feminine identity and in the sexual division of labor in order to contribute to the increasingly tenuous viability of their own or their parents' households. Women's migration evolved out of these multilayered transformations. Initially, Jewish women remained in Russia and Russian-Poland, maintained households and income-producing enterprises, and were sent for only later by male migrants who hoped to find a better life for themselves first. Frequently, oldest daughters accompanied their fathers, or were sent for first, in order to "keep house" in America. Gradually, over time, single women left Russia ahead of other family members. Some found employment for themselves among kin and within a coethnic community, and then sent money or tickets for additional family members to join them. Others transformed migration into an opportunity for a free-choice marriage and then established their own households. And others migrated to escape the gendered restrictions of women's family obligations altogether.

Italian women's migration, like that of Russian-Jewish women, was located at the center of the principal economic and political transformations of the mid- to late nineteenth century. In other words. Italian immigrant women were neither marginal to nor outside of social changes; nor were they otherwise exceptional women. Long before the time of the mass transatlantic migration, Italian women regularly participated in internal seasonal migrations within Europe, both as migrants themselves and as those who enabled the migration of others by maintaining the family's small holdings.

Although Italy was only nominally unified in 1861, and profound regional differentiation prevents the making of many generalizations, one of the most persistent patterns both in areas of high internal seasonal migration and temporary transatlantic migration was the increasing distribution of property rights and the growing expectation by the landless and the small holders of eventually finding the means to purchase more land. The prolonged agricultural depression at the end of the nineteenth century and the increased mechanization of industry, however, had different effects on the social composition of the population flows from each region. Not only was the relatively weak Italian state unable to prevent increased overseas migration at this time, but state policy indirectly promoted, regulated, and significantly affected the composition of the migrant flows to the Americas at the turn of the twentieth century. Unlike the Russian state, which selectively targeted and permanently expelled particular national minorities, the Italian state made great efforts toward retaining the allegiance of its predominantly temporary male breadwinning population abroad. The encouragement of temporary migration and the fostering of ties between adult male Italians abroad and families and communities in their native land was clearly tied to the significant earnings these emigrants remitted not only to their households but to Italian banks. These differences between Russian state and Italian state emigration policies had long-term consequences for women's experiences of immigration in the United States.

Italian women, like Russian-Jewish women, were faced with the burden of managing the intensifying economic constraints on their households and they responded similarly, in part, by increasing their paid and nonpaid income contributions. In some households, where daughters faced diminished economic options and the household lacked sufficient male earners, the motivation to emigrate was very strong. In other words, some heads of households were motivated to send daughters abroad and some daughters were highly motivated to leave. Although over time Italian women increased their share in the migration stream, it remained a predominantly male flow, unlike that of Russian Jews. Some Italian women migrated with a reserve of work experience and skills in agriculture, silk and clothing production, embroidery, and small business in order to earn enough for dowries; others followed emigrating husbands and fathers because their communities provided few alternatives for abandoned wives and mothers. Although few women migrated to America as an opportunity for self-actualization, few of those returned to Italy.

Within the United States Russian-Jewish and Italian wives and mothers faced distinctly different prospects, compared to each other and to younger single immigrant women. Among married immigrant women, I explored the notion that the remaking of gender, class, and racial/ethnic/national identities in America was central in determining the extent and kind of empowerment that they experienced. I found that immigration to the United States, an emerging core in the world-system at the turn of the century, was a generally disempowering experience for all women who entered as wives and mothers. Encumbered by child rearing and other nonwaged as well as waged activities in the household, immigrant wives and mothers, as is generally argued in studies on women from a life-course perspective, were rarely in a position to alter the gender balance of power either in their homes or outside. Empowerment and autonomy for immigrant women was thus inversely related to marriage and motherhood.

Though intensified subordination was the predominant pattern observed for married immigrant women, it is far too general and must itself be further explained and elaborated. It should be noted moreover that the major underlying point in examining the experiences of married women and mothers separately from single women was neither to find additional evidence to support this general finding nor to imply that all women necessarily pass through a chronological set of stages from childhood or girlhood to young adulthood when single, and then to marriage and motherhood in later adulthood where they progressively become disempowered. Rather, the point was to develop a strategy both for research and presentation that would avoid the stereotyped thinking and tautological methods customary in much research on immigrant women that initially separates women according to ahistorical nationality/ethnicity/race criteria and then claims that national/ethnic/racial differences underlay different migration experiences and outcomes. Too often migration research has presumed, rather than questioned, that "culture" is at the root of the differences between women. Rather than working with this reductionist, essentialist, and basically static notion of culture and cultural difference, my underlying objective has been to interrogate the specific categories of women's gender, national/race/ethnic, and class identities as they were constructed and reconstructed through the migration process, that is, to examine the categorization process in world-historical context beginning with global processes as they stratify sending regions.

Much more interesting than the discovery that married women and mothers, both Russian-Jewish and Italian, shared a generally negative outcome of migration to America was the finding of significant and patterned variations among these groups of women. Despite their shared gender and life-cycle status, and their shared origin as emigrants from peripheral regions of the nineteenth-century world-economy, Russian-Jewish and Italian women were channeled toward different and relatively unequal positions in the United States social structure. The variations among the women were related to a global *process* of racial/ethnic and gender transformation, itself dependent upon a complex relationship between a woman's politically based vulnerability prior to migration, her reception by the U.S. state, the impact of Americanizers upon her household and family arrangements, and the nature of her income-producing work. I examined this process in three interrelated areas: first, in the meanings and impact of racial nativism on Russian-Jewish and Italian immigrant wives and mothers; second, in the critically different experiences each had with predominantly female middle-class Americanizers and Americanizing institutions; and third, in the outcomes of their distinct modes of incorporation into coethnic communities and work forces.

Late nineteenth- and early twentieth-century racial nativism affected the reception of immigrant women differently than immigrant men, married women and mothers differently than single women, and Russian-Jewish and Italian women of the "new immigration" differently than women of the "old immigration." In particular, the racial nativist discourse about fertility and motherhood became an important part of the framework for relations between immigrant women, the U.S. state and a diversity of Americanizers. The "race suicide" alarm nourished fears that institutions of American civilization, particularly motherhood and the family, were in mortal danger of subversion from peoples with uncontrolled rates of child bearing. The racialization of Russian-Jewish and Italian women in the late nineteenth and early twentieth centuries occurred, in part, through these debates in the press, in Congress, and eventually in the decisions to selectively regulate and then nearly curtail southern and eastern European immigration.

Immigrant women's most immediate experiences of incorporation in the United States, as well as their future prospects, were fundamentally shaped by their relationships with Americanizers of dominant races and classes and by the nature of the preexisting coethnic communities in which they became the newest members. Married women and mothers emerged as an especially important concern and target of the movement to assimilate southern and eastern European immigrants. In the eyes of Americanizers, immigrant mothers were the guardians both of the present home and of future generations of American citizens. For social settlement workers, motherhood and family life were too essential to a democratic culture to leave them in the hands of the untrained and unassimilated. Impressed by studies on rationalization in the factory, middle-class female Americanizers made concerted efforts at a parallel transformation of the immigrant homemaking enterprise.

The relationship that developed between middle-class female Americanizers and Russian-Jewish and Italian immigrant women can best be characterized by the concept of *maternalism*; that is to say it was a relationship between women that degraded and insulted, as it protected and nurtured. It was based on a fundamental lack of respect for the female recepient of assistance as an autonomous adult, although certainly reformers differed from one another in the extent of their maternalist benevolence.

Despite their own subordinate status as women, the power of social settlement workers to reproach and to intervene in immigrant lives was enhanced by their own class and racial/ethnic/national identities. Moreover, as social settlement work produced and reproduced the perception of a childlike and vulnerable immigrant mother, it simultaneously validated and strengthened the new status and prestige of middle-class female professionals. Rather than promoting autonomy for individual immigrant women, or immigrant group mobility, Americanizing social reformers played an important role in institutionalizing social inequality between women, especially by nationality/race/ethnicity and class and between women and men in households and families. Americanization efforts, like social settlement work, in the short run generally complemented selective immigration restriction by attempting to alter the most undesirable behavior of new immigrant women, without curtailing the "golden stream," or contesting in any meaningful way the system of social stratification.

The domestic ideal of these social reformers often came into conflict with the ideals, needs, and practices of the eastern and southern European working-class women whom they tried to persuade to perform housework more productively and child care more efficiently. Immigrant wives and mothers continued with difficulty to pursue and implement their own gender ideals. Despite innumerable courses in middle-class Anglo-American child care, decorative handsewing, and household budgeting, as well as the harassment of "friendly home visitors," many immigrant women made efforts to provide income for their families in America just as they had learned to do from female kin in Europe, but were unable to practice there. They continued to muster all available hands, including their own, to contribute multiple types of income, waged and nonwaged, to the household. By maneuvering, manipulating, and sometimes subverting the intentions of Americanizers, many immigrant women were able to imaginatively maintain both their households and their self-respect, thus in some sense resisting the process of disempowerment. Some took to the streets in demonstrations and consumer boycotts. Others were quietly exploited by male heads of households and exploited less senior family members in turn, in the attempt to live up to European-constructed ideals of womanhood and motherhood.

While both Russian-Jewish and Italian immigrant wives and mothers came into some contact with middle-class female Anglo-American reformers, there was a significant difference between their experiences. The presence of coethnic (e.g., middle-class Americanized German-Jewish) associations specifically oriented to incorporating newly arrived immigrant women blunted the hard edge of racial nativism and the ethnic bias of the Americanization process for Russian-Jewish immigrant women. Of course, as demonstrated, middle-class coethnic reformers could be equally maternalistic, condescending, and impractical when material assistance was required. Italian immigrant women, however, faced the racial nativism and maternalism head-on, without substantial support or protection from a coethnic community organized specifically to receive immigrant women or families. This was, more than anything else, the consequence and the legacy of a transnational migration system dominated by the temporary circulation of low-wage adult male labor and promoted by the newly organized but weak Italian state.

Initially, I expected that a single woman's migration to New York City at the turn of the century would have increased her potential "to become a person," to not only imagine but frequently to realize her self-determined goals. However, in contrast to much of the literature on single wage-earning European immigrant women and my own expectations, I found that young women's potential for greater self-determination rested on much more than reaching the point in their life cycle where they could begin to produce income. Quite like the situation of their mothers or married sisters, significant and patterned differences regarding the emancipatory possibilities of immigration existed among unmarried women, based on a complex relationship between their politically constructed identity (ethnicity/race/nationality), the nature of their reception by both dominant U.S. institutions and a coethnic community, and their family/household position in relation to other members. Further, like married women and mothers, single women were not passive observers of their fates but, rather, active participants and strategists, imagining alternatives, weighing possibilities, and devising a multitude of means for realizing goals. Each woman's experience of immigration evolved out of her own way of negotiating between and reconciling structurally constrained options and possibilities.

Turn-of-the-century racial nativism, as promoted and practiced by both state authorities and various Americanizers, attempted without complete success, however, to construct a subordinate gender and sexual identity for young unmarried women. These agencies differentiated between Russian-Jewish and Italian women in both their attitudes and treatment. Racial nativist stereotypes, sexism, and class bias all intersected in the construction of a working-class "immigrant girl problem" for Americanizers at the turn of the century. The association of unmarried immigrant women with white slavery and prostitution emerged as the counterpart in tone, theme, and urgency to the racial nativist preoccupation with the fertility of immigrant mothers. In contrast to much of the data they collected, antiprostitution reformers and state authorities continally portrayed those involved in the traffic as primarily new immigrants, mostly eastern European Jews, stigmatizing and subjecting these women to closer surveillance and scrutiny where possible. Social settlement workers and Americanizers aimed, instead, to induce greater self-management and self-control on the part of the women. As these middle-class Americanizers sought to incorporate single immigrant women into their dichotomized and inflexible framework of appropriate female sexuality and acceptable womanhood, they warned young women of the dangers in the new world, in the labor market, in the new commericalized leisure activities, in short—in the public sphere.

Recommendations by Americanizers, social reformers, and the U.S. Immigration Commission to suppress or otherwise prevent prostitution demonstrated also the underlying and mounting social anxieties over turn-of-the-century changes in family ar-rangements (especially middle-class women's behavior) and the changing morality of youth (especially young working-class women). In iden-tifying unmarried working-class immigrant women as potential or actual prostitutes, state authorities and Americanizing social reformers attempted not only to regain control over women's more seemingly self-determined behavior but to induce self-regulation in compliance with middle-class American gender expectations. The preoccupation with unmarried women's gender and sexuality can also be read from the other side, as evidence of the increased poten-tial for self-determination that some immigrant women had been seeking from their families and households in industrializing New York. For at least a moment in their lives, if not longer for some, many women found the space to experiment with different class and gender images, to try out and play with new ways of being female, quite unlike the paths marked for them by their old world mothers and married sisters.

At the turn of the century, various social groups and institutions in New York became implicated in the attempt to channel single immigrant women into distinct sectors of the wage-earning work-force. The emergence of industrial/vocational classes for single women can be considered the counterpart to the instruction in homemaking and mothercraft married women received. And, in a similar manner, the organization and impact of these schools reflected the distinct social origins of their students, including the very different migration systems that had brought them to America.

Three underlying but contradictory goals informed industrial and vocational education programs for single immigrant women. The two most often stated goals were (1) to provide young women access to jobs and an economic independence previously unavail-able and (2) to keep women morally "fit for motherhood." Mid-dle-class advocates for vocational education attempted to imple-ment a third underlying and equally contradictory objective when it came to some unmarried working-class immigrant women— that of developing docile, loyal, disciplined, low-waged workers. The point of vocational education for immigrant women was to inculcate the values and skills perceived by middle-class reformers as appropriate to their national/racial/ethnic, class, and gender identities. Immigrant women from peripheral and semiperipheral regions of the world-economy were not, with few exceptions, expected or trained by middle-class female reformers to become pioneers in well-paid professions. They were instead—depending on their race/ethnicity—channeled into training for domestic service or specific branches of the needle trades or into courses on budgeting for households and small businesses, and they were lectured in sex hygiene.

The organization and impact of vocational/industrial education differed significantly between Russian-Jewish and Italian young women. Russian-Jewish immigrant women faced a well-organized and affluent nominally coethnic community, or "ethnic economic enclave," upon arrival in New York City. Accustomed to pooling resources and extending credit to poorer German-Jewish businessmen, this wealthy contingent of Americanized German-Jewish financiers, garment manufacturers, and department store owners developed a number of institutions to assist in the "adjustment" of new Jewish immigrants. Training single immigrant women for self-support, but channeling them into the lowest-waged sectors of the clothing trades in an ethnic economic enclave as loyal coethnics, was one form of this assistance. In response to this mixed blessing, Russian-Jewish women developed a reputation within the industry as troublesome and unruly workers and trade union agitators.

Gradually young Italian immigrant women replaced Russian-Jewish women in the garment trades. They faced a different set of racial/ethnic stereotypes and practices that shaped their incorporation into the labor market. Italian immigrant women were not able to rely on the support, however mixed, of an ethnic economic enclave. The coethnic community they found upon immigration and the household system they constructed was organized according to a migration system based primarily on the temporary circulation of low-waged adult male laborers and artisans. Instead of a reputation for leading strikes, young Italian women were regarded by their American and Jewish employers and their non-Italian coworkers as especially tractable and cheap labor. Their low wages remained a mandatory component of a low-waged household necessarily composed of multiple earners, and constituted one of the constraints on their labor market behavior. But most important, they were channeled into these areas of employment, not by an affluent and well-organized class of coethnics but by similarly placed friends and relatives.

Yet, despite their very different relationships with reformers, coethnic institutions, employers, and families, single immigrant women—both Italian and Russian-Jewish—were united by their various efforts to negotiate space for the pursuit of their developing goals and needs and to reconcile these with the constraints of Americanizers and households pressed for waged income. In the narrow space between increased household pressure to deliver waged income and the expressed interest by reformers and state authorities in protecting their morality, some young immigrant women were able to experience a new leverage to pursue more self-defined goals. Even, or especially a mainstay to household support, did on occasion demand the right to a personality and a dream of her own.

SOME REFLECTIONS ON THE MEANINGS OF TRANSNATIONAL MIGRATION

Migration to the United States for Russian-Jewish and Italian women at the turn of the century was only one part of the lengthy transnational process, in the words of one immigrant woman, of "becoming a person." Russian-Jewish immigrant, Anzia Yezierska, repeatedly used in her autobiographical fiction the vernacular expression "becoming a person" to encompass an immigrant woman's yearning to become a more active agent in control of her life. "How it burns in me to work myself up for a person" conveys both the internal struggle ("hunger") and external strategizing involved in achieving personhood, as well as the increased social importance and power derived as a consequence of "mak[ing] from myself a person that can't be crushed by nothing nor nobody" ([1920] 1985:46, 64).

Was international migration then a means simply for women, individually and/or collectively, to fulfill these goals? Did Yezierska and other immigrant women, from Russia and from Italy, interpret their diverse migration experiences and outcomes as metaphors of their journeys toward greater self-determination and empowerment? International migration did indeed become a part of each immigrant woman's life struggle to make herself a person, to revise and/or transcend the social relationships constraining her to varying degrees, but the process was, at the same time, much broader than the development of an single individual.

Population movements at the turn of the century and in the present day represent the human side in the ongoing development of economic, political, and social relations between zones in the world-system. While it has certainly been possible to describe migration as the movement of units of low-waged labor power, or as the unequal exchange of commodities between distinct nation states in a world-economy, these approaches explain only one side of the migration coin—from the vantage point of the world-system. A more comprehensive and holistic approach to the study of immigration must include and account for the perspectives of the individual immigrants, at the point of origin, at the point of destination, and joined together in a global context. This is not a question of privileging a micro approach over a macro approach. It is a matter of their unity. The flexibility and malleability characteristic of human beings who dream, imagine, plan, create, and change because of, and often in spite of, the course of social relationships, global and otherwise, has always been the fuel of macro-social systems.

For women, global migration and becoming a person are two sides of the same coin. Becoming an immigrant and becoming a person involved each woman's participation in the uncertain web of global social relations, based on gender, class, and racial/ethnic/ nationality identities in flux. In this much broader sense, the study of women's transnational migration becomes a prism in which it is possible to simultaneously observe the transformation of individual lives *and* the transformation of social relationships in the world-system. Neither the meaning of migration for an individual woman nor the meaning of migration for the world-system can be understood without understanding both.

What are the broader ramifications and implications of a historical comparative study of Russian-Jewish and Italian immigrant women in turn-of-the-century New York? Various scholars of contemporary international migration have commented in recent years on the emergence of a new kind of migrating population and a new experience of migration (Glick Schiller et al. 1992). "Transnationalism," or the processes by which "transmigrants" build networks, activities, and patterns of life that encompass both their host and home societies in a context of global capitalism, and use these networks and multiple identities to protect and uplift themselves, may in fact, as this study has shown, not be new at all. What is new and promising are the increasing attempts by scholars of international migration to build bridges between previously polarized disciplines and paradigms, construct a common language and research agenda, and most importantly, put a multidimensional human being at the center of research. Recent theoretical insights have much to offer to historical research on past migrations; and comparative studies, such as this one, may suggest, I hope, more fruitful paths of understanding the various experiences of "the central or defining figure of the twentieth century," the migrant.

NOTES

INTRODUCTION:
STARTING FROM HOME

1. See Wittig [1971] 1985:89.

2. I am scarcely the only member of my generational cohort to explore the meanings of eastern European Jewish origins for contemporary Jewish-American women. Among the various reflections on this theme, see in particular: Kim Chernin's (1983) *In My Mother's House*; R. Ruth Linden's (1993) "My Grandmother's Samovar" in her book *Making Stories, Making Selves*; and many of the selections in Faye Moskowitz' (1994) edited collection, *Her Face in the Mirror*. In a poignant essay, "Mi Puente/My Bridge," anthropologist Ruth Behar (1994) describes how immigration affected her complex sense of identity (Polish/Turkish/Cuban/American-Jewish), by recalling her 1992 visit to her childhood home in Cuba.

3. A number of studies, review essays, and anthologies exploring immigrant women's lives were published in the 1970s and 1980s, but, as historian Donna Gabaccia has noted the lack of common ground, or a common theoretical and methodological language, has marginalized scholarship on immigrant women (1991:74). For authors who make similar or related points see Ward 1993; Tienda and Booth 1991; Pedraza 1991; Yans-McLaughlin 1990; Morawska 1990; Glick Schiller et al. 1992.

CHAPTER 1.
WOMEN AND INTERNATIONAL MIGRATION

1. Quoted in Sanderson 1988:i.

2. Mills 1959:3, 6.

3. Gordon 1986b:25.

4. For studies of racism and sexism that take a world-systems approach see Joan Smith et al. 1988. For a critique of world-system analysis with regard to gender inequality, see Ward 1993.

5. See, for example, Glenn 1994; Scott 1986; Acker 1992; Harding 1991. Paula England, ed. (1993) has assembled a collection of essays,

dialogues, and debates on the various sociological understandings of gender differentiation and gender inequality.

6. See in particular Collins 1990; King 1988; Glenn 1986, 1991, 1992; Andersen and Collins ed. 1992; Anthias and Yuval-Davis 1992.

7. See Geschwender 1978; Steinberg 1989; Nagel 1994; and Omi and Winant 1986 for critical reviews of the assimilation and cultural pluralist theoretical frameworks. See the collected essays in Takaki 1987 for examples of the various theoretical perspectives on race and ethnicity in the U.S.

8. For examples of recent efforts to understand the social and historical construction of whiteness, see Ware 1992; Frankenberg 1993; and Roediger 1994.

9. See for example the *Dictionary of Races or Peoples*, vol. 5, Reports of the Immigration Commission, 1911, and Grant 1916. I am indebted to Shirley Yee, Dept. of Women's Studies, University of Washington, Seattle, for pointing out the relevance of Grant's work to this argument.

10. I am grateful to Ruth Frankenberg, Department of American Studies, University of California, Davis for giving me a copy of Diane Paul's (1981) article, and for sharing her ideas on the social construction of whiteness with me.

11. Pessar 1986 was one of the first within a recent outpouring of sociological research on contemporary international migrations to critique the tendency of scholars to overlook women entirely in the migration process, or to neglect the role of gender.

12. For examples of research that explicitly problematized the impact of male out-migration on women remaining in the sending region see Brouwer and Priester 1983; Ahern, Bryan, Baca 1985; Baca and Bryan 1985; Deutsch 1987.

13. Reporting on the results of an 1890 census taken by the Baron de Hirsch Society, historian Moses Rischin writes ". . . of 111,690 of an estimated 135,000 Jews on the Lower East Side [the society] counted 60,313 children and 22,647 wage earners, with 28,730 unspecified, mostly women" (1977:81). From the overabundance of examples of this type of literature see also Barton 1975; Briggs 1978; Cinel 1982a, 1982b; Howe 1976; Kessner 1977; Pozzetta 1971; U.S.,WPA, 1938.

14. For a critical review of the modernization literature as it pertains explicitly to migration, see Pessar 1986 and Portes and Walton 1981:21–65.

15. For examples of the argument that migration resulted in the destruction of preindustrial cultural values and practices, see Handlin 1951; see also Ware 1935.

16. For some examples of stereotypes see Breckinridge 1921; and Warner and Srole 1943, v.3:108. For critical comments on the stereo-

typing, see Schwartz 1983:67–68; Seller 1981; Morokvasic 1983; and Deutsch 1987.

17. In the desire to recover evidence of women's agency and power in history, it may be useful to recall the cautionary words of feminist historian Linda Gordon: "History needs a subjective, imaginative, emulative process of communication. But . . . at the same time one can never and should never completely put oneself in the place of one's historical subjects. This is hindsight . . . [I]t is the attempt to ignore the time that has passed between oneself and one's subject, to ignore one's historical place. See Linda Gordon interview in *Radical History Review*, June 1981. See also The Personal Narratives Group 1989:22–23.

18. See Bodnar 1979, 1982, 1985; Cohen 1978; Gabaccia 1984a, 1984b, 1986; Hareven 1982; Smith 1985; Vecoli 1964.

19. Some of the analytical contradictions within the cultural continuity model are discussed by Kessler-Harris 1974 and L. Tilly 1974 in their review of Yans-McLaughlin's arguments.

20. For examples of this approach see Ginsburg and Lowenhaupt Tsing eds. 1990; and Glenn et al. ed. 1994.

21. See Weinberg 1988 for examples of the cost of household survival to immigrant mothers and daughters. For contemporary examples see Westwood and Bhachu eds. 1988. In a critical review of Bodnar's immigration history, *The Transplanted* (1985), Gabaccia draws attention to the author's tendency "to underplay if not to ignore hierarchy, conflict, and power struggles within families" (Gabaccia 1988b:244).

22. For examples of the diversity within the historical-structural and world-systems approaches to migration see Bach and Schraml 1982; Portes and Bach 1985; Bonacich and Cheng 1984; Buroway 1976; Castells 1975; Castles and Kosack 1972, 1973; History Task Force, Centro de Estudios Puertoriquenos 1979; Marks 1989; Petras 1987; Piore 1979; Portes 1978; Portes and Walton 1981; Sassen 1988; Sassen-Koob 1980b, 1981, 1985, 1988; Ward 1975; Wood 1982.

23. One noteworthy exception is Ewa Morawska's (1989) research on the mass labor migrations of Poles to western Europe and the United States. Her explicit purpose is however to integrate the push-pull and world-systems frameworks. See also Sassen-Koob 1980a; and Hoerder 1991.

24. For three exceptions among historical structural approaches who do incorporate "women's voices," see Glenn 1986; Di Leonardo 1984, and Lamphere 1987.

25. For valuable rethinking and reformulations of the household concept and its relation to women, gender relations, and international migration that does not entirely "throw the baby out with the bathwater," see Grasmuck and Pessar 1991; Kibria 1993; and Hondagneu-Sotelo 1994. Sociologist Kathryn Ward (1993) has critiqued world-

systems theory for excluding women and considerations of gender in a thought-provoking essay, which has important implications for understanding the relationship between women and international migration. For a response by world-systems theorists on the continued usefulness of the household concept for understanding long-term wage differentials between core, periphery, and semiperiphery, and the formation of differently remunerated labor forces in the world-economy, i.e., questions that comprised the initial purpose behind the deployment of the concept, see Smith, Wallerstein, Friedman Kasaba et al. 1992 and Dickinson 1995. These most recent works within world-systems theory also address questions of age, racial/ethnic, and gender stratification within and across the core-periphery divide.

26. See Arrighi, Hopkins, Wallerstein 1983; Wallerstein 1987; and Smith, Collins, Hopkins, and Muhammad 1988. One promising and exciting new development in migration studies is the effort to develop a "transnational perspective on migration." Scholars working within this emerging framework have developed a research agenda to (1) explore how transnational migration is shaped by and contributes to the global capitalist system; (2) rethink the analytical concepts used in migration studies; and (3) analyze how "transmigrants" construct their racial, ethnic, class, national, and gender identities as they move between countries of origin and countries of settlement (Glick Schiller et al. 1992).

CHAPTER 2.
"WHY DID WE HAVE TO LEAVE?"

1. See Fisher 1976:13–14.
2. See Chernin 1983:106.
3. Excellent reviews of the rapidly growing literature on immigrant/ethnic social and economic networks may be found in Morawska 1990, 1991; Portes and Rumbaut 1990; Tilly 1990; Light et al. 1994.
4. For critiques of cultural and gender essentialism, see especially Barrett 1987; Harding 1986; Di Leonardo 1984; and Steinberg 1989.
5. The Pale of Settlement, as of 1897, included the three provinces of Lithuania (Vilna, Grodno, Kovno), the three provinces of Bievlorussia/White Russia (Minsk, Vitebsk, Moheelev), the five provinces of Southwestern Russia (Volhynia, Poldolia, Kiev, Chernigov, Poltava), the four provinces of Southern/New Russia (Bessarabia, Kherson, Yekaterinoslav, Taurida), and the ten provinces of Russian Poland (Warsaw, Kalisz, Kielce, Lomza, Lublin, Petrikau, Plock, Radom, Suvalki, Siedlec). See Rubinow [1907] 1975:491; Dubnow 1918:39–40.
6. For Wallerstein, the roughly 100-year period of Russia's incorporation into the capitalist world-economy was marked by the emergence

of three important trends: the massive expansion of cash-crop agriculture destined for sale on the world market; the drastic reduction, if not elimination, of local manufacturing industry; and the beginning of migrant labor flows to work on both the cash-crop lands and diminished food-crop lands (1989:138).

7. Curiously, despite the pogroms, the internal migrations of Jews continued from the relatively untroubled but poorer northwest Pale to the comparatively higher-waged southwest sections. Most Jewish overseas migration prior to the 1903–1905 attacks originated in the northwest Pale. See Rubinow [1907] 1975:492, 530. This was as true for those who migrated to Britain as it was for those who entered the United States. See Feldman 1994.

8. Historian Suzanne Sinke (1992) has described a related phenomenon among young German women who migrated to the United States at the turn of the century. For them, participation in an "international marriage market" was a strategy they hoped would increase their marital choices and offer them more control over their own destinies.

CHAPTER 3.
"TAKE ME TO AMERICA"

1. See Mathias and Raspa 1985:272.

2. See Paolucci 1977:35.

3. Reportedly, between 1880 and the beginning of World War I, for every ten Italians who departed for the U.S., five returned to Italy (Cinel 1982b:43). Of these, it is unclear how many returnees remigrated to America later.

4. On Italian male labor migration to the United States, see the studies by Barton 1975; Briggs 1978; Caroli 1973; Cinel 1982a, 1982b; Foerster 1919; Kessner 1977; Piore 1979.

5. For examples of research on Italian immigrant women among the various disciplines, see Cohen 1977, 1978, 1982, 1992; Di Leonardo 1984; Ewen 1985; Furio 1979; Gabaccia 1984a, 1984b, 1986, 1988a, 1988b, 1991; Mathias and Raspa 1985; Maglione and Fiore 1989; Schwartz 1983; Smith 1985; Yans-McLaughlin 1977, 1990.

6. For a related phenomenon among German women migrating to the United States during the same period, see the account by historian Suzanne Sinke (1991).

7. Monica Boyd (1989) was among the first to note the near invisibility of women in social science research on family and personal networks in contemporary migrations and to urge the development of approaches that recognize how the sexual division of labor shapes the determinants and consequences of migration networks. Her insights

200 MEMORIES OF MIGRATION

have been followed up by many of the contributors to Gabaccia (1992), which also include students of women's migrations in the nineteenth century.

8. Ets 1970:xi.

9. Examples of this perspective include Covello 1972; Fenton 1975; and Foerster 1919.

10. See in particular Arrighi and Piselli 1987; Barton 1975; Bell 1979; Briggs 1978; Cinel 1982a, 1982b; and Gabaccia 1988a.

11. The expression, "women of the shadows," is from Ann Cornelisen's book of the same name (1976). However, my use of this term is different from Cornelisen's, who was concerned with making the lives of contemporary southern Italian women more visible. As used here, this characterization of Italian women is but the female counterpart of the racialized representation of southern Italian males. According to Fenton ([1957] 1975:25), "Despite his limited outlook and his fatalism, the typical south Italian peasant was a self-reliant and manly individual."

12. Gabaccia (1984a) explores Sicilian social ideals about kinship and other issues through a collection of proverbs collected by Giuseppe Pitre in the years preceding mass migration.

13. Italy may be divided up into areas of low and high emigration. High emigration areas included all the regions north of the Po River; the three provinces of Modena, Parma, and Piacenza; the province of Lucca; except for Apulia, all the regions of the south, such as Abruzzi, Campania, Basilicata, and Calabria; and coastal Sicily. Of course, each province differed from the other in terms of specific migration patterns, as did regions even within a single province. See Cinel 1982a:23–24, 45.

14. In their study of Calabria, one of the poorest regions in southern Italy, Arrighi and Piselli (1987) report that internal migration may have begun as early as 1450.

15. Covello (1972:191) exemplifies this approach. "There was little opportunity or need for individual initiative within the communal family group, or within the contadino community, because all activities and patterns of thought were based upon traditional folkways and customs. Thus there were social stabiity and order in the contadini community— stability and order which sprang from the static character of the social body, and were preserved by reason of the cultural and economic isolation of South Italy."

16. In some regions, returning emigrants, perhaps out of pride and the desire for increased social status, insisted on buying the same tract of land they had previously worked as sharecroppers or laborers, regardless of its price (Cinel 1982a:76–77).

17. This revealing statement was the response of the president of an agricultural society in Cosenza to Adolfo Rossi, Commissioner of Emigration in 1908. Cited in Cinel 1982a:41.

18. Brazilian companies, in providing passage for wives and children, had inadvertently effected the decline of remittances to Italy. Constantino Ianni, Brazilian-born son of Italian emigrants, maintained that economic considerations eventually drove the Italian government to prohibit subsidized migration to Brazil. This, then, had the effect of turning migration, particularly of single men, towards the U.S. (Caroli 1973:95). See also Baily 1990.

19. Summing up the results of 300 family budgets in northern Italy about 1880, one economist observed that "regardless of how hard they try, even though both women and children work, few families reach the end of the year in the black if they rely exclusively on the land. Most families are heavily in debt either to the local grocery store or to moneylenders. Tenants are often unable to pay the rent, and landowners have to provide them with food to prevent starvation. It is difficult to say whether there are domestic solutions to these problems" Cited in Cinel 1982a:98.

20. The Emigration Act of 1901 also assigned the responsibility of forwarding remittances from Italians living outside the country to the Banco di Napoli (Caroli 1973:57).

21. During the period of the "Brazilian Fever," a subtle competition developed between Austrian Poland, Russian Poland, and Italy over profit from the flow of labor to Brazil. Authorities in Austrian Poland increasingly recognized possibilities for profiting commercially from the circulation of labor, in terms of its effect on economic development in Galicia. But a successful development strategy hinged on the government's ability to manage and influence the terms of the population outflow, including the maintenance of ties with Polish immigrants abroad. The fever was contagious, though, and soon it appeared that everyone (except Austria-Hungary and Russia) was profiting from the labor flow. The two chief agencies promoting emigration from eastern Galicia in 1890–92 were those of Silvio Nodari and one Gergoleta, both of whom had offices in Udine, Italy. Having acquired a mailing list of villages in eastern Galicia, these two agents were able to recruit emigrating peasants for their ships directly. For a small fee they promised to send them "free" steamship tickets from Genoa to Rio de Janeiro (Murzdek 1977:105).

22. On the value of remittances see Cinel 1982a:75–76; Caroli 1973:58–59, 96.

23. Sicilians, male and female, comprised one of every four Italian emigrants to the United States. See Gabaccia 1986:95.

24. For a comparison of the daily work experiences of women of different classes and occupational groups in nineteenth-century Sicily, see Gabaccia (1984a:38–48).

25. Noether (1978:7) sees southern Italian and Sicilian women's involvement in the strikes and agitation among farm workers in the

1890s as further evidence of their increasing participation in the rural agricultural labor force. Gabaccia (1988a:62) also notes Sicilian women's widespread participation in jacqueries, or spontaneous protests, in the countryside in the 1890s, but adds that women and children were completely excluded from the workplace protests of wage earners. This reflected the monopoly poor Sicilian men had acquired over wage earning by the 1890s.

26. See Noether (1978:6) for regional distributions of the percentage of Italian women in the agricultural labor force. See also Gabaccia 1987:173.

27. For further discussion of regional variations in Italian women's domestic service employment, see Cohen 1992:20–21 and Tilly 1974: 453–54.

28. Even when migrating Italian women came to the United States alone, they tended to join parents, kin, or fiancés. For more discussion on this common practice among Italian immigrant women in New York, see Cohen 1992:39–42; in Chicago, see Meyerowitz 1988:11, 12, 17.

29. Rosa Cavalleri's life story was recorded by a social settlement worker, Marie Hall Ets, who befriended her in the Chicago Commons in the late 1920s. See *Rosa: The life of an Italian Immigrant* by Marie Hall Ets 1970.

30. It seems likely that Mamma Lena was simply participating in the common practice of restricting girls' behavior as they reached adolescence, but in this case, overreacting due to the circumstances of Rosa's (Inez') birth. Nonetheless, this was Rosa's first real memory of being sent away from home to work, and it undoubtedly influenced her later experiences of long-distance migration.

CHAPTER 4.
"SO, WE HAVE CROSSED HALF THE WORLD FOR THIS?"

1. See Alfred Kazin's memoirs, 1951:66–67.
2. See Covello 1972:214–15.
3. See Orsi 1985:146 for this valuable metaphor.
4. Between the Civil War and the turn of the century, the U.S. rose from fourth place in industrial production, behind England, France, and Germany, to an unrivaled first place. Not only did the number of manufacturing establishments more than double, but production increased four-fold. By 1900, the United States produced one-third of the world's total industrial output, nearly equaling in value that of England, France, and Germany combined (Calavita 1984:39).
5. See also Montgomery 1977:96–110; Rosenblum 1973:59–79.
6. For Higham, in the early twentieth century, "when sentiments

analogous to those already discharged against Negroes, Indians, and Orientals spilled over into anti-European channels, a force of tremendous intensity entered the stream of American nativism" (1955: 132).

7. In the introduction to their forty-two volumes of findings, the Immigration Commission acknowledged that "the chief basis of the Commission's work was the changed character of the immigration movement to the United States during the past twenty years" (USIC 1911, 1:14).

8. Characterizing Italian emigration at the turn of the twentieth century, journalist Erik Amfitheatrof wrote: "The land literally hemorrhaged peasants." Quoted in F. Cordasco and E. Bucchioni 1974:3.

9. Based on the New York State Manuscript Census, Miriam Cohen estimated that in 1905 the average Italian woman of foreign birth could expect to have at least 6.2 children, making her one of the most fertile groups of women in the country at the time (Cohen 1978:98–101). See also Williams 1938:105. In 1900, the New York Tenement Commission noted that Russian-Jewish and Italian families ranged in size from 4.7 to 5.3 members (Kessner 1977:133).

10. For discussion on feminism and eugenics at the turn of the century, see Gordon 1976:ch. 6–7. See also Davin 1978 and Klaus 1993.

11. As early as 1881, Charlotte Adams acknowledged that the belief "that the Italians are an idle and thriftless people is a superstition which time will remove from the American mind. A little kindly guidance and teaching can mold them into almost any form" (Adams [1881] 1974: 130).

12. For social backgrounds of female social reformers, especially social settlement workers, see the discussions in Kessler-Harris 1982:112–19; Matthaei 1982:173–86; Ewen 1985: 76–91. Mary Kingsbury Simkhovitch's *Neighborhood: My Story of Greenwich House* (1938) provides a glimpse into the activities and consciousness of one woman who devoted her life to the settlement house movement.

13. See especially Judith Rollins, *Between Women: Domestics and Their Employers* (1985:178–203); and Evelyn Nakano Glenn, *Issei, Nisei, War Bride: Three Generations of Japanese American Women in Domestic Service* (1986:153–64).

14. In 1915, the Union Settlement, in predominantly Italian and Russian-Jewish south Harlem, explained what the past twenty years of its existence had meant to "one of our little neighbors, a motherless Italian girl." Rescued by settlement workers from a "friendly saloon-keeper" in whose care her father had left her when he went to work, the grateful girl dutifully and appropriately replied, "You know my father's my father, but the Union Settlement is my mother" (Union Settlement, "Twenty Years in South Harlem, 1895–1915," New York City, December, 1915, pp. 13–14).

15. For a clear statement of the Progressive family ideal see Payne 1988:ch. 4; and May 1984:351–71.

16. The differences among female social reformers of the early twentieth century regarding what was fit work for women and what was not, and the contradictions between their ideals and their own lives is too vast a subject in itself to adequately discuss here. It is, however, important not to overlook the heterogeneity among female Americanizers and not to collapse the distinctions between those who promoted the entry of single women into temporary careers before motherhood, those who demanded paid jobs for all women, those who claimed that homemaking was not a real job, and those who argued that housekeeping and child rearing was "a business as big as the affairs of men" and women's "true vocation" (Rodgers 1978:ch. 7).

17. Researchers have shown increasing interest in the economic significance of the ethnic networks that immigrants mobilize and make use of in their resettlement and adaptation. Recent discussion has focused on the distinction between an "ethnic economy" perspective (based on the "middleman minority" concept) and an "ethnic economic enclave" perspective (based on the labor market segmentation model). See Light et al. 1994 for discussion of this debate. For studies on the economic value of specific ethnic community networks, see also Light 1972; Bonacich and Modell 1980; Portes and Bach 1985; Light and Bonacich 1988; Gold 1992.

18. The importance of coethnic community resources for new immigrant arrivals has a long tradition of study in the history and sociology of immigration (Morawska 1990). There has, however, been considerably less recognition or research on immigrant women's participation in these ethnic networks. Very few studies have addressed the role of married women's nonwaged labor in ethnic associations or in immigrant family businesses, where it has often meant the difference between economic success or failure. Still fewer studies have considered the effect that participation in the ethnic economy or in an ethnic economic enclave has had on the subordination of immigrant women, where it may empower them as independent entrepreneurs or, conversely, subordinate them to male-owned family businesses and coethnic institutions. For examples of this small but growing literature on immigrant women's role in this sector, see Westwood and Bhachu 1988; Boyd 1989; Fernandez-Kelly and Garcia 1990; Dallalfar 1994.

19. New York City, by 1915, was said to have somewhere between 2,000 and 3,000 narrowly localized Italian societies (Pozzetta 1971:19).

20. Foerster argues that male Italian workers without families could survive hard times, as in 1916, by living off savings, but once they formed families, they were forced to appeal to charity (Foerster 1919: 406–7).

21. Sicilian immigrant women, according to Gabaccia, were especially committed to rebuilding close kin ties in New York City. In a densely settled Sicilian district on Elizabeth Street in 1905, close relatives (*casa* kin) formed stem- and joint-family households in nearly one of every five apartments. That women were central to forming these extended household networks is evidenced by the fact that two-thirds of the stem-family households originated with a daughter who married and brought her husband into her parent's home to begin raising children (Gabaccia 1984b:46).

22. On the concept of "ethnic economic enclave," see Portes 1981; Portes and Bach 1985:38–48; Gold 1992.

23. In an obvious case of underreporting, the 1911 Immigration Commission found only 28 of 330 female heads of households (8.5%) in business for profit in New York City (USIC 1911, I, 2:218).

CHAPTER 5.
"THE RIGHT TO A PERSONALITY"

1. Kula et al. 1986:182–83
2. NYSFIC 1915,V:2654–55
3. It is not possible to distinguish either the marital status or the precise age of most migrating women due to the way the data was collected. Nonetheless, between 1886 and 1898, 44 percent of Russian-Jewish immigrants were female and over the age of sixteen (Kuznets 1975:100). From 1899–1924, nearly 46 percent of all Jewish immigrants to the U.S. were female (Hersch 1969:483). Among Italian arrivals in the U.S. between 1881 and 1920, women averaged only 25 percent, gradually increasing their share to 40 percent by the 1930s (Furio 1979:10; Martellone 1984:405).
4. See Lamphere 1987:29–31 for a valuable discussion on the strengths and shortcomings of a "strategy approach" to women's labor force participation.
5. The literature exploring middle-class women's participation in public policy making and social welfare provision under the rubric of "maternalism" has enjoyed a rapid expansion in recent years. Excellent examples of this scholarship, including contrasting definitions and descriptions of "maternalism" are found in Boris 1994; Koven and Michel 1993.
6. My thinking about female working-class sexuality and the charges of promiscuity and prostitution directed against young unmarried immigrant women at the turn of the century has benefitted enormously from analyses concerning different eras and regions. Christine Stansell's (1986) chapter "Women on the Town: Sexual Exchange and

Prostitution," concerning women in New York City between 1850 and 1860, and Aihwa Ong's (1987) discussion of the use of sexual imagery in constructing work discipline among Malaysian women employed in world factories have especially shaped my questions and views. Neither author, however, has explored how work discipline might be related to the process of racialization or the construction of ethnicity.

7. By "white slavery," Progressives generally meant "the selling of [non-Black] women's bodies for the purposes of prostitution." Reflecting their views on the causes of prostitution, many reformers maintained that white slavery was based on the use of coercion or force to bring a woman into prostitution and to prevent her from leaving it. Correspondingly, a white slaver was defined as "any man or woman who traffics in the sexual life of any woman or girl for financial reward or gain" (Rosen 1982:113). The term *white slavery* curiously originated in early industrializing Britain as a synonym for the "wage slavery" of young women (Bristow 1982:36). As with the racial nativist movement to restrict immigration, the campaign to control prostitution began with outlawing "the importation of Chinese women for immoral purposes" in California in 1870. This legislation presaged the Chinese Exclusion Act of 1882. The consequences for Chinese immigrant women, however, did not include the elimination of prostitution but, rather, the driving of the traffic underground and an increase in the prices of Chinese prostitutes. Moreover, the stigma of "sexual slavery" continued to haunt and disempower all Chinese immigrant women in the United States. See Cheng 1984; and Amott and Matthaei 1991:201–3.

8. The targeting of Jews among antiprostitution reformers occurred also in Britain in the 1830s. Dr. Michael Ryan, a London reformer, wrote in his *Philosophy of Marriage* in 1839 that "especially at the eastern end of town . . . the infernal traffic in question is still carried on to a great extent, principally by Jews. These white-slave dealers trepan young girls into their dens of iniquity, sell them to vile debaucheries . . . " (Quoted in Bristow 1982:35). Jewish community leaders in Europe and the United States worried about the striking parallels between the increasing numbers of blood libel and "white slavery" accusations at the turn of the century. Both charges involved violence to a defenseless young person. Historian Edward Bristow has argued persuasively that "white slavery was the sexualization of blood libel" and that the accusation of the latter was sufficient to provoke the Kishinev pogrom of 1903 (Bristow 1982:46). See also chapter 3 in Linda Gordon Kuzmack's (1990) comparison of the antiwhite slavery campaign in England and the United States, in terms of how Jewish feminists on both sides of the Atlantic responded to the antisemitic singling out of Jewish prostitutes and procurers.

9. "Treating" usually involved an exchange of sexual favors for gifts, treats, and a good time, but never money. Therefore, to most young

women of the time, treating was distinguishable from prostitution and, in certain contexts, still viewed as respectable behavior for a young unmarried working-class woman. See Peiss 1983:81–82.

10. What seemed to especially concern the antivice and antiprostitution group of Jewish communal leaders known as the Committee of Fifteen in New York (1902) was the increased flexibility in women's behavior. The Committee condemned less-restrictive relations between men and women for making it possible for young women "to experiment with immorality without losing such social standing as they may have . . ." Quoted in Rosen 1982:43.

11. Not all social reformers agreed that there was a connection between poverty or women's low-waged employment opportunities and prostitution. For a debate of the issues among contemporaries, concerning especially the notion of a minimum wage for women, see "Memorandum on the Relationship Between Low Wages and the Vice Problem," pp. 389–417, in New York State, Factory Investigating Commission, *Fourth Report*, vol. I (1915).

12. The industrial school supported by Richman was representative of the traditional gendered curriculum, in terms of maintaining the separation between manual training for boys and domestic science for girls. Richman herself was equally representative of the condescending while benevolent attitude of Americanized middle-class German-Jews toward recent Russian-Jewish arrivals. Richman envisaged her mission as one of instilling proper moral values into the children of immigrants and their "backward" parents (Berrol 1980:49, 42). Her work while director of the Educational Alliance and superintendent (from 1903) of the Lower East Side schools aroused the wrath of many "new immigrant" parents and local community leaders (Howe 1976:230–31). In the spring of 1908, the New York City Board of Education was presented with a number of petitions from the community demanding, although without success, that Richman be transferred to another district. In the eyes of petitioners, Richman, a "self-constituted censor of our morality and . . . patron saint of the slum seekers" had "degraded and lowered parents in the eyes of their children, [and had taken] advantage of every opportunity to suggest to the children that their parents were criminals . . ." Quoted in Rischin 1977:239; Berrol 1980:35.

13. At the same time, the New York State Factory Investigating Commission remarked that "in the case of home making schools, owing to the fact that women are not paid a wage in the home, no statistics as to the economic value of the training are obtainable" (N.Y. St. Fac. Inv. Com. IV, 1915:1432).

14. Russian-Jewish immigrant writer Anzia Yezierska was a resident at the Clara de Hirsch Home for Girls between 1900 and 1902. Despite feeling suffocated for freedom given the Home's inflexible regi-

men, she nonetheless accepted a scholarship from the school to attend Columbia University (Hendriksen 1988:17).

15. For an excellent description of an analogous relationship between female Anglo missionaries and Hispanic women in New Mexico and Colorado from 1880 through 1940, see Deutsch 1987:735–37.

16. In her address on directing immigrant girls into wage employment at the 1893 Jewish Women's Congress in Chicago, Julia Richman advised the establishment of "a training school for servants, from which we could supply competent cooks, laundresses, nursemaids, waitresses." In her characteristically benevolent but condescending posture toward working-class Russian-Jewish immigrants, Richman revealed part of the domestic service training program's "hidden curriculum." "The girls are gradually acquiring habits of greater refinement and culture. Table manners and personal habits will improve, and with their improvement a long stride will have been taken away from the old landmarks of ignorance and vulgarity." Quoted in Sinkoff 1988:583.

17. In her meticulous study of female Jewish garment workers, Susan Glenn (1990) argues that labor protest was the central means by which immigrant daughters experimented, rebelled, and at least temporarily expanded the presence of women in America beyond the household. For Glenn, factory work rather than domesticity defined young women's consciousness. Drawing on craft traditions and an identification with work rooted in eastern European Jewish culture, young women combined these with the most positive features of womanhood in American culture to forge a Jewish New Womanhood. This process, according to Glenn, is critical to understanding the high degree of Jewish women's labor activism, compared to other groups of wage-earning immigrant women, especially young Italian immigrant women. Miriam Cohen (1992) explains persuasively in a study that focuses on two generations of Italian women in New York City that while "paid labor itself was not new for southern Italian women living in New York . . . the work experience provided little freedom on the job . . . or much leisure time after hours. The nature of the work, the location of the job, its hours and wages, plus familial responsibilities after work meant that women had little opportunity to develop a social life independent of the family or to participate in community and political organizations" (Cohen 1992: 196–97).

18. For a detailed comparison of the changing composition of contributors to households (by age, gender, and ethnicity) and the changing types of income they provided (waged, nonwaged, etc.) in New York City from 1870–1975 see Kathie Friedman Kasaba, "New York City: The Underside of the World's Capital" in J. Smith, I. Wallerstein, et al., *Creating and Transforming Households: The Constraints of the World-Economy* (Cambridge, 1992).

CONCLUSION

1. Salman Rushdie, *Imaginary Homelands* (New York: Granta Books/Viking, 1991).

BIBLIOGRAPHY

Abbott, Edith. 1919. *Women in Industry*. New York: D. Appleton.

Acker, Joan. 1992. "From Sex Roles to Gendered Institutions." *Contemporary Sociology* 21:565–69.

Adams, Charlotte. 1881. "Italian Life in New York." In F. Cordasco and E. Bucchioni, eds., *The Italians: Social Backgrounds of an American Group*. Clifton, N.J.: August M. Kelley, 1974.

Addams, Jane. 1904. "Hull House and Its Neighbors." In L. Tomasi, ed., *The Italian in America*. New York: Center for Migration Studies, 1972.

Ahern, Susan, Dexter Bryan, and Reynaldo Baca, "Migration and La Mujer Fuerte." *Migration Today* XIII, 1, 1985:15–20.

Amott, Teresa, and Julie Matthaei. 1991. *Race, Gender, and Work: A Multicultural Economic History of Women in the United States*. Boston: South End Press.

Andersen, Margaret L., and Patricia Hill Collins, eds. 1992. *Race, Class, and Gender*. Belmont, Calif.: Wadsworth.

Anthias, Floya, and Nira Yuval-Davis. 1992. *Racialized Boundaries: Race, Nation, Gender, Colour and Class and the Anti-Racist Struggle*. London and New York: Routledge.

Anthony, Katharine. 1914. *Mothers Who Must Earn*. New York: Survey Associates, Inc., Russell Sage Foundation.

Antin, Mary. [1899] 1970. *From Plotzk to Boston*. New Jersey: Literature House.

———. [1911] 1969. *The Promised Land*. Boston: Houghton Mifflin.

Aronovici, C. 1908. "Italian Immigration." *University Settlement Studies* 2, 3:26–31.

Aronson, I. M. 1977. "The Prospects for the Emancipation of Russian Jewry during the 1880s." *Slavonic and East European Review* LV, 3 (July):348–63.

Arrighi, Giovanni, Terence K. Hopkins, and Immanuel Wallerstein. 1983. "Re-thinking the Concepts of Class and Status-Group in a World-System Perspective." *Review* 6, 3 (Winter):283–304.

———, and Fortunata Piscelli. 1987. "Capitalist Development in Hostile Environments: Feuds, Class Struggles, and Migrations in a Peripheral Region of Southern Italy." *Review* X, 4 (Spring).

Baca, Reynaldo, and Dexter Bryan. 1985. "Mexican Women, Migration, and Sex-Roles." *Migration Today* XIII, 3:14–18.

Bach, Robert, and Lisa Schraml. 1982. "Migration, Crisis, and Theoretical Conflict." *International Migration Review* XVI, 2 (Summer):320–41.

Baily, Samuel L. 1990. "Cross-Cultural Comparison and the Writing of Migration History: Some Thoughts on How to Study Italians in the New World." In *Immigration Reconsidered*, ed. V. Yans-McLaughlin, pp. 241–53. New York: Oxford University Press.

Banfield, Edward. 1958. *The Moral Basis of a Backward Society*. Glencoe, Ill.: Free Press.

Barolini, Helen, ed. 1985. *The Dream Book: An Anthology of Writings by Italian American Women*. New York: Schocken Books.

Barrett, Kate Waller. [1915] 1920. "The Immigrant Woman." In P. Davis, ed., *Immigration and Americanization*. Boston: Ginn.

Barrett, Michele. 1987. "The Concept of 'Difference'." *Feminist Review* 26 (July):29–41.

Barton, J. 1975. *Peasants and Strangers: Italians, Rumanians and Slovaks in an American City, 1890–1950*. Cambridge, Mass.: Harvard University Press.

Baum, Charlotte, Paula Hyman, and Sonya Michel. 1976. *The Jewish Woman in America*. New York: Plume Books/New American Library.

Beard, Mary Ritter. [1915] 1972. *Woman's Work in Municipalities*. New York: Arno Press.

Behar, Ruth. 1994. "Mi Puente/My Bridge." *Bridges* 4, 1 (Winter/Spring): 63–70.

Bell, Rudolph M. 1979. *Fate and Honor, Family and Village: Demographic and Cultural Change in Rural Italy since 1800*. Chicago and London: University of Chicago Press.

Berend, Ivan, and Gyorgy Ranki. 1982. *The European Periphery and Industrialization 1780–1914*. Cambridge: Cambridge University Press.

Bergland, Betty. 1988. "Immigrant History and the Gendered Subject: A Review Essay." *Ethnic Forum* 8, 2, 24–39.

Bernheimer, Charles D. 1908. "Lower East Side Dwellers." *University Settlement Studies* 4, 1, *Twenty-First Annual Report* (March):26–32. Russell Sage Foundation Collection. Cohen Library. The City College of the City University of New York.

Berrol, Selma. 1980. "When Uptown Met Downtown: Julia Richman's Work in the Jewish Community of New York, 1880–1912." *American Jewish History* LXX, 1 (Sept.):35–51.

Bhachu, Parminder. 1993. "Identities Constructed and Reconstructed: Representations of Asian Women in Britain." In G. Buijs, ed., *Migrant Women*. Providence, R.I., and Oxford, U.K.: Berg.

Bisno, Abraham. 1967. *Abraham Bisno, Union Pioneer*. Madison: University of Wisconsin Press.

Bodnar, John. 1979. "Immigration and Modernization: The Case of Slavic Peasants in Industrial America." In M. Cantor, ed., *American Working Class Culture*. Westport, Conn.: Greenwood Press.

————. 1982. *Worker's World: Kinship, Community, and Protest in an Industrial Society, 1900–1940*. Baltimore and London: Johns Hopkins University Press.

————. 1985. *The Transplanted: A History of Immigrants in Urban America*. Bloomington: Indiana University Press.

Bonacich, Edna. 1973. "A Theory of Middleman Minorities." *American Sociological Review* 38:583–94.

Bonacich, Edna, and John Modell. 1980. *The Economic Basis of Ethnic Solidarity*. Berkeley: University of California Press.

————, and Lucie Cheng. 1984. "Introduction: A Theoretical Orientation to International Labor Migration." In Cheng and Bonacich, eds., *Labor Immigration Under Capitalism: Asian Workers in the U.S. Before WWII*. Berkeley: University of California Press.

Boris, Eileen. 1993. "The Power of Motherhood: Black and White Activist Women Redefine the 'Political'." In *Mothers of a New World*, ed. S. Koven and S. Michel, pp. 213–45. New York and London: Routledge.

————. 1994. *Home to Work: Motherhood and the Politics of Industrial Homework in the United States*. New York: Cambridge University Press.

Boyd, Monica. 1989. "Family and Personal Networks in International Migration: Recent Developments and New Agendas." *International Migration Review* XXIII, 3 (Fall):638–70.

Boxer, Marilyn J., and Jean H. Quataert, eds. 1987. *Connecting Spheres: Women in the Western World, 1500 to the Present*. New York: Oxford University Press.

Breckenridge, Sophinisba. 1921. *New Homes for Old*. New York: Harper Brothers.

Brettell, Caroline B., and Rita James Simon. 1986. "Immigrant Women: An Introduction." In R. Simon and C. Brettell, eds., *International Migration: The Female Experience*. New Jersey: Rowman and Allanheld.

Briggs, John W. 1978. *An Italian Passage: Immigrants to Three American Cities, 1890–1930*. New Haven and London: Yale University Press.

Bristow, Edward J. 1982. *Prostitution and Prejudice: The Jewish Fight Against White Slavery, 1870–1939*. Oxford: Clarendon Press.

Brouwer, Lenie, and Marijke Priester. 1983. "Living in Between: Turkish Women in Their Homeland and in the Netherlands." In A. Phizacklea, Rouledge and Kegan Paul, eds., *One Way Ticket*. London: Routledge and Kegan Paul.

Bryner, Edna. 1916. *The Garment Trades*. Cleveland, Ohio: Survey Committee of the Cleveland Foundation.

Buijs, Gina, ed. 1993. *Migrant Women: Crossing Boundaries and Changing Identities*. Providence, R.I., and Oxford, U.K.: Berg.

Burawoy, Michael. 1976. "The Function and Reproduction of Migrant Labor: Comparative Material from Southern Africa and the United States." *American Journal of Sociology* 81 (March):1050–87.

Cafagna, Luciano. 1973. "The Industrial Revolution in Italy, 1830–1914." In Carlo Cipolla, ed., *The Fontana Economic History of Europe, The Emergence of Industrial Societies*, Pt. 1. London: Fontana/Collins.

Calavita, Kitty. 1984. *U.S. Immigration Law and the Control of Labor: 1820–1924*. London, England, and Orlando, Fla.: Academic Press.

Caroli, Betty Boyd. 1973. *Italian Repatriation from the United States, 1900–1914*. New York: Center for Migration Studies.

Castells, Manuel. 1975. "Immigrant Workers and Class Struggles in Advanced Capitalism: The Western European Experience." *Politics and Society* 5:33–66.

Castles, Stephen, and Godula Kosack. 1972. "The Function of Labor Immigration in Western European Capitalism." *New Left Review* 73 (May/June):3–21.

———, and G. Kosack. 1973. *Immigrant Workers and Class Structure in Western Europe*. New York: Oxford University Press.

Centro de Estudios Puertorriquenos, History Task Force. 1979. *Labor Migration Under Capitalism: The Puerto Rican Experience*. New York: Monthly Review Press.

Chapin, Robert Coit. 1909. *The Standard of Living Among Workingmen's Families in New York City*. New York: Charities Publication Committee, Russell Sage.

Cheng, Lucy. 1984. "Free, Indentured, Enslaved: Chinese Prostitutes in Nineteenth-Century America." In L. Cheng and E. Bonacich, eds., *Labor Immigration Under Capitalism*. Berkeley:University of California Press.

Chernin, Kim. 1983. *In My Mother's House*. New York: Harper and Row.

Child Labor Committee of New York. 1913/14. "A Ten Year's War Against Child Labor in New York State, 1902–1912." New York City: Russell Sage Foundation Collection. Cohen Library. The City College of the City University of New York.

———. n.d. "Child Labor—the Street" by Ernest Poole; and "Child Labor—Factories and Stores" (no author). New York: Russell Sage

Foundation Collection. Cohen Library. The City College of the City University of New York.

Cinel, Dino. 1982a. *From Italy to San Francisco:The Immigrant Experience*. Stanford, Calif.: Stanford University Press.

———. 1982b. "The Seasonal Emigrations of Italians in the Nineteenth Century: From Internal to International Destinations." *Journal of Ethnic Studies* X, 1 (Spring):43–68.

Claghorn, Kate Holladay. 1901. "The Foreign Immigrant in New York City." *Report of the Industrial Commission on Immigration*, vol. XV, ch. IX:449–92. Washington D.C.: Government Printing Office.

———. [1904] 1972. "Immigration and Dependence." In Lydio Tomasi, ed., *The Italian in America: The Progressive View, 1891–1914*. New York: Center for Migration Studies.

Clark, Sue Ainslie, and Edith Wyatt. 1911. *Making Both Ends Meet: The Income and Outlay of New York Working Girls*. New York: Macmillan.

Cohen, Miriam. 1977. "Italian-American Women in New York City, 1900–1950: Work and School." In Milton Cantor and Bruce Laurie, eds., *Class, Sex, and the Woman Worker*. Westport, Conn.: Greenwood.

———. 1978. "From Workshop to Office: Italian Women and Family Strategies in New York City, 1900–1950." Ph.D. dissertation, University of Michigan.

———. 1982. "Changing Education Strategies Among Immigrant Generations: New York Italians in Comparative Perspective." *Journal of Social History* 15 (March):443–66.

———. 1992. *Workshop to Office: Two Generations of Italian Women in New York City, 1900–1950*. Ithaca, N.Y.: Cornell University Press.

Collins, Patricia Hill. 1990. *Black Feminist Thought: Knowledge, Consciousness, and the Politics of Empowerment*. Boston: Unwin Hyman.

——— 1991. "Learning from the Outsider Within: The Sociological Significance of Black Feminist Thought." In *Beyond Methodology*, ed. M. M. Fonow and J. A. Cook. Bloomington: Indiana University Press.

Conk, Margo. 1985. "Immigration Reform and Immigration History." In Lionel Maldonado and Joan Moore, eds., *Urban Ethnicity in the U.S.* Beverly Hills, Calif.: Sage.

Consumer's League of New York City. 1915. "The Work of the Consumer's League of the City of New York," *Annual Report*. New York City: Russell Sage Foundation Collection. Cohen Library. The City College of the City University of New York.

———. 1919. "Is This Living?" New York City: Russell Sage Foundation Collection. Cohen Library. The City College of the City University of New York.

Cordasco, Francesco, and Eugene Bucchioni. 1974. Introduction. In F. Cordasco and E. Bucchioni, eds., *The Italians: Social Backgrounds of an American Group*. Clifton, N.J.: Augustus M. Kelley.

Cornelisen, Ann. 1976. *Women of the Shadows: The Wives and Mothers of Southern Italy*. New York: Dell.

Covello, Leonard. 1958. *The Heart Is the Teacher*. New York: McGraw-Hill.

————. 1972. *The Social Background of the Italo-American School Child*. Totawa, N.J.: Rowman and Littlefield.

Cowan, Neil M., and Ruth Schwartz Cowan. 1989. *Our Parents' Lives: The Americanization of East European Jews*. New York: Basic Books.

Dallalfar, Arlene. 1994. "Iranian Women as Immigrant Entrepreneurs." *Gender and Society* 8, 4 (December):541–61.

Davin, Anna. 1978. "Imperialism and Motherhood." *History Workshop* 5:9–65.

Davis, Philip, ed. 1920. *Immigration and Americanization*. Boston: Ginn & Co.

Deutsch, Sarah. 1987. "Women and Intercultural Relations: The Case of Hispanic New Mexico and Colorado." *Signs* 12, 4:719–39.

Dickinson, Torry. 1984. "Gender Division Within the U.S. Working Class: Households in the Philadelphia Area, 1870–1945." In J. Smith, I. Wallerstein, and H. Evers, eds., *Households and the World-Economy*. Beverly Hills, Calif.: Sage.

Dickinson, Torry D. 1995. *CommonWealth: Self-Sufficiency and Work in American Communities, 1830 to 1993*. Lanham, Md.: University Press of America, Inc.

Di Leonardo, Micaela. 1984. *The Varieties of Ethnic Experience: Kinship, Class, and Gender Among California Italian-Americans*. Ithaca, N.Y.: Cornell University Press.

Diner, Hasia. 1983. *Erin's Daughters in America: Irish Immigrant Women in the Nineteenth Century*. Baltimore and London: Johns Hopkins University Press.

Drachsler, Julius. [1920] 1970. *Democracy and Assimilation*. Westport, Conn.: Negro Universities Press.

Dubnow, S. M. 1918. *History of the Jews in Russia and Poland*, vol. II. Philadelphia: Jewish Publication Society of America.

Dunbar, Olivia Howard. [1913] 1917. "Teaching the Immigrant Woman." In Winthrop Talbot, ed., *Americanization*. New York: H. W. Wilson.

Dye, Nancy Schrom. 1980. *As Equals and As Sisters: Feminism, The Labor Movement, and the Women's Trade Union League of New York*. Columbia: University of Missouri Press.

Eaton, Isabel. 1895. "Receipts and Expenditures of Certain Wage Earners in the Garment Trades," *Quarterly Publications of the American Statistical Association* (June) 1895.

Eisenstein, Sarah. 1983. *Give Us Bread But Give Us Roses.* London and Boston: Routledge and Kegan Paul.

England, Paula, ed. 1993. *Theory on Gender/Feminism on Theory.* New York: Aldine De Gruyter.

Ernst, Robert. 1949. *Immigrant Life in New York City, 1825–1863.* New York: Columbia University, King's Crown Press.

Ets, Marie Hall. 1970. *Rosa: The Life of an Italian Immigrant.* Minneapolis: University of Minnesota Press.

Ewen, Elizabeth. 1985. *Immigrant Women in the Land of Dollars: Life and Culture on the Lower East Side, 1890–1925.* New York: Monthly Review Press.

Feldman, David. 1994. *Englishmen and Jews: Social Relations and Political Culture, 1840–1914.* New Haven: Yale University Press.

Fenton, Edwin. 1975. *Immigrants and Unions, A Case Study: Italians and American Labor, 1870–1920.* New York: Arno Press.

Fernandez-Kelly, Maria Patricia, and Anna M. Garcia. 1990. "Power Surrendered, Power Restored: The Politics of Work and Family Among Hispanic Garment Workers in California and Florida." In *Women, Politics, and Change,* ed. L. Tilly and P. Gurin, pp. 130–49. New York: Russell Sage.

Fisher, Minnie. 1976. *Born One Year Before the 20th Century.* New York: Community Documentation Workshop.

Foerster, Robert F. 1919. *The Italian Emigration of Our Times.* Cambridge: Harvard University Press.

Foner, Nancy. 1985. "Sex Roles and Sensibilities: Jamaican Women in New York and London." In *International Migration: The Female Experience,* ed. Rita J. Simon and Caroline B. Brettell. Totowa, N.J.: Rowman and Allanheld.

Frank, Dana. 1985. "Housewives, Socialists, and the Politics of Food: The 1917 New York Cost-of-Living Protests." *Feminist Studies* II, 2 (Summer):255–85.

Frankel, Lee K. 1905. "Philanthropy: New York." In C. Bernheimer, ed., *The Russian Jew in the U.S.* Philadelphia: John C. Winston.

Frankenberg, Ruth. 1993. *White Women, Race Matters: The Social Construction of Whiteness.* Minneapolis: University of Minnesota Press.

Fridkis, Ari Lloyd. 1981. "Desertion in the American Jewish Immigrant Family: The Work of the National Desertion Bureau in Cooperation with the Industrial Removal Office." *American Jewish History* LXXI, 2 (December):285–99.

Friedman, Kathie. 1984. "Households as Income-Pooling Units." In J. Smith, I. Wallerstein, and H. Evers, eds., *Households and the World-Economy.* Beverly Hills, Calif.: Sage.

Friedman Kasaba, Kathie. 1988. "'A Tailor is Nothing without a Wife, and Very Often a Child': Gender and Labor-Force Formation in the

New York Garment Industry, 1880–1920." In J. Smith, J. Collins, T. K. Hopkins, and A. Muhammed, eds., *Racism and Sexism in the World-System*. New York: Greenwood.

———. 1992. "New York City: The Underside of the World's Capital." In J. Smith, I. Wallerstein, K. Friedman Kasaba, et al., *Creating and Transforming Households: The Constraints of the World-Economy*. Cambridge, U.K.: Cambridge University Press.

Friedman, Reena Sigman. 1982. "Send Me My Husband Who Is in New York City: Husband Desertion in the American Jewish Immigrant Community, 1900–1926," *Jewish Social Studies* 44, 1 (Winter):1–17.

Furio, Columba M. 1979. "Immigrant Women and Industry: A Case Study, the Italian Immigrant Women and the Garment Industry, 1880–1950." Ph.D. dissertation, New York University.

Gabaccia, Donna R. 1984a. *From Sicily to Elizabeth Street: Housing and Social Change among Italian Immigrants, 1880–1930*. Albany: State University of New York Press.

———. 1984b. "Kinship, Culture, and Migration: A Sicilian Example." *Journal of American Ethnic History* 3, 2 (Spring):39–53.

———. 1986. "Neither Padrone Slaves nor Primitive Rebels: Sicilians on Two Continents." In D. Hoerder, ed., *Struggle a Hard Battle: Essays on Working-Class Immigrants*. DeKalb: Northern Illinois University Press.

———. 1987. "In the Shadows of the Periphery: Italian Women in the Nineteenth Century." In M. Boxer and J. Quataert, ed., *Connecting Spheres*. New York and Oxford: Oxford University Press.

———. 1988a. *Militants and Migrants: Rural Sicilians Become American Workers*. New Brunswick, N.J.: Rutgers University Press.

———. 1988b. "The Transplanted: Women and Family in Immigrant America." *Social Science History* 12, 3 (Fall):243–52.

———. 1989. *Immigrant Women in the United States, a Selectively Annotated Multidisciplinary Bibliography*. Westport, Conn.: Greenwood.

———. 1991. "Immigrant Women: Nowhere at Home?" *Journal of American Ethnic History* 10, 4 (Summer):61–87.

———, ed. 1992. *Seeking Common Ground: Multidisciplinary Studies of Immigrant Women in the United States*. Westport, Conn.: Praeger.

Ganz, Maria. 1920. *Rebels: Into Anarchy and Out Again*. New York: Dodd, Mead.

Gebhart, John C. 1924. *The Health of a Neighborhood: A Social Study of the Mulberry District*. New York: New York Association for Improving the Condition of the Poor.

Geschwender, James. 1978. *Racial Stratification in America*. Dubuque, Iowa: William C. Brown.

Gibbs, Winifred Stuart. 1917. *The Minimum Cost of Living: A Study of Families of Limited Income in New York City.* New York: Macmillan.

Gillett, Lucy H. 1924. "Adapting Nutrition Work to a Community." New York: New York Association for Improving the Condition of the Poor, Publication no. 134. Russell Sage Foundation Collection. Cohen Library. The City College of the City University of New York.

Ginsburg, Faye, and Anna Lowenhaupt Tsing, eds. 1991. *Uncertain Terms: Negotiating Gender in American Culture.* Boston: Beacon.

Glanz, Rudolf. 1976. *The Jewish Woman in America: Two Female Immigrant Generations 1820–1929*, vol. I, *The Eastern European Jewish Woman.* New York: KTAV Publishing House.

Glenn, Evelyn Nakano. 1986. *Issei, Nisei, War Bride: Three Generations of Japanese American Women in Domestic Service.* Philadelphia: Temple University Press.

———. 1991. "Racial Ethnic Women's Labor: The Intersection of Race, Class, and Gender Oppression." In *Gender, Family, and Economy*, ed. R. L. Blumberg, pp. 173–201. Newbury Park, Calif.: Sage.

———. 1992. "From Servitude to Service Work: Historical Continuities in the Racial Division of Women's Work." *Signs* 18, 1 (Fall):1–43.

Glenn, Evelyn Nakano, Grace Chang, and Linda Rennie Forcey, eds. 1994. *Mothering: Ideology, Experience, and Agency.* New York: Routledge.

Glenn, Susan. 1990. *Daughters of the Shtetl: Life and Labor in the Immigrant Generation.* Ithaca, N.Y.: Cornell University Press.

Glick Schiller, Nina, Linda Basch, and Cristina Blanc-Szanton, eds. 1992. *Towards a Transnational Perspective on Migration: Race, Class, Ethnicity, and Nationalism Reconsidered.* Annals of the New York Academy of Sciences, vol. 654. New York: New York Academy of Sciences.

Gold, Michael. 1930. *Jews Without Money.* New York: Horace Liveright.

Gold, Steve. 1992. *Refugee Communities: A Comparative Field Study.* Beverly Hills, Calif.: Sage.

Gordon, Milton. 1964. *Assimilation in American Life.* New York: Oxford University Press.

Gorelick, Sherry. 1981. *City College and the Jewish Poor: Education in New York, 1880–1924.* New Brunswick, N.J.: Rutgers University Press.

Gordon, Linda. 1976. *Woman's Body, Woman's Right: A Social History of Birth Control in America.* New York: Grossman.

———. 1986a. "Family Violence, Feminism, and Social Control." *Feminist Studies* XII, 3 (Fall):453–78.

————. 1986b. "What's New in Women's History." In Teresa de Laure-
tis, ed., *Feminist Studies/Critical Studies*. Bloomington: Indiana University Press.

Grant, Madison. 1916. *The Passing of the Great Race*. New York: Scrib-
ners.

Grasmuck, Sherri, and Patricia Pessar. 1991. *Between Two Islands:
Dominican International Migration*. Berkeley:University of California Press.

Greenberg, Louis. [1944] 1976. *The Jews in Russia: The Struggle for
Emancipation*, vol. 1: 1772–1880. New York: Schocken Books.

————. [1951] 1976. *The Jews in Russia: The Struggle for Emancipation*, vol. 2: 1881–1917. New York: Schocken Books.

Grinstein, Hyman B. 1945. *The Rise of the Jewish Community of New
York, 1654–1860*. Philadelphia: The Jewish Publication Society of
America.

Grose, Howard B. 1909. *Aliens or Americans?* New York: Young People's Missionary Movement.

Grossman, Gregory. 1973. "Russia and the Soviet Union." In Carlo M.
Cipolla, ed., *The Fontana Economic History of Europe: The Emergence
of Industrial Societies*, Part 2. Glasgow, U.K.: William Collins Sons.

Gutman, Herbert G. 1976. *Work, Culture and Society in Industrializing
America*. New York: Vintage.

Handlin, Oscar. 1951. *The Uprooted*. New York: Grosset and Dunlap.

Harding, Sandra. 1986. *The Science Question in Feminism*. Ithaca, N.Y.:
Cornell University Press.

————. 1991. *Whose Science? Whose Knowledge?: Thinking from
Women's Lives*. Ithaca, N.Y.: Cornell University Press.

Hareven, Tamara. 1982. *Family Time and Industrial Time*. New York:
Cambridge University Press.

Hartmann, Heidi. 1981. "The Unhappy Marriage of Marxism and Feminism: Towards a More Progressive Union." In Lydia Sargent, ed.,
Women and Revolution. Boston: South End Press.

Hartsock, Nancy, C. M. 1988. "Epistemology and Politics: Developing
Alternatives to Western Political Thought." Paper presented at the
International Political Science Association Meetings, August 1988.

Hendriksen, Louise Levitas. 1988. *Anzia Yezierska: A Writer's Life*.
New Brunswick, N.J.: Rutger's University Press.

Hersch, Liebmann. [1931] 1969. "International Migration of the Jews."
In W. F. Willcox, ed., *International Migrations: Interpretations* vol. 2.
Demographic Monographs, vol. 8. New York: Gordon and Breach
Science Publishers.

Herzfeld, Elsa G. 1905. *Family Monographs: The History of Twenty-
Four Families Living in the Middle West Side of New York City*. New
York: James Kempster.

Higham, John. 1955. *Strangers in the Land: Patterns of American Nativism, 1860–1925.* New Brunswick, N.J.: Rutger's University Press.

Hoerder, Dirk. 1991. "International Labor Markets and Community Building by Migrant Workers in the Atlantic Economies." In R. Vecoli and S. Sinke, ed., *A Century of European Migrations, 1830–1930.* Urbana and Chicago: University of Illinois Press.

———, and Horst Rossler, eds. 1993. *Distant Magnets: Expectations and Realities in the Immigrant Experience, 1840–1930.* New York and London: Holmes and Meier.

Hondagneu-Sotelo, Pierrette. 1994. *Gendered Transitions: Mexican Experiences of Immigration.* Berkeley: University of California Press.

Howe, Irving. 1976. *World of Our Fathers.* New York: Simon and Schuster.

Hyman, Paula E. 1980. "Immigrant Women and Consumer Protest: The NYC Kosher Meat Boycott of 1902." *American Jewish History* LXX, 1 (September):91–105.

Jenks, Jeremiah N., and W. Jett Lauck. 1920. "Social Problems of Recent Immigration." In P. Davis, ed. *Immigration and Americanization.* Boston: Ginn.

Kahan, Arcadius. 1978. "Economic Opportunity and Some Pilgrim's Progress: Jewish Immigrants from Eastern Europe in the U.S., 1890–1914." *Journal of Economic History* 38, 1 (March):237–45.

———. 1986. *Essays in Jewish Social and Economic History.* Chicago: University of Chicago Press.

Karp, Abraham J., ed. 1976. *Golden Door to America: The Jewish Immigrant Experience.* New York: Viking.

Katzman, David M., and Wm. M. Tuttle, Jr., eds. 1982. *Plain Folk: The Life Stories of Undistinguished Americans.* Urbana: University of Illinois Press.

Kazin, Alfred. 1951. *A Walker in the City.* New York: Harcourt, Brace.

Kennedy, Albert J., Kathryn Farra, and Associates. 1935. *Social Settlements in New York City.* New York: Columbia University Press.

Kessler-Harris, Alice. 1974. "Comments on the Yans-McLaughlin and Davidoff Papers." *Journal of Social History* VII, 4 (Summer):446–51.

———. 1982. *Out to Work: A History of Wage-Earning Women in the United States.* New York: Oxford University Press.

Kessner, Thomas. 1977. *The Golden Door: Italian and Jewish Immigrant Mobility in New York City, 1880–1915.* New York: Oxford University Press.

Kessner, Thomas, and Betty Boyd Caroli. 1978. "New Immigrant Women at Work: Italians and Jews in New York City, 1880–1905," *Journal of Ethnic Studies,* 5, 4 (Winter): 19–31.

Kibria, Nazli. 1993. *Family Tightrope: The Changing Lives of Vietnamese Americans.* Princeton, N.J.: Princeton University Press.

Kim, Illsoo. 1981. *New Urban Immigrants: The Korean Community in New York*. Princeton, N.J.: Princeton University Press.

King, Deborah. 1988. "Multiple Jeopardy, Multiple Consciousness: The Context of a Black Feminist Ideology." *Signs* 14:42–72.

Klaus, Alisa. 1993. "Depopulation and Race Suicide: Maternalism and Pronatalist Ideologies in France and the United States." In *Mothers of a New World*, ed. S. Koven and S. Michel, pp. 188–212. New York and London: Routledge.

Koven, Seth, and Sonya Michel, eds. 1993. *Mothers of a New World: Maternalist Policies and the Origins of Welfare States*. New York and London: Routledge.

Kramer, Sydelle, and Jenny Masur, eds. 1976. *Jewish Grandmothers*. Boston: Beacon.

Kugelmass, Jack. 1986. "Native Aliens: The Jews of Poland as a Middleman Minority." Ph.D. dissertation, New School for Social Research.

Kula, Witold, Nina Assorodobraj-Kula, and Marcin Kula, eds. 1986. *Writing Home: Immigrants in Brazil and the United States, 1890–1891*. Boulder, Colo.: East European Monographs.

Kuzmack, Linda Gordon. 1990. *Woman's Cause: The Jewish Woman's Movement in England and the United States, 1881–1933*. Columbus: Ohio State University Press.

Kuznets, Simon. 1975. "Immigration of Russian Jews to the U.S.: Background and Structure." In Donald Fleming and Bernard Bailyn, eds., *Perspectives in American History*, IX. Cambridge, Mass.: Charles Warren Center for Studies in American History, Harvard University.

Kyrk, Hazel. 1933. *Economic Problems of the Family*. New York: Harper.

Lamphere, Louise. 1987. *From Working Daughters to Working Mothers: Immigrant Women in a New England Industrial Community*. Ithaca, N.Y.: Cornell University Press.

LaRuffa, Anthony L. 1988. *Monte Carmelo: An Italian-American Community in the Bronx*. New York: Gordon and Breach.

Leeds, Anthony. 1976. "Women in the Migratory Process: A Reductionist Outlook." *Anthropological Quarterly* 49:69–76.

Light, Ivan. 1972. *Ethnic Enterprise in America*. Berkeley: University of California Press.

Light, Ivan, and Edna Bonacich. 1988. *Immigrant Entrepreneurs*. Berkeley: University of California Press.

———, and Parminder Bhachu, eds. 1993. *Comparative Immigration and Entrepreneurship*. New Brunswick, N.J.: Transaction.

———, Georges Sabah, Mehdi Bozorgmehr, and Claudia Der-Martirosian. 1994. "Beyond the Ethnic Enclave Economy." *Social Problems* 41, 1 (February):65–80.

Linden, R. Ruth. 1993. "My Grandmother's Samovar." In *Making Stories, Making Selves* by R. R. Linden, pp. 19–25. Columbus: Ohio State University Press.

Lodge, Henry Cabot. [1900] 1920. "Immigration—A Review." In *Immigration and Americanization*, ed. Philip Davis, pp. 50–60. Boston: Ginn.

Lowenstein, Steven M. 1984. "Governmental Jewish Policies in Early Nineteenth Century Germany and Russia: A Comparison," *Jewish Social Studies* XLVI, 3–4 (Summer/Fall):303–20.

McBride, Paul W. 1975. *Culture Clash: Immigrants and Reformers, 1880–1920*. San Francisco: R and E Research Associates.

McClymer, John F. 1991. "Gender and the 'American Way of Life': Women in the Americanization Movement." *Journal of American Ethnic History* 10, 3 (Spring):3–20.

McLean, Francis H. 1898. "Food Stores and Purchases in the Tenth Ward." *University Settlement Society of New York*. New York: Russell Sage Foundation Collection. Cohen Library. The City College of the City University of New York.

Maglione, Connie A., and Carmen Anthony Fiore. 1989. *Voices of the Daughters*. Princeton, N.J.: Townhouse.

Mangano, Antonio. 1908. "The Effect of Emigration Upon Italy," *Charities and the Commons* XX (April).

———. [1917] 1971. *Sons of Italy: A Social and Religious Study of the Italians in America*. New York: Missionary Education Movement.

Marks, Carole. 1989. *Farewell—We're Good and Gone: The Great Black Migration*. Bloomington: Indiana University Press.

Martellone, Anna Maria. 1984. "Italian Mass Emigration to the United States, 1876–1930: A Historical Survey." *Perspectives in American History* n.s, I:379–423. Charles Warren Center for Studies in American History, Harvard University, Cambridge University Press.

Mathias, Elizabeth, and Richard Raspa. 1985. *Italian Folktales in America: The Verbal Art of an Immigrant Woman*. Detroit, Mich.: Wayne State University Press.

Matthaei, Julie A. 1982. *An Economic History of Women in America: Women's Work, the Sexual Division of Labor, and the Development of Capitalism*. New York: Schocken.

May, Martha. 1984. "The 'Good Managers': Married Working-Class Women and Family Budget Studies, 1895–1915." *Labor History*, 351–72.

Mendelsohn, Ezra. 1970. *Class Struggle in the Pale: The Formative Years of the Jewish Worker's Movement in Tsarist Russia*. Cambridge: Cambridge University Press.

Meyerowitz, Joanne J. 1988. *Women Adrift: Independent Wage Earners in Chicago, 1880–1930*. Chicago: University of Chicago Press.

Mills, C. Wright. 1959. *The Sociological Imagination*. New York: Oxford University Press.

Model, Suzanne. 1985. "A Comparative Perspective on the Ethnic Enclave: Blacks, Italians, and Jews in New York City." *International Migration Review* XIX, 1 (Spring):64–81.

Montgomery, David. 1977. "Immigrant Workers and Managerial Reform." In Richard L. Ehrlich, ed., *Immigrants in Industrial America 1850–1920*. Charlottesville: University Press of Virginia.

Moore, Deborah Dash. 1981. *At Home in America: Second Generation New York Jews*. New York: Columbia University Press.

Morawska, Ewa. 1987. "A Replica of the 'Old Country' Relationship in Ethnic Niche: East European Jews and Gentiles in Small-Town Western PA, 1880s–1930s." *American Jewish History* LXXVII, 1 (September):27–86.

———. 1989. "Labor Migrations of Poles in the Atlantic World-Economy, 1880–1914." *Comparative Studies in Society and History* 31, 2 (April):237–72.

———. 1990. "The Sociology and Historiography of Immigration." In *Immigration Reconsidered*, ed. V. Yans-McLaughlin, pp. 187–238. New York: Oxford University Press.

———. 1991. "Return Migrations: Theoretical and Research Agenda." In *A Century of European Migrations, 1830–1930*, ed. R. Vecoli and S. Sinke, pp. 277–92. Urbana and Chicago: University of Illinois Press.

More, Louise Bolard. 1907. *Wage Earners Budgets: A Study of Standards of Living in New York City*. New York: Henry Holt.

Morokvasic, Mirjana. 1983. "Women in Migration: Beyond the Reductionist Outlook." In A. Phizacklea, ed., *One Way Ticket: Migration and Female Labour*. London: Routledge and Kegan Paul.

———. 1984. "Birds of Passage Are also Women." *International Migration Review* 26:886–907.

Moskowitz, Faye, ed. 1994. *Her Face in the Mirror*. Boston: Beacon.

Murdzek, Benjamin. 1977. *Emigration in Polish Social-Political Thought, 1870–1914*. Boulder, Colo.: East European Quarterly, Columbia University Press.

Mussey, Henry R. 1903. "'Fake' Installment Business and Its Social Consequences." *Charities* X, 10 (March 7):236–44.

Nagel, Joanne. 1994. "Constructing Ethnicity: Creating and Recreating Ethnic Identity and Culture," *Social Problems* 41, 1:152–76.

National Council of Jewish Women. 1897. *Proceedings of the First Convention*. Philadelphia: Jewish Publication Society of America.

New York City Tenement House Department. *First Report*, vol. I. New York: 1902–1903.

New York State Department of Labor. 1903. *Twentieth Annual Report of the Bureau of Labor Statistics, 1902*. Albany.

New York State Factory Investigating Commission. 1915. *Fourth Report of the Factory Investigating Commission*. 5 vols. Albany.

Noether, Emiliana P. 1978. "The Silent Half: Le Contadine Del Sud Before the First World War." In B. B. Caroli, R. F. Marney, L. Tomasi, eds., *The Italian Immigrant Woman in North America*. Toronto: Multicultural History Society of Ontario.

Obolensky-Ossinsky, V. V. [1931] 1969. "Emigration from and Immigration into Russia." In W. F. Wilcox, ed., *International Migrations*, vol. 2, *Interpretations*. New York: Gordon and Breach Science Publishers.

Odencrantz, Louise C. 1919. *Italian Women in Industry: A Study of Conditions in New York City*. New York: Russell Sage.

Omi, Michael, and Howard Winant. 1986. *Racial Formation in the United States*. New York: Routledge.

Ong, Aihwa. 1987. *Spirits of Resistance and Capitalist Discipline: Factory Women in Malaysia*. Albany: State University of New York Press.

Orsi, Robert Anthony. 1985. *The Madonna of 115th Street: Faith and Community in Italian Harlem, 1880–1950*. New Haven, Conn.: Yale University Press.

———. 1990. "The Fault of Memory: 'Southern Italy' in the Imagination of Immigrants and the Lives of Their Children in Italian Harlem, 1920–1945." *Journal of Family History* 15, 2:133–47.

Paolucci, Anne. 1977. "Back in the Old Country." In *Poems Written For Sbek's Mummies, Marie Mencken, and Other Important Persons, Places, and Things*, by A. Paolucci, p. 35. New York: Griffon House.

Park, Robert. 1950. *Race and Culture*. New York: Free Press.

Passero, Rosara Lucy. 1978. "Ethnicity in the Men's Ready-Made Clothing Industry, 1880–1950: The Italian Experience in Philadelphia." Ph.D. dissertation, University of Pennsylvania.

Paul, Diane. 1981. "'In the Interests of Civilization': Marxist Views of Race and Culture in the Nineteenth Century." *Journal of the History of Ideas* 4, 1 (Jan.–March):115–38.

Payne, Elizabeth Anne. 1988. *Reform, Labor, and Feminism: Margaret Drier Robins and the Women's Trade Union League*. Urbana: University of Illinois Press.

Pearson, Raymond. 1983. *National Minorities in Eastern Europe, 1848–1945*. New York: St. Martin's.

Pedraza, Silvia. 1991. "Women and Migration: The Social Consequences of Gender." *Annual Review of Sociology* 17:303–25.

Peiss, Kathy. 1983. "'Charity Girls' and City Pleasures: Historical Notes on Working-Class Sexuality, 1880–1920." In A. Snitow, C. Stansell, and S. Thompson, eds., *Powers of Desire: The Politics of Sexuality*. New York: Monthly Review Press.

———. 1986. *Cheap Amusements: Working Women and Leisure in Turn-of-the-Century New York*. Philadelphia: Temple University Press.

Peled, Yoav, and Gershon Shafir. 1987. "Split Labor Market and the State: The Effect of Modernization on Jewish Industrial Workers in Tsarist Russia." *American Journal of Sociology* 92, 6 (May):1435–60.

The Personal Narratives Group, ed. 1989. *Interpreting Women's Lives: Feminist Theory and Personal Narratives*. Bloomington: Indiana University Press.

Pessar, Patricia. 1982. "The Role of Households in International Migration." *International Migration Review* 16, 2 (Summer):342–64.

———. 1985. "The Linkage Between the Household and Workplace of Dominican Women in the U.S." *International Migration Review* 18, 4 (Winter):1188–1211.

———. 1986. "The Role of Gender in Dominican Settlement in the U.S." In June Nash, Helen Safa, et al., eds., *Women and Change in Latin America*. South Hadley, Mass.: Bergin and Garvey.

Petras, Elizabeth McLean. 1987. *Jamaican Labor Migration: White Capital and Black Labor, 1850–1930*. Boulder, Colo.: Westview.

Piore, Michael J. 1979. *Birds of Passage: Migrant Labor and Industrial Societies*. Cambridge: Cambridge University Press.

Pope, Jesse E. 1905. *The Clothing Industry in New York*. Columbia: University of Missouri Press.

Portes, Alejandro. 1978. "Migration and Underdevelopment." *Politics and Society* 8:1–48.

———. 1981. "Modes of Structural Incorporation and Present Theories of Labor Immigration." In *Global Trends In Migration: Theory and Research on International Migration Population Movements*, ed. M. Kritz, C. B. Keely, and S. M. Tomasi, pp. 279–97. New York: Center for Migration Studies.

———, and John Walton. 1981. *Labor, Class, and the International System*. New York: Academic Press.

———, and Robert Bach. 1985. *Latin Journey: Cuban and Mexican Immigrants in the United States*. Berkeley: University of California Press.

———, and Ruben G. Rumbaut. 1990. *Immigrant America: A Portrait*. Berkeley:University of California Press.

Pozzetta, George E. 1971. "The Italians of New York City, 1890–1914." Ph.D. dissertation, University of North Carolina at Chapel Hill.

Ratti, Anna Maria. 1931. "Italian Migration Movements, 1876–1926." In Walter F. Willcox, ed., *International Migrations*, vol. II. New York: Gordon and Breach Science Publishers, 1969, ed. First published New York: National Bureau of Economic Research, 1931.

Reed, Alfred. [1912] 1920. "Social: Immigration and Health." In P. David, ed., *Immigration and Americanization*. Boston: Ginn.

Riis, Jacob. 1890. *How the Other Half Lives*. New York: Charles Scribner's.

Rischin, Moses. 1977. *The Promised City: New York's Jews, 1870–1914*. Cambridge, Mass.: Harvard University Press.

Rodgers, Daniel T. 1978. *The Work Ethic in Industrial America, 1850–1920*. Chicago: University of Chicago Press.

Roediger, David R. 1994. "Whiteness and Ethnicity in the History of 'White Ethnics' in the United States." In *Towards the Abolition of Whiteness* by D. Roediger, pp. 181–98. London and New York: Verso.

Rogger, Hans. 1976. "Government, Jews, Peasants, and Land in Post-Emancipation Russia," *Cahiers du Monde Russe et Sovietique 17*, 1 (Jan.–March):5–25; 2–3 (April–Sept.):171–211.

Rogow, Faith. 1993. *Gone to Another Meeting: The National Council of Jewish Women, 1893–1993*. Tuscaloosa: University of Alabama Press.

Rollins, Judith. 1985. *Between Women: Domestics and Their Employers*. Philadelphia: Temple University Press.

Rose, Elizabeth. 1994. "From Sponge Cake to Hamantashen: Jewish Identity in a Jewish Settlement House, 1885–1952." *Journal of American Ethnic History* 13, 3 (Spring):3–23.

Rosen, Ruth. 1982. *The Lost Sisterhood:Prostitution in America, 1900–1918*. Baltimore: Johns Hopkins University Press.

Rosenblum, Gerald. 1973. *Immigrant Workers: Their Impact on American Labor Radicalism*. New York: Basic.

Rosenwaike, Ira. 1972. *Population History of New York City*. Syracuse, N.Y.: University of Syracuse Press.

Rubinow, Isaac M. 1905. "Economic and Industrial Condition: New York." In C. S. Bernheimer, ed., *The Russian Jew in the United States*. Philadelphia: J. C. Winston.

———. [1907] 1975. *Economic Condition of the Jews in Russia*. Bulletin of the Bureau of Labor v.15, Department of Commerce and Labor, Washington D.C., New York: Arno.

Rudd, Joy. 1988. "Invisible Exports: The Emigration of Irish Women This Century." *Women's Studies International Forum* 2, 4:307–11.

Rushdie, Salman. 1989. *Satanic Verses*. New York: Viking.

———1991. *Imaginary Homelands*. New York: Granta Books/Viking.

Safa, Helen I. 1987. "Work and Women's Liberation: A Case Study of Garment Workers." In Leith Mullings, ed., *Cities of the United States: Studies in Urban Anthropology*. New York: Columbia University Press.

Sanderson, Stephen. 1988. *Macrosociology*. New York: Harper and Row.

Saroff, Sophie. 1983. *Stealing the State: An Oral History*. New York: Community Documentation Workshop.

Sassen-Koob, Saskia. 1980a. "Immigrant and Minority Workers in the Organization of the Labor Process." *Journal of Ethnic Studies* 8, 1 (Spring):1–34.

———. 1980b. "The Internationalization of the Labor Force." *Studies in Comparative International Development* 15, 4 (Winter):3–25.

———. 1981. "Towards a Conceptualization of Immigrant Labor." *Social Problems* 29, 1 (Oct):65–85.

———. 1985. "Notes on the Incorporation of Third World Women into Wage-Labor Through Immigration and Off-Shore Production." *International Migration Review* 18, 4 (Winter):1144–67.

Sassen, Saskia. 1988. *The Mobility of Labor and Capital: A Study of International Investment and Labor Flow*. Cambridge and New York: Cambridge University Press.

Schmitter Heisler, Barbara. 1993. "The Future of Immigrant Incorporation: Which Models? Which Concepts?" *International Migration Review* 26, 2:623–45.

Schwartz, Laura Anker. 1983. "Immigrant Voices from Home, Work, and Community: Women and Family in the Migration Process, 1890–1938." SUNY-Stonybrook, History Ph.D. dissertation.

Scott, Joan. 1986. "Gender: A Useful Category of Historical Analysis." *American Historical Review* 91 (December):1053–75.

Seller, Maxine, ed. 1981. *Immigrant Women*. Philadelphia: Temple University Press.

———. 1986. "The Uprising of the Twenty Thousand: Sex, Class, and Ethnicity in the Shirtwaist Makers Strike of 1909." In D. Hoerder, ed., *"Struggle a Hard Battle": Essays on Working-Class Immigrants*. DeKalb: Northern Illinois University Press.

———. 1987. "Defining Socialist Womanhood: The Women's Page of *The Jewish Forward* in 1919." *American Jewish History* 76, 4 (June):416–38.

Sherman, Mary. 1906. "Manufacturing of Foods in the Tenements." *Charities and the Commons* 15, 18 (Feb. 10):668–72.

Simkhovitch, Mary Kingsbury. 1938. *Neighborhood: My Story of Greenwich House*. New York: W. W. Norton.

Sinke, Suzanne. 1989. "A Historiography of Immigrant Women in the Nineteenth and Early Twentieth Centuries." *Ethnic Forum* 9, 1–2:122–45.

———, with Stephen Gross. 1992. "The International Marriage Market and the Sphere of Social Reproduction: A German Case Study." In

Seeking Common Ground, ed. D. Gabaccia, pp. 67–87. Westport, Conn.: Praeger.

Sinkoff, Nancy B. 1988. "Educating for 'Proper' Jewish Womanhood: A Case Study in Domesticity and Vocational Training, 1897–1926," *American Jewish History* 77, 4 (June):572–99.

Sklar, Kathryn Kish. 1993. "The Historical Foundations of Women's Power in the Creation of the American Welfare State, 1830–1930." In *Mothers of a New World*, ed. S. Koven and S. Michel, pp. 43–93. New York: Routledge.

Skocpol, Theda. 1979. *States and Social Revolutions*. Cambridge: Cambridge University Press.

Smith, Joan, Immanuel Wallerstein, Hans-Dieter Evers, eds. 1984. *Households and the World-Economy*. Beverly Hills, Calif.: Sage.

————, Jane Collins, Terence K. Hopkins, and Akbar Muhammed, eds. 1988. *Racism, Sexism, and the World-System*. New York: Greenwood.

Smith, Joan, Immanuel Wallestein, Kathie Friedman Kasaba, et al. 1992. *Creating and Transforming Households: The Constraints of the World-Economy*. Cambridge: Cambridge University Press.

Smith, Judith E. 1985. *Family Connections: A History of Italian and Jewish Immigrant Lives in Providence, Rhode Island, 1900–1940*. Albany: State University of New York Press.

Speranza, Gino C. [1906] 1974. "Political Representation of Italo-American Colonies in the Italian Parliament." In F. Cordasco and E. Bucchioni, eds., *The Italians: Social Backgrounds of An American Group*. Clifton, N.J.: August M. Kelley.

Stansell, Christine. 1986. *City of Women: Sex and Class in New York, 1789–1860*. New York: Alfred A. Knopf.

Steinberg, Stephen. 1989. *The Ethnic Myth*. Boston: Beacon Press.

Supple, Barry E. 1957. "A Business Elite: German-Jewish Financiers in Nineteenth-Century New York," *The Business History Review* 31, 2 (Summer):143–78.

Takaki, Ronald, ed. 1987. *From Different Shores: Perspectives on Race and Ethnicity in America*. New York: Oxford University Press.

Tananbaum, Susan L. 1994. "Biology and Community: The Duality of Jewish Mothering in East London, 1880–1939." In *Mothering*, ed. E. N. Glenn et al., pp. 311–32. New York: Routledge.

Tcherikower, Elias. [1945] 1961. *The Early Jewish Labor Movement in the United States*. New York: YIVO Institute for Jewish Research.

Tenenbaum, Shelly. 1993. *A Credit to Their Community: Jewish Loan Societies in the United States, 1880–1945*. Detroit, Mich.: Wayne State University Press.

Tentler, Leslie Woodcock. 1979. *Wage-Earning Women: Industrial Work and Family Life in the United States, 1900–1930*. New York: Oxford University Press.

Thomas, Brinley. 1954. *Migration and Economic Growth*. Cambridge: Cambridge University Press.

Tienda, Marta, and Karen Booth. 1991. "Gender, Migration, and Social Change." *International Sociology* 6, 1 (March):51–72.

Tilly, Charles. 1990. "Transplanted Networks." In *Immigration Reconsidered*, ed. V. Yans-McLaughlin, pp. 79–95. New York and London: Oxford University Press.

Tilly, Louise A. 1974. "Comments on the Yans-McLaughlin and Davidoff Papers." *Journal of Social History* 7, 4 (Summer):452–59.

Treese, Lorett. 1990. "'Why, It's Mother': The Italian Mother's Clubs of New York." *Italian Americana* 9, 1 (Fall/Winter):25–41.

Union Settlement Association. 1900–1910. *Annual Reports*. New York: Russell Sage Foundation Collection. Cohen Library. The City College of the City University of New York.

———. 1915. "Twenty Years in South Harlem, 1895–1915." New York: Russell Sage Foundation Collection. Cohen Library. The City College of the City University of New York.

U.S. Bureau of Labor. 1911. *Report on Condition of Woman and Child Wage Earners in the United States*. Senate Doc. 645, 61st Congress, 2nd session; vol. 2, *Men's Ready-Made Clothing*; vol. 9, *History of Women in Industry in the United States*, by Helen S. Sumner. Washington, D.C.: Government Printing Office.

U.S. Bureau of the Census. 1890. *Compendium* III. *Population*. Washington, D.C.: Government Printing Office, 1897.

———. 1890. *Manufacturing Industries*. Washington, D.C.: Government Printing Office.

———. 1910. States, III; Occupations, IV. *Population*. Washington, D.C.: Government Printing Office, 1914.

———. 1910. *Abstract with Supplement for New York*. Washington, D.C.: Government Printing Office, 1913.

———. 1960. *Historical Statistics of the U.S., Colonial Times to 1957*. Washington, D.C.: Government Printing Office.

U.S. Federal Writer's Project, New York City. 1938. *The Italians of New York*. Work Progress Administration, City of New York. New York: Random House.

U.S. Immigration Commission. 1911. *Abstracts of Reports of the Immigration Commission*, vols. I and II, 61st Congress, 3rd session, Senate Doc. No. 747. Washington, D.C.: Government Printing Office.

———. 1911. *Emigration Conditions in Europe*, Reports of the Immigration Commission, vol. 4, 61st Congress, 3rd session, Senate Doc. No. 748. Washington, D.C.: Government Printing Office.

———. 1911. *Dictionary of Races or Peoples*, Reports of the Immigration Commission, vol.5, 61st Congress, 3rd session, Senate Doc. 748. Washington, D.C.: Government Printing Office.

———. 1911. *Immigrants in Cities,* Reports of the Immigration Commission, vol. 26, Senate Doc. No. 338, 61st Congress, 2nd Session. Washington, D.C.: Government Printing Office.

———. 1911. *Fecundity of Immigrant Women,* Reports of the Immigration Commission, vol. 28, 61st Congress, Senate Doc. No. 282, 2nd Session. Washington, D.C.: Government Printing Office.

———. 1911. *Importation and Harboring of Women for Immoral Purposes,* Reports of the Immigration Commission, vol 37, Senate Doc. No. 753, 61st Congress, 3rd session. Washington, D.C.: Government Printing Office.

U.S. Industrial Commission. 1901. *Reports of the Industrial Commission on Immigration,* vol. XV. Washington, D.C.: Government Printing Office. Arno Press Reprint edition 1970.

University Settlement Society of New York. 1893. *Bulletin* (November). New York: Russell Sage Foundation Collection. Cohen Library. The City College of the City University of New York.

———. 1905–1908. *University Settlement Studies.* New York City: Russell Sage Foundation Collection. Cohen Library. The City College of the City University of New York.

Van Kleeck, Mary. 1910. "Child Labor in Home Industries." *Annals of the American Academy of Politics and Social Sciences* supplement, 26 (March):145–49.

———. 1913. *Artificial Flower Makers.* New York: Survey.

———. 1914. *Working Girls in Evening Schools.* New York: Survey.

———. 1917. *A Seasonal Industry: A Study of the Millinery Trade in New York.* New York: Russell Sage.

Van Vorst, Mrs. John, and Marie Van Vorst. [1903] 1974. *The Woman Who Toils.* Los Angeles: Institute of Industrial Relations, University of California.

Vecoli, Rudolph J. 1964. "Contadini in Chicago: A Critique of *The Uprooted.*" *Journal of American History* 51 (Dec.):404–17.

Wald, Lillian D. 1915. *The House on Henry Street.* New York: Henry Holt.

Waldinger, Roger. 1985. "Another Look at the International Ladies' Garment Workers' Union: Women, Industry Structure, and Collective Action." In Ruth Milkman, ed., *Women, Work, and Protest.* Boston: Routledge and Kegan Paul.

———. 1986. *Through the Eye of the Needle: Immigrants and Enterprise in New York's Garment Trades.* New York: New York University Press.

Walker, Francis A. [1899] 1920. "Restriction of Immigration." In Philip Davis, ed., *Immigration and Americanization.* Boston:Ginn.

Wallerstein, Immanuel. 1987. "The Construction of Peoplehood: Racism, Nationalism, Ethnicity." *Sociological Forum* 2, 2 (Spring):373–88.

————. 1988. "The Ideological Tensions of Capitalism: Universalism versus Racism and Sexism." In J. Smith, J. Collins, T. K. Hopkins, and A. Muhammed, eds., *Racism, Sexism, and the World-System*. New York: Greenwood.

————. 1989. *The Modern World-System III: The Second Era of Great Expansion of the Capitalist World-Economy, 1730–1840s*. San Diego, Calif.: Academic.

Ward, A. 1975. "European Capitalism's Reserve Army." *Monthly Review* 27, pt. 6.

Ward, Kathryn B. 1993. "Reconceptualizing World-System Theory to Include Women." In *Theory on Gender/Feminism on Theory*, ed. Paula England, pp. 43–68. New York: Aldine De Gruyter.

Ware, Caroline F. 1935. *Greenwich Village 1920–1930: A Comment on American Civilization in the Post-War Years*. Boston: Houghton Mifflin.

Ware, Vron. 1992. *Beyond the Pale: White Women, Racism, and History*. New York and London: Verso.

Warner, W. Lloyd, and Leo Srole. 1943. *Social Systems of American Ethnic Groups, Yankee City*, vol. 3. New Haven, Conn.: Yale University Press.

Watson, Elizabeth C. 1911. "Homework in the Tenements," *The Survey* 25 (Feb. 4):772–81.

Weatherford, Doris. 1986. *Foreign and Female*. New York: Schocken.

Weinberg, Sydney Stahl. 1988. *The World of Our Mothers: The Lives of Jewish Immigrant Women*. Chapel Hill: University of North Carolina Press.

Westwood, Sallie, and Parminder Bhachu, eds. 1988. *Enterprising Women: Ethnicity, Economy, and Gender Relations*. London: Routledge.

Willett, Mabel Hurd. 1902. *The Employment of Women in the Clothing Trade*. New York: Columbia University Studies in the Social Sciences; New York: AMS Reprint edition, 1968.

Williams, Phyllis H. 1938. *South Italian Folkways in Europe and America: A Handbook for Social Workers, Visiting Nurses, School Teachers, and Physicians*. New Haven, Conn.: Yale University Press, Publications of the Institute of Human Relations.

Wirth, Louis. 1928. *The Ghetto*. Chicago: University of Chicago Press.

Wischnitzer, Mark. 1948. *To Dwell in Safety: The Story of Jewish Migration Since 1800*. Philadelphia: Jewish Publication Society of America.

Wittig, Monique. [1971] 1985. *Les Guerillieres*. David Le Vay, trans. Boston: Beacon.

Wood, Charles. 1982. "Equilibrium and Historical-Structural Perspectives on Migration." *International Migration Review* 16, 2 (Summer):298–319.

Woods, Robert A., and Albert J. Kennedy. 1922. *The Settlement Horizon: A National Estimate*. New York: Russell Sage.

Yans-McLaughlin, Virginia. 1977. *Family and Community: Italian Immigrants in Buffalo, 1880–1930*. Ithaca, N.Y.: Cornell University Press.

———. 1990. "Metaphors of Self in History: Subjectivity, Oral Narrative, and Immigration Studies." In *Immigration Reconsidered: History, Sociology, and Politics*, ed. V. Yans-McLaughlin, pp. 254–90. New York: Oxford University Press.

Yezierska, Anzia. [1925] 1975. *The Bread Givers*. New York: Persea.

———. [1920] 1985. *Hungry Hearts*. New York: Persea.

INDEX